Periodizing Jameson

 FLASHPOINTS

The FlashPoints series is devoted to books that consider literature beyond strictly national and disciplinary frameworks, and that are distinguished both by their historical grounding and by their theoretical and conceptual strength. Our books engage theory without losing touch with history and work historically without falling into uncritical positivism. FlashPoints aims for a broad audience within the humanities and the social sciences concerned with moments of cultural emergence and transformation. In a Benjaminian mode, FlashPoints is interested in how literature contributes to forming new constellations of culture and history and in how such formations function critically and politically in the present. Series titles are available online at http://escholarship.org/uc/flashpoints.

SERIES EDITORS:
Ali Behdad (Comparative Literature and English, UCLA), Founding Editor; Judith Butler (Rhetoric and Comparative Literature, UC Berkeley), Founding Editor; Michelle Clayton (Hispanic Studies and Comparative Literature, Brown University); Edward Dimendberg (Film and Media Studies, Visual Studies, and European Languages and Studies, UC Irvine), Coordinator; Catherine Gallagher (English, UC Berkeley), Founding Editor; Nouri Gana (Comparative Literature and Near Eastern Languages and Cultures, UCLA); Susan Gillman (Literature, UC Santa Cruz); Jody Greene (Literature, UC Santa Cruz); Richard Terdiman (Literature, UC Santa Cruz)

A complete list of titles begins on p. 270.

Periodizing Jameson

*Dialectics, the University, and
the Desire for Narrative*

Phillip E. Wegner

NORTHWESTERN UNIVERSITY PRESS | EVANSTON, ILLINOIS

Northwestern University Press
www.nupress.northwestern.edu

Digital Printing

Library of Congress Cataloging-in-Publication Data

Wegner, Phillip E., 1964– author.
    Periodizing Jameson : dialectics, the university, and the desire for narrative /
Phillip E. Wegner.
        pages cm — (Flashpoints)
    ISBN 978-0-8101-2981-8 (pbk. : alk. paper)
        1. Jameson, Fredric. 2. Marxist criticism. 3. Postmodernism (Literature) 4. Marxian
school of sociology. 5. Dialectical materialism. I. Title. II. Series: FlashPoints
(Evanston, Ill.)
PN75.J36W44 2014
801.95092—dc23   2014012369

For two teachers
Fredric Jameson
and
John Hartzog

Jag ska försöka komma ihåg vad vi talat om.

—Riddaren Antonius Block, in Ingmar Bergman's *Det Sjunde Inseglet*
(*The Seventh Seal*)

The "desire for Marx" can therefore also be called a desire for *narrative*, if by this we understand, not some vacuous concept of "linearity" or even *telos*, but rather the impossible attempt to give representation to the multiple and incommensurable temporalities in which each of us exists.

—Fredric Jameson, introduction to *The Ideologies of Theory*, volume 1 (1988)

Contents

Acknowledgments

From 1987 until 1993, I had the privilege to study in Duke University's Graduate Program in Literature (referred to by us in those days as the GPL). There I had the opportunity to learn from a rare group of scholars and teachers—Barbara Herrnstein Smith, Michael Moses, Susan Willis, Toril Moi, Frank Lentricchia, Stanley Fish, Alice Kaplan, Linda Orr, Annabel Patterson, Thomas Robisheaux, Rick Rodderick, Marianna Torgovnick, Annabel Wharton, Terry Eagleton, Franco Moretti, and Darko Suvin, among others—and it was there that I first encountered Fredric Jameson, who ultimately became my dissertation director. It was an experience that shaped my subsequent work in a deep and lasting way. I hope what follows gives some sense of the intellectual energy and excitement of a time and place that remains special.

My interest in critical theory in general and Jameson's work in particular has continued to grow thanks to an exceptional community of intellectuals and friends who have shared so freely their wisdom over the course of the last quarter century. As I learned in my last two books, any list of their names will always be incomplete, and so I hope you recognize yourself and our conversations in the pages that follow; I have tried to remember what we talked about. A core group of my comrades from Duke have come together for a number of years as the Summer Institute collective—Susan Hegeman, Caren Irr, Carolyn Lesjak, Chris Pavsek, Michael Rothberg, and Rob Seguin—and our regular exchange of ideas has influenced this project from the outset. At the University of Florida,

I have been fortunate to have the opportunity to teach and write as part of a vibrant group of interdisciplinary scholars, deeply invested in the labors of theory, and I would like to acknowledge my many colleagues and students past and present, and especially the graduate students in my spring 2000 and spring 2007 seminars on Jameson's work: our common labors in these two classes are the wellspring of this book. Our colleague, friend, and mentor, John P. Leavey, Jr., deserves special acknowledgment for his example of a rigorous, engaged scholar, teacher, and leader; as does our contemporary and comrade, Kim Emery, for her courage and unwavering fidelity to justice. A good deal of the material in this book was first presented at UF's annual Marxist Reading Group (MRG) Conference—justifiably described by Cary Nelson as "one of the finest graduate student traditions in the country"—and I want to offer my heartfelt thanks to the multiple generations of students whose efforts have sustained this extraordinary event well into its second decade. I would also like to express my gratitude to the Marston-Milbauer professorship for providing support for this and other important events at UF in beleaguered times. A UF colleague, Jim Paxson, and one of my former students and a committed MRG member, Nicole LaRose, unexpectedly passed away shortly before this book came to its completion. I think both would have had interesting things to say about it, and I sorely miss the opportunity to speak with them.

I appreciate the close and detailed readings of and thoughtful comments on the entire manuscript generously offered by Crystal Bartolovich, Clint Burnham, John Hartzog, Calvin Hui, Kim Stanley Robinson, Rob Seguin, Rich Simpson, and especially the two anonymous readers at Northwestern. The FlashPoints series weathered a crisis in the time after our first conversations about the book, but throughout Ed Dimendberg remained committed to the project, and I thank him deeply for his perseverance and vision. Dick Terdiman has been wonderfully supportive in shepherding the manuscript through the editorial process, and Henry Carrigan, Peter Raccuglia, and Nathan MacBrien provided valuable support in bringing it to completion. The warmth and generosity of our hosts in Uppsala, Sweden, especially Dag Blanck and Danuta Fjellestsad, made the final work on the manuscript even more enjoyable.

The Society for Utopian Studies continues to be a source of inspiration, and I am thankful for the support and the friendships I have developed there, especially those with two others who have long engaged with the Utopian aspects of Fred's work, Tom Moylan and Peter Fitting. (My additional gratitude to Peter for prompting me to write the first version of what became this book's chapter on *Archaeologies of the Future*.) In addition to the annual conferences of these organizations, parts of this project were presented at talks at Duke, Northwestern, and Stanford universities, and at the Marxist Literary Group and Modern Literature conferences, and I thank these fine institutions for the opportunity to further refine these ideas.

Someone who has been part of this journey from the beginning—first as a classmate at Duke, then as a friend, a colleague at UF, and always an interlocutor—is Susan Hegeman, and whatever good comes from this is thanks to her. It has been a tremendous pleasure the last few years to watch Nadia and Owen grow to be admirers of Fred's work (or at least of Fred). My extended families continue to provide inestimable support in these new days bad and good.

This is a book about a gifted teacher, and hence I would like to dedicate it to two of the most influential teachers I have encountered over the last thirty years. John Hartzog, my undergraduate mentor at California State University, Northridge, first introduced me to the work of Fredric Jameson and then encouraged me to apply to the new program that Fred was just then helping bring together. The debts I owe to both of them for these gifts—another name for the impossible—can never be repaid.

A shorter version of the introduction and part I appeared as "Periodizing Jameson, or, Notes Toward a Cultural Logic of Globalization," in *On Jameson: From Postmodernism to Globalization* (Albany, NY: SUNY Press, 2006), 241–280. Material in the interlude was first published as "Greimas avec Lacan; or, From the Symbolic to the Real in Dialectical Criticism," *Criticism* 51, no. 2 (2009): 211–45. A version of chapter 6 was first published as "Jameson's Modernisms; or, the Desire Called Utopia," *Diacritics* 37, no. 4 (Winter 2007): 3–20. Special thanks are due to the editors of this book and these two outstanding journals—Caren Irr and Ian Buchanan, and Jonathan Flatley and Bruno Bosteels—both for permission to reprint this material and for offering me the opportunity to first share some of these ideas with a wider audience.

Preface: To Name the System

> The peculiar difficulty of dialectical writing lies indeed in its holistic, "totalizing" character: as though you could not say any one thing until you had first said everything; as though with each new idea you were bound to recapitulate the entire system.

This observation concerning the difficulty of dialectical writing, reading, and thinking—the three understood here as inseparable—was first offered by Fredric Jameson in his early book *Marxism and Form: Twentieth-Century Dialectical Theories of Literature* (1971).[1] It is an equally apt description of the challenges many readers face when encountering Jameson's now voluminous writings: in order to grasp any particular point he makes, it is as if we need to have the whole of his work before us. Indeed, one of the more common errors in critical engagements with Jameson's work lies in taking observations and claims he advances in isolation from their nested contexts—within the specific essay to be sure, but also within his larger project and the situation of their writing. My aim here is to provide readers with the tools necessary to begin to meet this challenge by offering the most comprehensive examination to date of a half-century of work by Jameson, one of the most significant contemporary dialectical writers and thinkers and indeed, one of the most significant American literary and cultural scholars.

Few living intellectuals are less in need of an introduction than Jameson. On the back covers of Jameson's recent books, Terry Eagleton praises him as "America's leading Marxist critic." Adam Roberts echoes this sentiment in writing that "Jameson remains the world's most famous American Marxist thinker."[2] Colin MacCabe is even more sweeping in his summation, describing Jameson as "probably the most important cultural critic writing in English today. The range of his analysis, from architecture to science fiction, from the tortuous thought of late Adorno to the *testimonio* novel of the third world, is extraordinary; it can truly be said that nothing cultural is alien to him."[3] And finally, in his fine assessment of "the usefulness of Jameson," Ian Buchanan maintains, "Jameson's work has done more to shape our consciousness of ourselves as an emergent global society than any other thinker."[4]

Indeed, Jameson has produced a tremendous amount of deeply influential scholarship, comprising more than twenty books and hundreds of essays, with a number of other major projects forthcoming in the near future. He has been a member of some of the most innovative literary and culture studies programs in the United States, at Harvard University (1959–67), University of California, San Diego (1967–76), Yale University (1976–83), University of California, Santa Cruz (1983–85), and, since 1985, Duke University, where he served for nearly two decades as the Chair of the Program in Literature. At all of these institutions, he contributed in inestimable ways to the education of multiple generations of younger scholars—myself included—many of whom have gone on to become influential and original thinkers in their own right.[5] The importance of Jameson's overall contribution was further confirmed in the fall of 2008 with the Norwegian parliament's naming him the fifth recipient of the Holberg International Memorial Prize, awarded to a scholar working in the fields of the arts and humanities, social sciences, law, or theology (the previous recipients are Julia Kristeva, Jürgen Habermas, Shmuel Eisenstadt, and Ronald Dworkin; and subsequent winners include Ian Hacking, Natalie Zemon Davis, Jürgen Kocka, Manuel Castells, and Bruno Latour); and again in 2011, with the Modern Language Association presenting him with only its sixth Award for Lifetime Scholarly Achievement.[6]

Although increasing attention to Jameson's intellectual project has produced a number of invaluable studies, this book is unique in a number of ways.[7] Jameson is, to paraphrase Louis O. Mink on the earlier dialectical historian and philosopher R. G. Collingwood—a figure who also has had a significant if uncommented upon influence on Jameson—

a systematic thinker in a time that has little use for systems, and thus, "each of his books must be seen as the discussion of a specific set of questions in the context of a *possible* system."[8] In *Valences of the Dialectic* (2009), Jameson notes that the "implied projection of a philosophical system," not only in his own work but in all dialectical thinking, "can be taken as a distorted expression of a rather different dialectical requirement, namely that of totality. In other words, the philosophical claim of unity turns out to be a symptomal transformation of the deeper claim or aspiration to totality itself."[9]

I will return shortly to the significance of this "aspiration to totality" in Jameson's project. However, rather than attempting to codify this possible system, my book's unity lies in its *narrative* presentation. *Periodizing Jameson* tells a story that is attentive to the significant transformations and reconsiderations that take place in Jameson's project from its inception through some of his most recent writings. In this regard, Mink's claims about Collingwood become apt once again: "his thinking went through a process of development and change in which earlier stages were modified but not entirely superseded by later ones, a process which is itself an illustrative example of the notion of dialectical change which was one of his own leading ideas."[10] One of the goals of this book will be to clarify the ways Jameson's work too exemplifies just such a process of dialectical change.

Although a definitive theorization of narrative awaits the publication of the opening, and last to be written, book of his six-volume magnum opus, *The Poetics of Social Forms,* the theme of narrative has been central throughout Jameson's intellectual career.[11] Indeed, as we shall see in subsequent chapters, his larger project turns on the changing fortunes of the ability to tell stories (*fabula*) in different historical situations, and his major works all contain rich and complex emplotments (*sujet*) in their own right.[12] In his landmark statement of Marxist dialectical criticism, *The Political Unconscious: Narrative as a Socially Symbolic Act* (1981), Jameson characterizes narrative as a mode of *presentation*—or to use the "untranslatable" German term that is so important for his project, *Darstellung*—taking the form of a "rhetorical movement of language and writing through time."[13] Conversely, a cognitive presentation—those found in "philosophy, science, and the like"—unfolds in terms of space; however, for Jameson one of the most important lessons of the French semiotician A. J. Greimas, of whom I will have occasion to say a good deal more in the following pages, is that the distinction is not an absolute one, and both narrative and cognitive texts are open to being rewritten in terms of the other (ideology in its most comprehensive sense, Jameson then notes, is "whatever in its very structure is susceptible of taking on a cognitive and a narrative form alternately").[14]

Earlier, in *The Prison-House of Language: A Critical Account of Structuralism and Russian Formalism* (1972), Jameson maintains—following the lead of Georg Lukács, a figure he engages with more extensively in the preceding *Marxism and Form*—that narration is to be understood as "our basic way of coming to terms with time itself and with concrete history."[15] Nearly a decade later, he expands further, and claims that the "all-informing process of *narrative*" is "the central function or *instance* of the human mind," a point he reiterates more recently in *Valences of the Dialectic*, noting, "I am at least postmodern enough to be willing to defend the proposition that everything is narrative (something which requires a defense against traditional positions based on truth, but also against the objections of comrades like Slavoj Žižek who feel that the relativity of narrative versions also menaces that unique conception of historical truth embodied in Marxism)."[16] A few pages later in *Valences* he further observes that the genius of Paul Ricoeur's *Time and Narrative* lies not only in its "vindication of narrative as a primary instance of the human mind, but also the equally daring conception of temporality itself as a construction, and a construction achieved by narrative itself."[17] Finally, in the Introduction to the two-volume collection of essays *The Ideologies of Theory* (1988), Jameson argues that narrative is not to be identified, as on occasion was claimed in the heyday of poststructuralism, with "some vacuous concept of 'linearity' or even *telos;*" instead, narrative is "the impossible attempt to give representation to the multiple and incommensurable temporalities in which each of us exists."[18] It is this complex and nuanced sense of the concept of narrative that is at play in all of Jameson's work.

At the same time, *Periodizing Jameson* works to demonstrate the value of many of these same conceptual and narrative modes of presentation—totalization, the content of the form, the four-fold hermeneutic, cognitive mapping, Utopia, transcoding, the semiotic square, and periodization—by setting them to work in a reading of his project. Such an approach requires both a fidelity to Jameson's work that is at once, paradoxically, a betrayal of it, and the kind of "articulated receptivity, of deep listening (*l'écoute*)" that Jameson himself describes as characteristic of the Lacanian discourse of the analyst. These are all strategies I will elaborate more in the Introduction.[19]

Finally, this book explores the ways each of Jameson's texts intervenes in a particular social, cultural, institutional, and political context, or *situation*, to use his preferred Sartrean term, that "can be reconstructed from the response, the attempts to resolve its contradictions or to escape its death grip, as well as from the constraints imposed on that 'socially symbolic act' in virtue of its reference to that specific historical situation and not some other one."[20] Jameson's own attention to the specific situations of his interventions is indicated by the fact that he has long provided the place of composition and date for his prefaces or introductions (Cambridge, Massachusetts, February 1961; La Jolla, March 1971; Durham, April 1990; Killingworth, July 2006). The development of Jameson's scholarship thus presents us with an exceptional opportunity to examine the adventures of perhaps the single most significant intellectual invention of the last half-century, the thing known as *theory*, as well as the potentials of and challenges to humanist intellectual work in the American university today.

This book is about Jameson's project to the degree it illuminates the contours of this volatile period in American cultural life; but even more, it attempts to speak the unique language it makes available to us. Such an approach is a deeply immanent one, using Jameson's ideas, terms, and concepts to think about his own work; or, to put this in the terms of Alain Badiou, this book unfolds as a persistent fidelity to the *event* of Jameson's ongoing project. Bruno Bosteels usefully formulates in this way his related project of *thinking with* Badiou's concepts: "rather than remaining at the level of exegesis, which always means somewhat desperately trying to stabilize the correct reading of a thinker, it is a question of taking up a transformative and critical sort of reading by way of a separate and localized—theoretical—intervention in the present that attempts to think of our actuality in the terms provided."[21] In this respect, my book has a kinship with a range of otherwise very different experiments in intellectual biography, including Toril Moi's groundbreaking study of the development of Simone de Beauvoir's thought, Geoff Bennington's exploration of Jacques Derrida's intellectual trajectory, Slavoj Žižek's extensive and ongoing recovery of the radicality of Jacques Lacan's corpus, Jodi Dean's formalization of Žižek's political thought, and Bosteels's reevaluation of Badiou as a dialectical thinker.[22] (Indeed, it may very well be the immanence of their approaches and the depth of their fidelity to their intellectual predecessors that accounts for the sometimes strong disagreements between the two champions, Žižek and Bosteels, of a renewed dialectical materialism.)[23]

Such a presentation invariably gives rise to questions about any ultimate assessment of Jameson's project offered in this book. In formulating a response, I would begin by pointing out that like any other reader, with my own history, experiences, tastes, and biases, there are places where I disagree with claims Jameson makes about specific texts, theorists, or cultural phenomena. Moreover, there is a very real sense in which the most productive building upon Jameson's project would begin by considering it as a failure, a point emphasized by Steven Helmling in his fine study of Jameson's work published more than a decade ago: "Most pointedly, for a Marxist critic, how can a 'revolutionary' critique be said to succeed in a period when revolution itself is failing?"[24] Jameson offers an answer to Helmling's query and an original reconsideration of the productivity of failure more generally in the book that remains perhaps his best known, *Postmodernism, or, The Cultural Logic of Late Capitalism* (1991), in what amounts to a stirring declaration of principles and even critical axioms:

> It is the failure of imagination that is important, and not its achievement, since in any case all representations fail and it is always impossible to imagine. This is also to say that in terms of political positions and ideologies, all the radical positions of the past are flawed, precisely because they failed. The productive use of earlier radicalisms such as populism, Gilman's feminism, or even these anticommodity impulses and attitudes that Lears and others have begun to explore lies not in their triumphant reassemblage as a radical precursor tradition but in their tragic failure to constitute such a tradition in the first place. History progresses by failure rather than by success, as Benjamin never tired of insisting; and it would be better to think of Lenin or Brecht (to pick a few illustrious names at random) as failures—that is, as actors and agents constrained by their own ideological limits and those of their moment of history—than as triumphant examples and models in some hagiographic or celebratory sense.[25]

Thinking of the theoretical projects of the post-1960s moment as I do in these pages as so many failures, hemmed in by the historical situation in which they unfold (situations, moreover, that today are no longer our own and can only ever be reconstituted after the fact, by way of reading again these interventions), is, paradoxically, both a way of marking their successes in moving history elsewhere—Brecht's bad new days—and, even more significantly, maintaining a fidelity to their "unfinished" Utopian agendas.

However, a number of things need to be said in light of such a confession. First, any such evaluation subtly shifts the focus of the analysis from Jameson's work to other, admittedly very important, issues. I do think it is legitimate when the topic is Theodor Adorno's writings or Greimas's semiotics or Andrei Tarkovsky's films or postmodern architecture to engage, sometimes critically, with Jameson's conclusions and claims. At the same time, I find too many "critiques" of Jameson's work to be premature, responding to a statement isolated from its contexts in a particular argument, his ongoing project, and the historical situation to which that work always needs to be understood as a measured response. Another of the aims of my book is to encourage readers to defer such premature judgments by highlighting the importance of grasping these multiple contexts. Jameson himself notes, that in terms of any theoretical argument or concept, "their intelligibility is incomplete without a keen awareness of the 'moment' of each, of the time of the problematic as a whole, of the shape and point in the life cycle of this particular exploding galaxy in which that technical term pulsates with its brightest life."[26] It is in the terms not only of the past but also of multiple futures "to come" that actions in the present can be understood, the three joined for the briefest of instances in the "lightning flash" of Walter Benjamin's dialectical image.[27] My motto here then would be close to that Bennington issues early in his study of Derrida: "Our task is not to take sides according to these possibilities, but to show up their insufficiency; not to say 'He is one or the other, you have to choose,' nor 'He's a bit of both, you must love and hate him for both reasons at the same time' (although these sentences are legitimate too) but something like 'Only Derrida can give us the means to understand this situation.'"[28]

Equally significantly, any too neat dismissal of Jameson's analyses (or Derrida's for that matter) risks falling into the ethical trap that Jameson, drawing in turn on the work of Friedrich Nietzsche, derides throughout his work as that which confuses difference—that is, different from the beliefs I already hold, the position I already occupy—with error, sin, or evil. The example of Jameson's work offers an alternative way of reading, or what we might call following Jameson's lead in his discussion of Bertolt Brecht, an alternate readerly *stance* (*Haltung*), one "beyond" the ethical fixation on the parsing of good and evil.[29] I will begin to outline something of this alternate stance in the next chapter, and then try to enact it within the pages that follow.

Such an approach offers not only a different way of understanding Jameson's work, but also of theoretical discourse more generally.

These lessons become especially valuable in light of the already tired assertion in recent years of a "post-theoretical turn." Rather than taking Jameson's work as a unified system and a body of claims about the world—in short, as a tool box filled with ingenious devices that one can deploy, and then toss aside when more up-to-date and relevant technology becomes available[30]—I want to suggest that we think it along the lines of a new language: a living and richly dialectical language with its own history and in constant dialogue with and imbibing of other languages surrounding it and the situation to which they all necessarily must respond.

In the process of learning any such new language, we occupy it, become immersed within it, in order to test it out and thereby discover how it enables us to move through the world in a different way. A good deal of our work after coming to occupy such a language lies in "the amount of translation we are able to effect out of the older terminology into the new."[31] Such an operation, what Jameson will later call *transcoding*, in turn produces "the relief of new problems and new interests."[32] Any post-theory would thus be understood as underwritten by its own disavowed theoretical project of rewriting and reinvention and its own exhilaration in the face of the new problems and interests to which it gives rise—as Jameson so effectively demonstrated was the case in the earlier "against theory" theoretical claims of New Historicism.[33] What distinguishes the post-theoretical theoretical turn is not only its directive to stop doing something, again much like earlier polemics against theory, but also its pointed refusal to take the time to learn other languages, or to acknowledge that one is "always already" (*toujours-déjà,* an Althusserian and Derridean concept that Jameson deploys in his work from *The Prison-House of Language* onward)[34] ensconced in a language as such: to paraphrase one of Derrida's most well-known theoretical axioms, *il n'y a pas de hors-théorie,* there is no outside theory, no unmediated access to the real of history. (That such a finally unknowable real exists, and moreover is the material thing that finally constrains and limits—but never determines—the effectivity of our interventions, is the point advanced in one of Jameson's own most familiar axioms, "history is what hurts."[35] In short, there is no outside of history, of context or a situation, either.)

Furthermore, as I will discuss in the second part of this book, the claim to post-theory has reinvigorated the project of theory in some unexpected ways. My book announces its fidelity and contributes to such a project by showing how Jameson's more than five decades of scholarship still offer us as scholars, teachers, and intellectuals an extraordinary model for effectively intervening in our world, a model that unfolds under the creative sign of the science fictional "what if?" rather than the constraints of the naturalist "what is." Ultimately every reader will have to determine for themselves the adequacy and usefulness of such an approach for their own engagements with cultural phenomena, past, present, and future. However, before such a determination can be made, it is crucial that we become fluent in the language under examination, so we don't confuse its specific and situated limitations and failures with our own.

The chapters in this book are divided into three sections. Following the Introduction, the first three chapters offer a decade by decade examination of Jameson's intellectual output from his inaugural book, *Sartre: The Origins of a Style* (1961), through his deeply influential *Postmodernism, or, The Cultural Logic of Late Capitalism,* and on into his groundbreaking work in the early 1990s on what was just then being widely referred to as globalization. The second set of three chapters focuses on some of Jameson's more recent and untimely writings in the context of his ongoing project and in relationship to such central concerns as the place of the event of revolution (and love) in Marxist cultural theory, the situation of academic and intellectual labor in the contemporary moment, and the politics of Utopia in our global situation. Bridging these two sections is an extended discussion of the changing uses by Jameson of one of his most well known intellectual tools, the "semiotic square" developed by Greimas, and the lessons it offers to contemporary critical theory more generally.

As noted earlier, I find in Jameson's work an important alternative method of reading, and in the first part of my introductory chapter I outline some of its major features. I then map the contours of the periodizing approach to Jameson's project that I take up in part I. Jameson suggests that the best textual manifestation we have of a period, dialectically conceived at once in a temporal and spatial manner—the twin slogans of his project being, I argue, the well known "Always historicize!" and the implicit "Always totalize!"—is to be found in what he names the "ideology of form." While much of the discussion of Jameson's writings has centered on their content, far less attention has been paid to their form, or their highly original *Darstellung.* I show that Jameson's thoroughgoing commitment to narrative is further manifest in the profound formal unity of his major books, as each can be understood to tell a story in its own right. However, such a synchronic or total-izing approach to Jameson's work has as its dialectical complement a diachronic perspective, wherein each individual text is understood as one point within another larger narrative sequence. In order to illumi-nate the contours of this sequence, I deploy as my fundamental plot device Jameson's periodizing schema of realism, modernism, and post-modernism. The reading that I offer here thus represents an experiment in intellectual biography, a strategy of narration through which both the developments in Jameson's work and the contexts in which they intervene can be understood in fresh new ways.

The story I have to tell begins in earnest in the first chapter of part I. The conclusions drawn in Jameson's first book, *Sartre: The Origins of a Style*—that modern society is unpropitious for the production of narratives—are reversed a decade later in, and more significantly *by,* the form of his next major intervention, *Marxism and Form.* I argue that *Marxism and Form* can be understood as organized by a "realist" critical aesthetic whose form, as Lukács argues of any realism, is nar-rative rather than descriptive. The plot of *Marxism and Form,* begin-ning with Adorno's dire vision of an administered society and coming to its climax with Sartre's dramatic reinvention of collective political agency in the first volume of *The Critique of Dialectical Reason* (1960), is furthermore rewriteable as a story about the fundamental intellectual and cultural transformations within the United States and the university that occur as we move from the Cold War 1950s to the enthusiasm and Utopian potential of the 1960s; and, within literary studies in particu-lar, the movement beyond the hegemony of the New Critical and "late modernist" formalist orthodoxies into the exuberance of the debates over theory that characterized the 1970s and 1980s.

In chapter 2, I explore the modernist form of Jameson's major inter-vention in the latter debates, *The Political Unconscious,* and the mode of investigation it makes available for contemporary literary and cul-tural criticism. Modernism, Jameson later maintains, must "be seen as uniquely corresponding to an uneven moment of social development," and I argue that within the academic context of *The Political Uncon-scious* we see a similar unevenness, as the then-dominant disciplinary structure confronts the new work advanced under the aegis of theory.[36] Indeed, it is specifically the interdisciplinarity of theory that strikes its readers in this moment with all the shock of the modernist new (as in Ezra Pound's quintessential modernist adage, "make it new"). This "the-oretical modernism" also replays many of the same issues, anxieties, and concerns of high modernism proper, and falls into crisis during the decade that follows the book's publication.

In chapter 3, I maintain that we find in the original formal structure of Jameson's *Postmodernism* a figuration of one of the central dilemmas of the postmodern condition: our inability to tell the stories necessary to position ourselves within emerging global realities. In order to begin to bring into focus such a radically new situation, a new form of presentation is necessary, and Jameson will find the intimations of such a *Darstellung* in Walter Benjamin's neo-Platonist notion of the *constellation,* as well as in its further refinement in the late work of Theodor Adorno, a model Jameson elaborates in the book that serves as *Postmodernism*'s "epistemo-critical" prologue, *Late Marxism: Adorno, or the Persistence of the Dialectic* (1990). *Postmodernism* examines a breathtaking range of different cultural forms and practices, a proliferation of objects that in turn reflects some of Jameson's central claims concerning the nature of postmodernism. However, often overlooked in discussions of Jameson's work at this point is the fact that in both the original 1984 essay and the later book he approaches these diverse cultural "texts" through two distinct optics. First, his engagement is aimed at developing what he calls a "symptomology" of various dimensions of the original experience of the postmodern; and second, he offers us a number of figures of a new "pedagogical political culture"—the narrative aesthetic practice he names *cognitive mapping.* The production of retooled practices of cognitive mapping is imperative, Jameson maintains, for a heretofore unimaginable politics to develop. Any successful cognitive mapping will thus need to shift in spatial scale from the national to the global level, and this shift also marks the opening of an original "period" in Jameson's thinking. This is very much evident in the formal structure of Jameson's two major film studies of the early 1990s, *Signatures of the Visible* (1990) and *The Geopolitical Aesthetic: Cinema and Space in the World System* (1992), wherein we see the effort to coordinate perspectives generated from different places across the globe in order to produce a more integrative narrative, and hence a more totalizing mapping of an emergent present.

This first set of chapters is followed by an extended interlude, wherein I explore the implications for a materialist dialectics of a reading of A. J. Greimas's semiotics, and its "supreme achievement," the semiotic square. I show how the reputedly closed structure of the square opens up when we read it "with" Jacques Lacan's "fundamental classification system" of the three orders of the Symbolic, Imaginary, and Real. Jameson is the best known English-language champion of Greimas's work, and this chapter maps the evolution of Jameson's use of this particular tool from *The Prison-House of Language* up through his most recent writings, arguing for a marked shift in his emphasis from Greimas's "complex" to his "neutral" term, the former corresponding to Lacan's Symbolic and the latter to the void of the real. I illustrate these different deployments through original readings of the plots of nineteenth century British novels by Mary Shelley, Walter Scott, and Jane Austen; the semiotic squares Jameson develops in his discussion of Hayden White's *Metahistory: The Historical Imagination in Nineteenth-Century Europe* (1973) and the popular film *Something Wild* (1986); contemporary theory by two of the most original dialectical thinkers working today, Slavoj Žižek and Michael McKeon; the recent critical and commercial hit film *Slumdog Millionaire* (2008); and finally, briefly, Walter Benjamin's *Ursprung des deutschen Trauerspiels* (*The Origins of German Tragic Drama*) (1928) and, most far-reaching of all, the problematic of Marxism itself.

The opening chapter of part II takes up where the interlude concludes and moves our story into the contemporary moment. Here the structure of my discussion shifts from the narrative and periodizing movements of part I and the interlude to the ways that the tools, commitments, and insights Jameson makes available enable us to intervene in the debates and concerns of the present situation. The first chapter of part II assesses the contributions that Jameson's work makes to the traditions of Marxist cultural studies. I begin by positing a correspondence between the four coordinates of the Marxist problematic outlined at the conclusion of the interlude—what I refer to with the terms *hegemony, reification, the mode of production,* and *the consciousness of the proletariat*—and what Badiou names the four "conditions" of any truth procedure: politics, art, science, and love. After tracing the emergence of these four nodes in Marx's own work, I argue that a Greimasian presentation of the relationships between them highlights the incompleteness of much of the work that today proceeds under the aegis of Marxist cultural criticism. While superb treatments of the first three conditions appear regularly throughout the tradition, including those found in Jameson's work, it is in its fourth condition that Marxist theory encounters its own void of the real, that which at once remains generative and foundational to its entire complex, and yet unnamable within it. What Lukács formulates as "consciousness of the proletariat" is a placeholder for the impossible effort to represent Marxism's *raison d'être,* the revolutionary or evental break with the capitalist mode of production. Thus, the question I confront here is in what ways might a contemporary Marxist cultural criticism similarly "think" from the perspective of the permanent scandal of the consciousness of the proletariat and revolution, Utopia and love or communism? It is here too that Jameson's work offers an invaluable example, as it repeatedly underscores and demonstrates the necessity for cultural criticism to sensitize itself to efforts to figure such an impossible otherness. The formulations he develops of this elusive fourth condition—Utopia, content of the form, cognitive mapping, and neutralization—change at different points in his project, and the rest of the chapter explores the relationships between some of these different presentations. It is only by taking up the challenge represented by this fourth condition, Jameson argues, that "a Marxist cultural study can hope to play its part in political praxis, which remains, of course, what Marxism is all about."[37]

The role of this praxis in interventions in the more local context of the contemporary university is the topic of the next chapter. I begin by looking at the trope of the "unfinished" that appears throughout *Valences of the Dialectic*. There are three different valences of this figure at work in this monumental undertaking. First, Jameson uses it to refer to projects whose realization still remains a task for the future. Secondly, he stresses the necessarily unfinished nature of projects, like the dialectic, whose labors are interminable. And finally, he offers a much darker invocation of the unfinished, as those formations that stand as the last specters haunting the imaginary of a final victory of global neoliberalism and the "end of history" itself. It is this complex dialectical sense of the unfinished that offers some productive ways to think about the university and our work in it as intellectuals, teachers, and activists. Three earlier books by Jameson—*Late Marxism* (1990), *Brecht and Method* (1998), and *A Singular Modernity* (2002)—develop a devastating portrait of current threats to humanist intellectual work, threats that take the form of a dialectic of institutional instrumentalization or corporatization, and a conservative appeal within our disciplines for a "return" to aesthetics, formalism, and disciplinarity. At the same time, these works by Jameson issue a call for a re-imagining of our intellectual and pedagogical practices along the lines of what he describes as Brecht's method. Such innovative intellectual schemas are indispensible, Jameson concludes in *Valences of the Dialectic*, in that in them we find a figuration of collectivity—the central project of what he describes elsewhere as a fourth moment in the ongoing project of theory—whose Utopian energies are much in need today.[38]

My final chapter explores in some detail the intervention that takes place in the climactic volume of *The Poetics of Social Forms,* Jameson's untimely 2005 study *Archaeologies of the Future: The Desire Called Utopia and Other Science Fictions.* In order to begin to sort out the diverse layers of this book, I take a page from its opening section, where Jameson offers a visual mapping of the various levels of the "Utopian allegory, of the investments of the Utopian impulse."[39] Here, Jameson returns to the mechanism of the four-fold medieval hermeneutic that he had first invoked in *Marxism and Form* and which he then develops further in the long opening chapter of *The Political Unconscious.* I show how the intervention of *Archaeologies* unfolds simultaneously on four allegorical levels. First, on the literal level, the book offers an investigation of the formal workings of science fiction, and thus provides us with the tools for rethinking both the modernism of the science fiction form in particular and its historical development more generally. Second, on the allegorical level, the discussion of science fiction becomes a way of exploring some of the dilemmas faced in the construction of any representation of Utopia. Third, on what is called the moral, or today the individual psychological, level, the book can be understood as a major intervention in and further extension of Jameson's ongoing intellectual project—including the completion, with the subsequent publication of the essays collected together in *The Modernist Papers* (2007), of the second half of *The Poetics of Social Forms* and its own internal dialectic. And finally, on the anagogical level, the book contributes to the vitally important work of reinventing the collective project of Marxism so that it might more effectively respond to the "historic originalities" of a post-Cold War "late capitalism." In this way, Jameson puts the question of Utopia back on the table in a moment that seems allergic to such radical totalizing visions.

The book concludes with a glance at what were at the moment of this book's completion, Jameson's two most recent book length studies, *The Hegel Variations* (2010) and *Representing* Capital: *A Reading of Volume One* (2011). Presented as the "completion" of the unfinished project of *Valences of the Dialectic,* these two short volumes, and *Representing* Capital in particular, are, among their other significant interventions, also very much about the problems of narrative closure, and so they offer an appropriate place at which I might conclude my own engagement with Jameson's ongoing project. (In fact, while this book was in production, Jameson published *The Antinomies of Realism* [2013], the third volume of *The Poetics of Social Form.*) The conclusions he draws about Marx's great work—it is "both finished and unfinished all at once. What this means in fact is that we can expect both boundaries and lines of flight simultaneously, climaxes along with unfinished business"—are only made possible by Jameson's unreserved commitment "to be dialectical."[40] Thus, the deepest lesson of these short books, as it is of all of his work, is the continued necessity of and unwavering fidelity to the strenuous labors of dialectical thinking and writing.

Uppsala, Sweden
March 2013

Periodizing Jameson

Introduction: Betraying Jameson

Caveat lector: this book will offer neither a survey of the work of Fredric Jameson "nor even an introduction to it (always supposing such a thing was possible in the first place)."[1] Rather, in the pages that follow, the book's argument unfolds in terms of what Alain Badiou calls a fidelity to the truth of Jameson's project, thinking through and along with his diverse and wide-ranging interventions in order to see what kinds of productive, and even unexpected, insights might emerge.

Any such fidelity is thus paradoxically, Slavoj Žižek argues, a form of betrayal. Žižek notes,

> The true betrayal is an ethico-theoretical act of the highest fidelity: one has to betray the letter of Kant in order to remain faithful to (and repeat) the "spirit" of his thought. It is precisely when one remains faithful to the letter of Kant that one really betrays the core of his thought, the creative impulse underlying it. One should bring this paradox to its conclusion: it is not only that one can remain really faithful to an author by way of betraying him (the actual letter of his thought); at a more radical level, the inverse statement holds even more—one can only truly betray an author by way of repeating him, by remaining faithful to the core of his thought. If one does not repeat an author (in the authentic Kierkegaardian sense of the term), but merely "criticizes" him, moves elsewhere, turns him around, and so forth, this effectively means that one unknowingly remains within his horizon, his conceptual field.[2]

Žižek's concept of repeating, very different from the notion of "return," is crucial as well for his own radical dialectical thought experiment, and I enact in the pages that follow a similar dialectic of fidelity and betrayal in my engagement with Jameson's work.[3]

Žižek's last observation concerning the stance of "criticism" is borne out in a number of assessments of Jameson's contributions, the particular form of ethical engagement they represent being, Clint Burnham suggests, "the dominant mode of literary interpretation in the Anglo-American world, both within theory (which is mostly engaged in a liberal-humanist mode) and outside of it."[4] Such a conventional ethical stance is amply evident in some strands of the recent "New Formalist" reactions against historicism, interdisciplinarity, and theory.[5] The assertion that Jameson's political and historical commitments mean that he is not attentive enough to form leads the critic to "unknowingly remain within his horizon," reinventing Jameson's project in a much-diminished fashion. Such an ethical approach begins by reducing the issue at stake to a zero-sum binary opposition—formalism *or* historicism, space *or* time, totality *or* the particular, Marxism *or* postmodernism, Hegel *or* Spinoza, Adorno *or* Brecht, First World *or* Third World, the global *or* the local, art *or* culture—and then accusing the opponent of falling into error by selecting the wrong (or irresponsible or even evil) option before finally celebrating one's own right (or responsible or good) choice.

The "ethical ideology" that underlies this binary imagination has long been a target of Jameson's critique. In *The Political Unconscious,* he argues,

> the concept of good and evil is a positional one that coincides with categories of Otherness. Evil thus, as Nietzsche taught us, continues to characterize whatever is radically different from me, whatever by virtue of precisely that difference seems to constitute a real and urgent threat to my own existence. . . . these are some of the archetypal figures of the Other, about whom the essential point to be made is no so much that he is feared because he is evil; rather he is evil *because* he is Other, alien, different, strange, unclean, and unfamiliar.[6]

More recently, Jameson emphasizes that "the challenge remains to avoid that ethical binary, which is the root form of all ideology."[7]

It is this ethical binary that Jameson's dialectical approach to cultural phenomena consistently refuses. For example, in the opening of the final chapter of *Postmodernism, or, The Cultural Logic of Late Capitalism* (1991), Jameson points out that some people find his combination of Marxism and postmodernism "peculiar or paradoxical," and, as a result, "conclude that, in my own case, having 'become' a postmodernist I must have ceased to be a Marxist in any meaningful (or in other words, stereotypical) sense." He then goes on to observe:

> It has happened to me before to have been oddly and comically identified with an object of study: a book I published years ago on structuralism [*The Prison-House of Language*] elicited letters, some of which addressed me as a "foremost" spokesperson for structuralism, while the others appealed to me as an "eminent" critic and opponent of that movement. I was really neither of those things, but I have to conclude that I must have been "neither" in some relatively complicated and unusual way that it seemed hard for people to grasp.[8]

Nearly a decade later, in a footnote to *Brecht and Method* (1998), Jameson again refuses the zero-sum ethical option:

> Someone so ill-advised as to have written enthusiastically about both Adorno and Brecht will presumably not be surprised by pressures to choose between them (what they share is evidently a sarcasm, a dialectical cynicism, about the present; what separates them is then the principle of hope). Instead of doing so, however, I recommend Brecht's own version, the parable of Gordian Knot:
>
> > . . . ach der Mann
> > Dessen Hand ihn knüpfte, war
> > Nicht ohne Plan, ihn zu lösen, jedoch
> > Reichte die Zeit seines Lebens, angefüllt
> > Leider nur aus für das eine, das Knüpfen.
> > Eine Sekunde genügte
> > Ihn durchzuhauen.
> > (XIII, 353–54)

> . . . Oh, the man
> Whose hand tied it was not
> Without plans to undo it, but alas
> The span of his life was only long enough
> For the one thing, the tying.
> A second sufficed
> To cut it.
> (*Poems,* 119)[9]

The "relatively complicated and unusual" approach to these problems Jameson refers to above is, of course, his own dialectical thought process, a mode of thinking and writing he has observed that is alien to the institutions we currently inhabit, and better understood as "a speculative account of some thinking of the future which has not yet been realized."[10]

Anyone with even the most passing familiarity with Jameson's project will recognize that this speculative form of thinking and writing involves an immense effort of borrowing from and refunctioning (*Umfunktionierung*) of various aspects of a staggeringly diverse range of theories to generate his highly original and productive uses.[11] Jameson elsewhere names such a practice, following the lead of A. J. Greimas, *transcoding:* "less a question of finding a single system of truth to convert to, than it will of speaking the various theoretical codes experimentally, with a kind of Whorf-Sapir view toward determining what can and cannot be said in each of those theoretical 'private languages'."[12] These labors make Jameson, in Burnham's wonderful phrase, one of the few fully "'dialogic' theorists."[13] Burnham further maintains that Jameson's unique reading strategy involves not ignoring or critically dismissing other approaches to any particular text—and thereby falling into the trap of the ethical criticism I outlined above—but rather making "the sediment of previous readings part of the text, or least to take [them] . . . as starting points for his own interpretation."[14]

In developing his concept of the dialogic theorist, Burnham seems to deploy, without making it explicit, the generative machinery of the Greimasian semiotic square, a device used from the early 1970s on throughout Jameson's work.[15] Burnham's four internal terms—Greimas's S, −S, −S̄, and S̄—are the familiar Bakhtinian ones of "monologism" and "dialogism," and the equally well-known Kuhnian figures of "paradigm shifts" and "normal science."[16] This then generates four possible ways we can characterize the labors of contemporary literary or cultural studies scholars. Burnham maintains that most "high-profile literary theorists," by which he means those who effect Kuhnian paradigm shifts in contemporary cultural scholarship, "tend to produce a monologic discourse; while the work of other theorists is acknowledged, *this is primarily to correct/supplement* that work."[17] Directly opposed to these theorists are the figures Burnham names the "technicians," whose work is "unrelentingly dialogic."[18] Moreover, in a reversal of Kuhn's normative hierarchy, Burnham argues "that it is the work of scholars in the 'normal' teaching and writing about literary theory today that the so-called research of the field takes place."[19] More common are the "'monologic' technicians" who "prove to be quite boring—think of the pedant in your own faculty department for verification of this." Conversely, Burnham concludes, true dialogic theorists are "quite rare, for their allegiance to the methodology of the technicians-proletariat, as it were, almost ensures a marginalization of their work."[20]

In my essay "Lacan avec Greimas: Formalization, Theory, and the 'Other Side' of the Study of Culture," which is a further expansion of the work begun in this book's interlude, I show how the "four discourses" first theorized by Jacques Lacan in his 1969–70 seminar XVII, *The Other Side of Psychoanalysis*—the discourses of the master, the hysteric, the university, and the analyst—can be re-presented through Greimas's semiotic square.[21] A combination of the schema produced in that essay along with the one implicitly generated in Burnham's discussion would appear as in figure 1. All of this suggests an additional potentially productive correspondence between Lacan's discourses and Burnham's figures of the academic worker.

In the concluding section of his essay "Imaginary and Symbolic in Lacan," originally published in *Yale French Studies* in 1977, Jameson too takes up Lacan's four discourses in a manner that exemplifies the dialogic openness characteristic of all of his work. Jameson first suggests "these positions seem to me to have *interesting equivalents* in that other 'unity-of-theory-and-practice' which is Marxism."[22] What occurs here is one of the most characteristic and significant gestures in Jameson's method, one I will also deploy throughout my book: the act of *positing (setzung)* heretofore unexpected "equivalents," "correspondences," "resonances," "likenesses" (or in Jameson's more characteristic litote or double negative form, "not unlike"), "relationships" ("not unrelated"), "coincidences" ("not uncoincidentally"), "similarities," "family likenesses," and "kinships" between otherwise disparate objects, texts, and theories. The positing of these equivalences—not unlike what appears

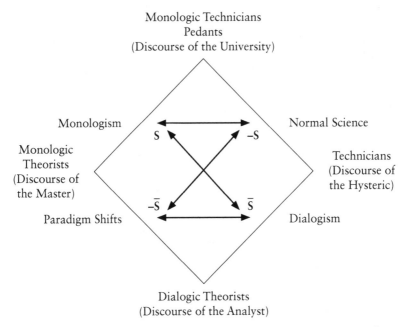

Monologic Technicians
Pedants
(Discourse of the University)

Monologism   Normal Science

Monologic
Theorists   Technicians
(Discourse of   (Discourse of
the Master)   the Hysteric)

Paradigm Shifts   Dialogism

Dialogic Theorists
(Discourse of the Analyst)

Figure 1. Clint Burnham, *The Jamesonian Unconscious: The Aesthetics of Marxist Theory.*

at times to be ungrounded assertions, the "all" statements that are characteristic of Jameson's and all the great theorists' projects (we have encountered a few of these already in the preceding pages)—function as *axioms,* or R. G. Collingwood's "absolute presuppositions," which Jameson suggests cannot "be evaluated or 'proven' or disproven."[23] Louis O. Mink similarly maintains, "Absolute presuppositions, whether taken singly or as belonging to constellations, are not subject to proof or disproof."[24] In one of the key essays that helped prepare the ground for *The Political Unconscious,* Jameson further develops this position in observing (and note again the deployment of the trope of the litote, creating emphasis by "denying the contrary," a dialectical rhetorical figure also central for Thomas More's *Utopia*),[25]

> The dilemma of any "historicism" can then be dramatized by the peculiar, unavoidable, yet seemingly unresolvable alternation between Identity and Difference. This is indeed the first arbitrary decision we are called on to make with respect to any form or object from out of the past, and it is a decision which founds that contact: so that on the one hand, as

with Sartrean freedom, we cannot *not* opt for one or the other of these possibilities (even when for the most part we remain oblivious of a choice made in an unthematized and unreflexive way), while on the other, the decision itself, since it inaugurates the experience, is something like an absolute presupposition that is itself beyond any further philosophical argumentation (thus, we cannot appeal to any empirical findings about the past, since they are themselves grounded on this initial presupposition).[26]

The thematization or self-reflection on these choices is the operation Jameson earlier describes as *metacommentary,* a gesture similarly fundamental for any developing theoretical discourse: "every individual interpretation must include an interpretation of its own existence, must show its own credentials and justify itself."[27] In a manner especially relevant to our discussion here, Jameson writes in *The Prison-House of Language,*

> I believe it is axiomatic that a philosophy which does not include within itself a theory of its own particular situation, which does not make a place for some essential self-consciousness along with the consciousness of the object with which it is concerned, which does not provide for some basic explanation of its own knowledge at the same time that it goes on knowing what it is supposed to know, is bound to end up drawing its own eye without realizing it.[28]

More recently, Jameson has gone further, and suggests that while the Hegelian act of positing (*setzung*) does seem to have some nearness to the notion of presuppositions, as both "somehow always [take] place 'in advance' of other kinds of thinking and other kinds of acts and events," the latter "would seem to anchor us firmly in mental operations and in thinking as such." Thus, Jameson notes,

> rather than thinking in terms of axioms, belief, presuppositions, and other such conceptual ballast, it might be better to try to convey the specificity of positing in terms of theatrical settings or pro-filmic arrangements, in which, ahead of time, a certain number of things are placed on stage, certain depths are calculated, and an optical center also carefully provided, the laws of perspective invoked in order to strengthen the

illusion to be achieved. Even though the suggestion of fic-
tionality and of calculated illusion remains very strong in
this example, it might well help to convey the kind of analysis necessary to explain the effects of a spectacle provided in
advance: how the sets were put together, what the lines of
flight are, the illusion of specific depths, the lighting in fore-
ground and background, etc.[29]

The demonstration of the interest and value of these various positings,
axioms, absolute presuppositions, and existential decisions, and hence
their ultimate evaluation, lies in the new things they enable us to do and
the original insights they make possible. Jameson illustrates this last
point in *The Political Unconscious* when he observes, "Lévi-Strauss's
work suggests that the proposition whereby all cultural artifacts are to
be read as symbolic resolutions of real political and social contradictions deserves serious exploration and systematic experimental verification," something that he goes on to do in the rest of the book.[30]

Moreover, there is another kinship to be drawn between the practices
of positing correspondences and the allegorical hermeneutic that plays
such a significant role in Jameson's critical project from its introduction
in *Marxism and Form* onward. Indeed, immediately following on the
heels of the statement from *The Political Unconscious* I quoted in the
previous paragraph, Jameson further notes, "the most readily accessible
formal articulation of the operations of a political *pensée sauvage* of
this kind will be found in what we will call the structure of a properly
political *allegory*, as it develops from networks of topical allusion in
Spenser or Milton or Swift to the symbolic narratives of class represen-
tatives or 'types' in novels like those of Balzac."[31] Allegorical readings
too are inaugurated by the positing of what may be surprising and unexpected correspondences between different narratives. These are not,
to be sure, arbitrary or willful connections, as the initial act of effect-
ing the movement between the narratives or levels depends upon the
uncovering of a hinge between the two that then triggers the process of
interpretation. For example, in J. Lee Thomson's classic film noir thriller
Cape Fear (1962), it is the iconography of the film's villain, Max Cady
(played with such delirious abandon by Robert Mitchum)—his urban
slang-filled speech, his pork-pie hat, his frequenting of jazz clubs, and
indeed his criminality—that signals the allegorical reflection also taking
place in the film on the racial and sexual dangers unleashed by desegre-
gation.[32] Or as I will show in the interlude, it is the very composition of

the body of the creature in Mary Shelley's *Frankenstein* that indicates the novel's allegorical meditation on the responsibilities of intellectuals in the unstable revolutionary context of early nineteenth century Europe. In James Whale's 1931 film adaptation, itself based on a 1927 stage version of Shelley's novel, the allegorical coding shifts again, as the newly prominent role played by the character of Frankenstein's father helps transform the narrative into another of the myriad efforts in this moment imaginatively to resolve the crisis of the British empire. The aim in any such allegorical interpretation is not to resolve contradictions between the two narrative levels, let alone dissolve one into the other—indeed, the productivity of the encounter is contingent on maintaining their differences.

If the positing of the initial correspondence cannot be proven or disproven, the system of "enunciations" or *proof* that arises from them, its rigor, coherence, thoroughness, and most importantly, usefulness, can be. Ian Stewart notes that within the related context of mathematics, "a proof is a path through the maze, starting from the axioms."[33] Stewart goes further and emphasizes the narrative dimension of any proof:

> The upshot is that a proof, in practice, is a mathematical story with its own narrative flow. It has a beginning, a middle, and an end. It often has subplots, growing out of the main plot, each with its own resolution. The British mathematician Christopher Zeeman once remarked that a theorem is an intellectual resting point. You can stop, get your breath back, and feel you've got somewhere definite. The subplot ties off a loose end in the main story. Proofs resemble narratives in other ways: they often have one or more central characters—ideas rather than people, of course—whose complex interactions lead to the final revelation.[34]

Stewart's observation concerning the narrative dimension of proof also suggests a nearness with dialectics. It is in terms of the story produced, the intellectual resting point or the dialectical pause, Stewart concludes, that a responsible engagement should lie: "A proof is a story told to and dissected by people who have spent much of their life learning how to read such stories and find mistakes or inconsistencies."[35] The same approach should be taken in regard to any allegorical reading, or indeed any theoretical discourse: the responsible reader first needs to identify the absolute presuppositions of the story to be told, and then carefully follow the twists and turns of the plot that arises from them. The simple refusal of these initial starting points as wrong, impossible, or even evil is the kind of failure of imagination that Roland Barthes identifies as the elevation of "one's blindness or dumbness to a universal of perception:" "You don't want to understand the play by Lefebvre the Marxist." However, Barthes then pointedly concludes, "you can be sure that Lefebvre the Marxist understands your incomprehension perfectly well, and above all (for I believe you to be more wily than lacking in culture) the delightfully 'harmless' confession you make of it."[36]

Such an imaginative act of uncovering unexpected correspondences enables Jameson to suggest that the discourse of the master—itself an absolute presupposition for Lacan's late work—finds its equivalence in Marxism in "charismatic authority, and of the historical originality and innovations of key individuals, from Marx himself and Lenin, to Mao Tse-tung and Fidel Castro." The Marxist version of the discourse of the university is on the other hand pedantic in its orientation, concerned as it is first and foremost with "the authority of letter, texts, doctrine: the scholastic weighing and comparing of juridical formulas; the concern with coherency and system; and the punctilious textual distinction between what is orthodox and what is not." The discourse of the hysteric corresponds "to a commitment to existential authenticity;" and in "politics, this stance often corresponds to essentially anarchist positions and to what Lenin uncharitably called 'infantile leftism,' a revolutionary but also existential purism, in which political acts must also—immediately—constitute political expressions, the expressions of the passions of indignation and justice."[37] (In *Valences of the Dialectic,* Jameson similarly notes, "To be sure, the anarchist strain in Marx is not to be underestimated.")[38] Finally, this leaves the Marxist equivalent of the discourse of the analyst, "the subject position that our current political languages seem least qualified to articulate:"

> This is not, unlike the discourse of the master, a position of authority (although those dutifully enumerated as masters above have always possessed extraordinary "analytic" sensitivity to the deepest currents of collective desire, which it was also their task to unbind, to articulate, and to demystify); rather it is a position of articulated receptivity, of deep listening (*L'écoute*), of some attention beyond the self or the ego, but one that may need to use those bracketed personal

functions as instruments for hearing the Other's desire. The active and theoretical passivity, the rigorous and committed self-denial, of this final subject position, which acknowledges collective desire at the same moment that it tracks its spoors and traces, may well have lessons for cultural intellectuals as well as politicians and psychoanalysts.[39]

Another evocation of this deep listening is to be found in the Swedish author Karin Boye's moving dystopian novel *Kallocain* (1940)—a work published only months before Boye, as with Benjamin, committed suicide in her despair over the rising tide of fascism: "I have a definite impression that until that moment I had never in my life listened. What I had called listening before was essentially different from this; then my ears had functioned in their place, my thoughts in theirs, my memory registered all in detail, and still my interest had been somewhere else, I don't know where. Now I was conscious of nothing except what she was telling me. I was absorbed in it; I *was* Linda."[40] Deep listening is, I have argued elsewhere, also the stance of Hegel, whom Alexandre Kojève describes as the first of the "auditor-historian-philosophers," or at least, "the first to be so consciously."[41] These lessons from Hegel, as with so many others, are ones that Jameson has taken to heart, and this stance of "deep listening" has been characteristic of his diverse contributions to the collective project not only of Marxism but critical and cultural theory more generally.

Ian Buchanan points out that in regard to post-1945 theory, "Perhaps uniquely, Jameson is at once historian, critic, and contributor to this movement."[42] In his Introduction to *Postmodernism,* Jameson writes, "Theory—I here prefer the more cumbersome formula 'theoretical discourse'—has seemed unique, if not privileged, among the postmodern arts and genres in its occasional capacity to defy the gravity of the zeitgeist and to produce schools, movements, and even avant-gardes where they are no longer supposed to exist."[43] Jameson defines "theoretical discourse" in his two-volume collection of essays, *The Ideologies of Theory* (1988), "as a historical form of language production in its own right, a discursive phenomenon or genre developed in the last few decades, with only the most distant structural affinities to apparently related forms of writing associated with traditional philosophy or other disciplines."[44] The shift to such a post-disciplinary form of language production occurs in the period of the 1960s:

> The "discovery" of the Symbolic, the development of its linguistic-related thematics (as, e.g., in the notion of understanding as an essentially synchronic process, which influences the construction of relatively ahistorical "structures," such as the Althusserian one described above), is now to be correlated with a modification of the practice of the symbolic, of language itself in the "structuralist" tests, henceforth characterized as "theory," rather than work in a particular traditional discipline.[45]

Of this new form of language production, Steven Helmling, in his discussion of the dialectic of "success and failure" in Jameson's project, dramatically claims "that more exhilarating, not to say 'sublime,' effect of large powers dilating to the largest scope they can encompass belongs almost entirely to figures like Jameson and Derrida, who enact it far more impressively than any contemporary poet, novelist, painter, sculptor, filmmaker or musician I can think of."[46]

What both Jameson and Helmling bear out is the fact that theory represents what I refer to in part II as an "untimely modernism." The concept of the untimely is taken from Friedrich Nietzsche, who with it underscores the aims of his corrosive challenge to the reigning presuppositions of his moment: "acting counter to our time and thereby acting on our time and, let us hope, for the benefit of a time to come."[47] With this term, I mean to underscore the "uneven" persistence in theory of modernism's global projects of social and cultural transformation (make it new, revolution of the word, the New Man and the New Woman) into the very different context of postmodernism.[48] Jameson offers the ground for such an approach when, in the Introduction to *Postmodernism,* he argues that if we follow the lead of his student Michael Speaks and hold that "there is no pure postmodernism as such, then the residual traces of modernism must be seen in another light, less as anachronisms than as necessary failures that inscribe the particular postmodern project back into its context, while at the same time reopening the question of the modern itself for reexamination."[49]

In chapter 2, I argue that modernism appears in an indirect fashion in Jameson's major work in the 1970s and 80s, and something similar could be said of my book as a whole: among its other interventions then, I imagine it as also a contribution to and engagement with the work being done under the aegis of the new modernist studies.[50] Moreover, given that the untimely experimental interdisciplinary project of theory has always represented a fundamental challenge not only to how we do our work but to the institutions in which such labors take place, such an approach also offers an avenue by which we might assess the potentials of and challenges for innovative and committed humanist intellectual work, what Helmling characterized in the passage I cited above as "dilating to the largest scope they can encompass," in a contemporary American university experiencing dramatic and unprecedented change and conservative retrenchments of various sorts.

The first part of this book undertakes another borrowing from Jameson's project. In the opening line of *The Political Unconscious,* Jameson presents to his readers what he describes as the "moral" of the book, and, as many would no doubt concur, of all his work: "Always historicize!"[51] However, to this "one absolute and we may even say 'transhistorical' imperative of all dialectical thought" we need to add another: "Always totalize!" Burnham notes, "For Jameson, the world's postmodern fragmentation demands a totalizing response and virtually posits that totality in its nexus of fragments."[52] The *practice* of totalizing—not to be confused, as Jameson himself tirelessly points out, with the totality itself—is a synthetic and narrative one. Jameson later suggests that the process of totalization "often means little more than the making of connections between various phenomena, a process which . . . tends to be ever more spatial."[53] The effect is, as Evan Watkins contends, not "toward some larger overarching pattern, but rather around the mazy web of effects made visible from the proliferation of contacts emerging at every turn of the argument"—that is, to use another figure that has become prominent in our digital era, to produce networks or constellations of cultural phenomena.[54] It is thus this double optic, at once historical and spatial, diachronic and synchronic, subjective and objective, that, as Jameson already argues in *Marxism and Form,* marks the originality of Marxism in particular, and of dialectic thought more generally, and which, as he shows in *The Prison-House of Language,* distinguishes this practice from the then dominant formalisms and structuralisms.

Such a double perspective moves us in *The Political Unconscious* into an exploration of "cultural periodization" as another fundamental dialectical paradox: an attempt to think the open-ended process of history through the synchronic or spatial concept of totality. Discussions of periodization, Jameson goes on to argue, ultimately unfold into larger questions about the nature of the "representation of History itself." And we are always ultimately dealing with representations, the thing itself is unknowable: "history—Althusser's 'absent cause,' Lacan's

'Real,' " Jameson maintains in *The Political Unconscious* in one of his other absolute presuppositions (and which could also be understood as a before-the-fact reply to the New Historicism), "is *not* a text, for it is fundamentally non-narrative and nonrepresentational; what can be added, however, is the proviso that history is inaccessible to us except in textual form, or in other words, that it can be approached only by way of prior (re)textualization."[55] Moreover, prefiguring the later biopolitical and affective turn in theory, Jameson notes a few pages later that we also encounter the history-thing on a somatic, corporeal level: "History is what hurts, it is what refuses desire and sets inexorable limits to individual as well as collective praxis, which its 'ruses' turn into grisly and ironic reversals of their own intentions." He then concludes, "But this History can be apprehended only through its effects, and never directly as some reified force. This is indeed the ultimate sense in which History as ground and untranscendable horizon needs no particular theoretical justification: we may be sure that its alienating necessities will not forget us, however much we might prefer to ignore them."[56]

Not unexpectedly then, these questions of representation can be understood to have a synchronic and diachronic dimension, concerned, respectively, with the composition of any particular period, and the unfolding of the "succession" of these variously constituted periods through time.[57] In terms of the former, one of the fundamental misunderstandings concerning a periodizing *Darstellung,* Jameson later argues, is that it "implies some massive homogeneity about a given period."[58] Rather, he maintains that any period logic be thought of as a cultural "*dominant,*" a conception, not unlike Raymond Williams's reformulation of the classical Marxist metaphor of the base and superstructure (the latter about which Jameson has further interesting things to say in *Valences of the Dialectic*), "which allows for the presence and coexistence of a range of very different, yet subordinate features," and which in turn stresses the particular class and group interests served by the ideologies of this dominant, as it engages in a continuous struggle with and attempts to assert its hegemony over "other resistant and heterogeneous forces."[59]

This constitutive unevenness of any cultural period is also a key feature of the second dimension of Jameson's model, the placement of every period within a larger historical or diachronic sequence: the "survivals from older modes of cultural production," the "anticipatory" traces of those which have "not-yet" emerged into the light of historical day, and the diverse articulations of the dominant all jostling up against one another in a particular configuration of relationships, a well-nigh permanent "cultural revolution," that defines the complex and continuously shifting identity of any cultural moment.[60] It is this very complexity that thwarts any reductive typologizing operation imagined to accompany a periodizing approach to cultural production.

Jameson takes up the question of periodization once again in *A Singular Modernity: Essay on the Ontology of the Present* (2002), the opening section of the fourth volume of the projected six-volumes of *The Poetics of Social Forms*. Jameson acknowledges that periodization is, for contemporary sensibilities at least, an act that is "intolerable and unacceptable in its very nature, for it attempts to take a point of view on individual events which is well beyond the observational capacities of any individual, and to unify, both horizontally and vertically, hosts of realities whose interrelationships must remain inaccessible and unverifiable."[61] Nevertheless, he maintains, "We cannot not periodize:" these forms are as "inevitable" as they are unacceptable, a quintessential part of our modernity. On this basis, Jameson elaborates what he calls the "four maxims" for any discussion of the concept of modernity:

1. One cannot not periodize.

2. Modernity is not a concept but rather a narrative category.

3. The one way not to narrate it is via subjectivity (thesis: subjectivity is unrepresentable). Only situations of modernity can be narrated.

4. No "theory" of modernity makes sense today unless it comes to terms with the hypothesis of a postmodern break with the modern.[62]

These maxims also serve as the fundamental axioms or absolute presuppositions of all periodizing narratives, including the one I elaborate in the following pages, with the particular concept of "modernity" above replaced in each case with that of the "period." (A period is not a concept but rather a narrative category; no "theory" of a period makes sense unless it comes to terms with the hypothesis of a break.)

Jameson also sketches out a number of corollaries to these axioms. First, any "periodization necessarily constructs a frame around itself, and builds on the basis of a subtle interplay between two forms of negation, the contrary and the contradictory, between differentiation and outright opposition, between the locally distinguished and the absolute negation, antagonistic and non-antagonistic, the non- and the anti-."[63] Second, whereas the focus on seamless historical change "slowly turns into a consciousness of a radical break . . . the enforced attention to a break gradually turns the latter into a period in its own right."[64] Finally, "each break officially posited seems to bring a flurry of new ones in its wake."[65]

Already in *The Political Unconscious,* Jameson suggests that the best textual manifestation we have of a period, dialectically conceived in this temporal and spatial manner, is to be found in what he names the *ideology of form:* "the determinate contradictions of the specific messages emitted by the varied sign systems which coexist in a given artistic process as well as in its general social formation . . . formal processes as sedimented content in their own right, as carrying ideological messages of their own, distinct from the ostensible or manifest content of the works."[66] In his more recent book *The Modernist Papers* (2007), Jameson further develops this insight, calling for a critical method that is at once sensitive to the "form of the content"—social representations that "can be said to encompass everything called ideology in the most comprehensive acceptation of the word"—and the "content of the form"—"the only productive coordination of the opposition between form and content that does not seek to reduce one term to the other, or to posit illicit syntheses and equally illicit volatilizations of an opposition whose tensions need to be preserved."[67]

While much of the discussion of Jameson's own work has centered on the various "ostensible or manifest content" of his texts, less attention has been paid to the question of their form. Indeed, when the issue of form is raised at all it is more often than not to decry the "difficulty," "denseness," or even "obscurity" of his prose. The defense in turn focuses upon the specific form of thinking that occurs in the production, or writing, of dialectical *sentences:* as Helmling puts it in the conclusion of his illuminating meditation on the Jamesonian sentence,

> Jameson dramatizes his own project, testing, trying, interrogating the very possibility of critique in the sentence-by-sentence activity of (his) writing it and (our) reading it—a resourceful, ingenious, continuously surprising proof or probe of the chances of critical ("dialectical") thinking itself, in a writing whose improbable (impossible?) success is to make of its own failure the most trenchant possible critique of culture.[68]

Here Helmling follows Jameson's lead in *Marxism and Form,* where he writes, "For insofar as dialectical thinking is thought about thought,

thought to the second power, concrete thought about an object, which at the same time remains aware of its own intellectual operations in the very act of thinking, such self-consciousness must be inscribed in the sentence itself."[69]

Dialectical thinking and writing—not only in the unfolding of the sentence but in the movement between sentences and paragraphs and in the incorporative sweep of the argument as a whole—are inseparable.[70] Writing thus here needs to be understood in an expanded Derridean sense, as an inscriptional coding at once prior to and inclusive of speech; in this way, Jameson emphasizes the thoroughgoing materiality of all dialectical thinking, its narrative structure as it unfolds through time, and its totalizing sweep as its hammers together unanticipated relationships between its various moments. In a classical dialectical reversal, the demand for clarity and simplicity in prose is then unmasked as thoroughly ideological, and difficulty and density posited as "a conduct of intransigence," "the price . . . to pay for genuine thinking," and even the potential source of a "purely formal pleasure."[71] Jameson later maintains that in this way dialectical thought/writing is always to be conceived of as an experiment in presentation, "a thought mode of the future."[72]

While such attention to the structure and movement of the individual sentences—that is, to Jameson's *style*—illuminates central dimensions of his intellectual project, as well as its place within a larger tradition of dialectical thinking, it risks occluding another level of formal organization and experimentation to be found in Jameson's texts. In *Valences of the Dialectic*, Jameson observes a fundamental "incommensurability of plot and style in the novel, in which neither the macro-level of the narrative nor the micro-level of the language can be reduced to the other." "This kind of dialectic," he further points out, "is therefore not so much dualistic as it is revelatory of some ontological rift or gap in the world itself, or, in other words, of incommensurables in Being itself."[73] The goal of dialectical thinking and writing is not to "resolve" this contradiction, as some more mechanical or clichéd versions would have it, Hegel himself already decrying in the Preface to the *Phenomenology of Spirit* the degraded "lifeless schema" of the Fichtean thesis-antithesis-synthesis dialectic that he never advocates.[74] Rather, "the very vocation of the dialectic"—and the concept of the *vocation* of thought and writing is also an important one throughout Jameson's work—is "to hold two distinct dynamics, two distinct systems of law or well-nigh scientific regularities, together within the unity of a single thought."[75] In order to engage in such a dialectical reading of Jameson's own project, I want to bring attention to his plots, or "the macro-level of narrative" evident within and between each of his particular books.

In his Foreword to Jean-François Lyotard's *The Postmodern Condition*, Jameson notes that the "insistence on *narrative analysis* in a situation in which the narratives themselves henceforth seem impossible is [a] declaration of intent to remain political and contestatory." Narrative, he stresses, is a fundamental part of any Marxist scholarship and politics, because "on the political and social level, indeed, narrative in some sense always meant the negation of capitalism."[76] Such a contestation becomes increasingly significant, he will later suggest, precisely in a cultural situation, such as our own, increasingly dominated by the image, the visual, and a retreat to the aesthetic.[77] (At the same time, Jameson remains one of the most significant champions of the spatialized or visual form of thinking represented by structuralism more generally and Greimas's semiotics in particular, an issue I will take up in some detail in the middle section of this book). Jameson's own thorough-going commitment to narrative is also manifest in the profound formal unity of his major books, as each can be understood to form a coherent narrative in its own right—they can, or perhaps we should say they should, be read as comprising something like theoretical novels.

However, such a synchronic or totalizing approach to each of Jameson's books, stressing the connections between what often appear as the discreet elements (essays and chapters), has as its dialectical complement a diachronic perspective, wherein each individual text is understood as one moment within a larger periodizing sequence. This sequence is in fact Jameson's own well-known one of realism, modernism, and postmodernism, and in the first section of this book I use this sequence as a way of reading the transformations that take place in the first four decades of Jameson's intellectual career.

Jameson suggests the basis for such an approach in his first book dedicated to film, *Signatures of the Visible* (1990). A similar dialectic of synchrony and diachrony, of totalization and historicization, is to be found at work in the form of this book. The various essays collected in part I, all published previously, represent, when considered together, an initial experiment in a new kind of mapping of capitalism's world system; whereas the long original essay "The Existence of Italy," comprising part II, offers what Jameson himself describes as "the most sustained rehearsal of the dialectic of realism, modernism and postmodernism that I have so far attempted, and which I have hitherto misrepresented by staging one or the other in isolation."[78]

In "The Existence of Italy," Jameson deploys this tripartite schema as a means of thinking about the transformations that occur within the particular and foreshortened history of sound film, "the 'realisms' of the Hollywood period, the high modernisms of the great *auteurs,* the innovations of the 1960s and their sequels."[79] If the historical narrative of sound film can be shown to replicate the tripartite sequence "at a more compressed tempo," then, Jameson argues, a similar proposition

> could also be argued for other semi-autonomous sequences of cultural history such as American Black literature, where Richard Wright, Ralph Ellison, and Ishmael Reed can be taken as emblematic markers; or for the history of rock, where the social moment of Elvis or rhythm-and-blues—and behind that, Black music—unpredictably develops into the "high modernisms" of the Beatles and the Stones, and thereafter into rock postmodernisms of the most appropriately bewildering kinds.[80]

In order for these "recapitulations" not to seem "paradoxical or willful," we must introduce into the schema the issue of *scale:* from the most abstract economic perspective, each of these three stages corresponds to "structural stages" within the historical development of the capitalist mode of production; while "in social terms, the moment of realism can be grasped rather differently as the conquest of a kind of cultural, ideological, and narrative literacy by a new class or group; in that case, there will be formal analogies between such moments, even though they are chronologically distant from each other."[81] Moreover, such transformations in the formal practices of any particular social group are to be understood not simply as a matter of individual will, but rather as concrete responses, symbolic actions, to the particular historical situations in which these groups are located. A periodizing narration of these microchronologies is thus also a powerful means of bringing into focus the contours of much larger cultural and social histories.

I explore this proposition on another even more finely tuned scalar level, that of Jameson's intellectual project. I read the "ideology of the form" of the major statements produced at the end of each of the first three decades of his career—*Marxism and Form* (1971), *The Political Unconscious* (1981), and *Postmodernism* (1991)—as embodiments, respectively, of a realist, modernist, and postmodernist critical aesthetic.[82]

I use Jameson's own descriptions of these practices as instructions to the reader on how to grasp the formal structure and unity of his major texts. These descriptions thereby function in a way akin to what Jameson describes as the "literary institutions" of genres:

> social contracts between a writer and a specific public, whose function is to specify the proper use of a particular cultural artifact. . . . In the mediated situation of a more complicated social life—and the emergence of writing has often been taken as paradigmatic of such situations—perceptual signals must be replaced by conventions if the text in question is not to be abandoned to a drifting multiplicity of uses (as *meanings* must, according to Wittgenstein, be described).[83]

Jameson goes on to point out that as any particular text becomes more distant from its "immediate performance situation," the context in which it initially intervenes, "it becomes ever more difficult to enforce a given generic rule on their readers. No small part of the art of writing, indeed, is absorbed by this (impossible) attempt to devise a foolproof mechanism for the automatic exclusion of undesirable responses to a given literary utterance."[84] In my discussion, I would like to help restore something of this context, and thereby enable later readers to encounter anew these "always-already-read" texts—"we apprehend them through sedimented layers of previous interpretations"—with the freshness and drama that was the experience of many of their first readers.[85]

The publication of each of these works occurs exactly one decade after its predecessor, and much of Jameson's work in the period between them takes the form of a working through and trial run of the ideas and strategies presented in these major texts. From this perspective, for example, we can read the essays collected in the original two volumes of *The Ideologies of Theory* as bringing together some of the most significant preparatory material for both *The Political Unconscious* and *Postmodernism*. By this, I do not mean to offer any neat categorization of every work of Jameson. Indeed, as Michael Hardt and Kathi Weeks point out, there is a "rare combination of continuity and openness to change" in Jameson's intellectual project, such that a number of the concepts and problematics "we associate with a later stage of Jameson's work, such as cognitive mapping, [were] already present in embryo decades earlier."[86] I very much concur with this insight, and offer a good deal of evidence of it in the pages that follow. However, one of the payoffs of such a dialectical periodizing modeling of Jameson's intellectual project is that it enables us to make connections between diverse texts and recognize different manifestations of central concepts in ways that might not have been evident earlier. Moreover, such an approach will ultimately enable me to extend the discussion further, and uncover in Jameson's work following the publication of *Postmodernism* the intimations of a "fourth" period beginning in the 1990s, wherein we see the outline of a formal narrative strategy appropriate to grapple with the cultural logics of post–Cold War globalization—what in the same moment Giovanni Arrighi theorizes as a new phase in the history of finance capitalism, and Hardt and Antonio Negri more dramatically see as witnessing the shift from imperialism to both the global logics of empire and the new forms of resistance they name the multitude.[87]

The reading that I offer here is thus very much intended as an experiment in intellectual biography, a strategy of narrative presentation (*Darstellung*) through which the history of Jameson's writings "can be clarified, or at least usefully estranged."[88] Finally, however, I also want to return to his insights about the relationship between transformations that occur in the microchronologies of various cultural practices and the histories of the social groups or publics who make up their producers and consumers. It will be my contention here that a reading of Jameson's unique intellectual project that takes up the twinned dialectical imperatives "always historicize" and "always totalize" can at the same time offer us new ways of representing changes that occur in the intellectual and institutional contexts in which Jameson himself operates. The story I offer is thus also very much that of the adventures of both the new thing called theory that emerges during the course of these decades, and the intellectual public for which theory stands as a premier cultural achievement, a public whom Helmling aptly characterizes as composed of "the sort of intellectually ambitious reader who sought out Joyce or Goethe in their day . . . the sort of reader who today will find the challenges of Derrida or Jameson more demanding, the difficulties more difficult in pertinent 'contemporary' ways, the rewards proportionally more complicatedly satisfying."[89] My book is thus also meant as a challenge to the premature claims of the "death of theory" and the institutional and disciplinary retrenchments that invariably follow upon the heels of such claims.

However, at this point, we are still at the other end of the story, and in the next chapter I want to begin by telling a tale about theory's rise to prominence and its profound effects on the institutions we inhabit— a tale, needless to say at this point, in which Jameson's work plays a vital role.

PART I

Mediations; or, The Triumph of Theory

CHAPTER 1

The Return of Narrative (1960s)

Jameson opens his professional intellectual career and the decade of the 1960s with the publication of *Sartre: The Origins of a Style* (1961), a revision of the dissertation he completed while a doctoral student at Yale University. In this first book, Jameson inaugurates an engagement with a group of twentieth century intellectuals that will continue into his most recent publications. As the book's title suggests, the literary writings of Jean-Paul Sartre are the most central concern here, making this the first of the four book length studies he has published to date on the writings of an individual intellectual, the other three being focused on Wyndham Lewis, Theodor Adorno, and Bertolt Brecht.[1] However, in the original Foreword to *Sartre*, Jameson also notes "the thinking of this book owes a heavy debt to the works of Theodor W. Adorno and Roland Barthes," a fact he feels it necessary to point out because in the U.S. at this time "for want of translation their books are little known"—a situation Jameson's work will play no small part in changing.[2] This initial group of touchstone figures will expand throughout the next decade to also include, most significantly, the "Western Marxist" dialectical thinkers, Walter Benjamin, Ernst Bloch, Herbert Marcuse, and Georg Lukács, followed shortly by the Russian Formalists and French Structuralists. Jameson notes in a more recent interview that in the English-language context, he "was probably the first to write on Adorno, on Bloch, maybe even Benjamin, and on Sartre's critique. That's a service that I'm still rather proud of."[3] The influence of these early interventions is borne out by Martin Jay, who observes, "If the moment when Adorno's work became more than merely an enticing rumor for the American New Left could be dated, it would probably be 1967 with the publication of an essay entitled 'Adorno: or, Historical Tropes' by the Marxist literary critic Fredric Jameson in the journal *Salmagundi*."[4]

In an Afterword appended to the republication of *Sartre* in 1984—the same year as the appearance in *New Left Review* of perhaps Jameson's most well-known essay, "Postmodernism, or, The Cultural Logic of Late Capitalism"—Jameson notes that "the basic proposition of this study turned around the question of narrative, or more exactly, around the relationship between narrative and narrative closure, the possibility of storytelling, and the kinds of experience—social and existential—structurally available in a given social formation."[5] The conclusion he draws through his early engagement with Sartre's work is that modern society is unpropitious for the production of narratives, and it is for this reason that he opens the book with a discussion of Sartre's most well-known play, *No Exit*: this play "reflects the condition of a society without a visible future, a society dazzled by the massive permanence of its own institutions in which no change seems possible and the idea of progress is dead."[6]

As a kind of compensation for this dual closure of history and narrative, Sartre stages events on the level of form itself: "Each of these sentences is a complete event; the past definite hermetically closes off each of the verbs."[7] It is these formal efforts that then connect Sartre and his contemporaries to an earlier high modernism: "Sartre's works face the same situation, the same cluster of aesthetic problems, that the older generation of moderns attempted to solve in a different way: the place of chance and facticity in the work of art, the collapse of a single literary language, a period style, the expression of a relatively homogenous class, into a host of private styles and isolated points in a fragmented society."[8] The difference for Sartre's generation is that they have the additional burden of coming to grips with the achievements, and failures, of their predecessors: "The very existence of such a generation, with the multiplicity of new roads traced, the apparent exhaustion of the possibilities of direct experimentation, constituted a new situation for the writers following it: a situation to which many of Sartre's contemporaries responded with an attempt to revive archaic forms."[9] However, this is a project that in the present seems doomed to failure. For Sartre's "literature of consciousness" is the subjective inversion to a naturalism obsessed with the objective description of the world. Both practices bookend the moment of modernism proper; and like modernism, neither the extreme literatures of naturalism nor of consciousness find themselves capable of healing the fundamental divisions that mark the situation of the modern world that gave rise to such a "crisis of narratable experience" in the first place.[10]

While this is a fundamental characteristic of the situation that Jameson four decades later in *A Singular Modernity* will refer to as "late modernism," this first effort, a form of the Sartrean original choice of being that he discusses in these pages, will mark in a profound way all of his later work. Already, for example, we see a depth of attention to what he more recently characterizes as the content of the form, down to the most micrological dimension of punctuation:

> The colon permits not an abstract description of the process of seeing something and then realizing what it is, a description that would use weak and faded words like "realize" and "it occurred to him suddenly," but a concrete presentation of the event in which we participate ourselves. We are suddenly lifted out of the realistic world of the rest of the novel, lifted higher and higher into fantasy the length of the whole sentence, until suddenly the single withheld word is released and the world immediately settles back to normal again.[11]

Moreover, even at this early juncture, amply on display is Jameson's synthetic totalizing approach to any cultural text: "It is obvious that the literary results we have been considering in these pages would not take place and would not even be possible in every kind of work, in every kind of style: they are not 'techniques' but parts of an indivisible whole, the language reflecting the themes, which are in turn materializations of what is already in the language itself."[12]

If *Sartre* sets into place a number of the concerns and strategies that we will see deployed throughout Jameson's project, the conclusions rendered here on the contemporary world will be reversed in dramatic fashion in his next book, published exactly a decade later, *Marxism and Form: Twentieth-Century Dialectical Theories of Literature* (1971). What Jameson means by narrative at this juncture becomes most explicit in *Marxism and Form*'s key chapter on the writings of Lukács. The emblematic opposition for Lukács—one of the most ill-treated and misunderstood of the major twentieth century left intellectuals, and a figure Jameson tirelessly champions up to the present—lies between the work of Honoré de Balzac and Emile Zola, between the full flourishing of European bourgeois realism and the increasingly constricting and fragmented vision of naturalism, and most importantly, between what Lukács describes as *narration* and description. "Realism itself," Jameson notes, "comes to be distinguished by its movement, its storytelling and dramatization of its content."[13] Thus, while the photographic precision and positivistic attention to detail would seem at first glance to make Zola's work superior to that of his precursor (and indeed, this is the conclusion drawn by one of Jameson's teachers at Yale, Erich Auerbach, in the latter's magisterial *Mimesis: The Representation of Reality in Western Literature* [1953]), a closer examination reveals that Zola

> has succumbed to the temptation of abstract thought, to the mirage of some static, objective knowledge of society. Implicitly he has admitted the superiority of positivism and science over mere imagination. But from Lukács' point of view, for which narration is the basic category and abstract knowledge a second best only, this means that the novel in Zola's hands has ceased to become the privileged instrument of the analysis of reality and has been degraded to a mere illustration of a thesis.

In contrast, "Balzac does not really know what he will find beforehand."[14] This means the very process of the unfolding of narration is, in Balzac's deployment, one of discovery, a means of constructing a fresh and estranging vision of figures both characteristic of a given period and always in the process of change.

In such a reading, realist narration becomes something akin to the dialectical process orientation evident in Hegel's *Phenomenology of Spirit,* where the central protagonist of *Geist* can never really know its destination until it has laboriously ascended each of the steps of the dialectical ladder: "consciousness must work its way through a long road. . . . one must endure the length of this road, since every moment is necessary."[15] Moreover, in this very process comes the possibility of a confrontation with a totality unavailable to the schematizing, dissecting social vision of the naturalist writer: for while the totality is never available for depiction or description, an effective figuration of its contours and lines of force and conflict can be called into life through the process of narration. Realist representation then is not a mimetic correspondence of individual characters and "fixed, stable components of the external world . . . but rather, an analogy between the entire plot, as a conflict of forces, and the total moment of history itself considered as a process."[16] If we already see at work here both dimensions of Jameson's version of the dialectic—an awareness of historical process (Always historicize!) and an emphasis on the relationship between elements of the social totality (Always totalize!)—it is because the "closed realm of literature, the experimental or laboratory situation which it constitutes, with its characteristic problems of form and content, and of the relationship of superstructure to infrastructure, offers a microcosm in which to observe dialectical thinking at work."[17]

The different strategies deployed by the emblematic figures of Balzac and Zola, narration and description, are not the result of simple choice. Rather, each represents concrete responses to the very different situations in which each is located: "if it is the material substructure, the social situation that takes precedence over mere opinion, ideology, the subjective picture someone has of himself, then we may be forced to conclude that under certain circumstances a conservative, a royalist, a believing Catholic can better seize the genuine forces at work in society than a writer whose sympathies are relatively socialistic."[18] Ironically, it is this insight that Lukács himself seems to have forgotten in his scathing assault on the various practices of modernism.[19] Jameson thus concludes that "realism," or authentic narrative itself, "is dependent on the possibility of access to the forces of change in a given moment of history."[20]

Various aspects of this description of the formal strategies of the realist narrative can be applied in some very productive ways to a reading of *Marxism and Form* itself. In his Preface to the book, Jameson begins by noting the fundamental differences between what he attempts to do here and more familiar approaches to this material:

> At the same time, if the chapters that follow do not present any of the rigor of technical philosophical investigation, their status as language remains ambiguous: for they are also far from being simplified introductory sketches, or journalistic surveys of the various positions and key ideas of a writer, anecdotal narratives of his situation and his relationship to the problems of his time. Not that these things are uninteresting or without their usefulness; but from my point of view, they remain on the level of sheer *opinion* only, which is to say of intellectual attitudes seized from the outside. I have felt the

> dialectical method can be acquired only by a concrete work-
> ing through of detail, by a sympathetic internal experience
> of the gradual construction of a system according to its inner
> necessity.[21]

There is a kinship between the central emphasis of this passage and the descriptions of the realist narrative offered in the Lukács chapter. The positivistic assumptions at the basis of the "introductory sketch," "jour-nalistic survey," and "anecdotal narrative" make them formal kin to a naturalist representation (and indeed, these approaches to the history of ideas emerge in the very moment of naturalism) as they attempt to grasp the raw material from an "outside" systematizing perspective. A productive comparison might be generated here with the narrative strat-egies deployed in two of the other major surveys of this material, Perry Anderson's *Considerations on Western Marxism* (1976) and Martin Jay's *Marxism and Totality: The Adventures of a Concept from Lukács to Habermas* (1984), both of which offer more accessible "introductions" to the work of these thinkers than Jameson's book. What distinguishes *Marxism and Form* from these other approaches is "its movement, its storytelling and dramatization of its content," the way it meticulously works through its various objects, constructing its totality according to the logic of the raw material itself. Eschewing both the confident sweeping survey and abstract conceptual generalizations of Anderson, or the chronological sequence of Jay—indeed, in Jameson's story, the work of the brash younger scholar (T. W. Adorno) precedes that of his seniors (Ernst Bloch and Lukács)—the chapters of *Marxism and Form* are ordered like those in a realist novel, each figure appearing on stage when, and only when, necessitated by the development of the work's plot. Crucially then, one can say that Jameson, in this book, "does not really know what he will find beforehand," and only discovers his object as its story unfolds.

The plot of *Marxism and Form* is a rich and exhilarating one. We be-gin the narrative with the version of the dialectic criticism developed by Adorno. Jameson's central object here is Adorno's *Philosophy of Mod-ern Music,* a text he will later describe as belonging to the "exceedingly rare" genre of the "dialectical history." The central narrative feature shared by the three works he claims make up this genre—the others being Roland Barthes's *Writing Degree Zero* and Manfredo Tafuri's *Ar-chitecture and Ideology*—"is the sense of Necessity, of necessary failure, of closure, of ultimate unresolvable contradictions and the impossibility of the future, which cannot have failed to oppress any reader of these texts."[22] Adorno's vision is thus one of a complete domination of the subject, individual or collective, by the object, the global system of contemporary capitalist society: "the total organization of the economy ends up alienating the very language and thoughts of its human population, and by dispelling the last remnant of the older autonomous subject or ego."[23] The structure of the modern musical form, as much as that of Adorno's own dialectical history, mirrors back to the listener or reader the terrible closure of this emergent reality: "the total organizational principle of Schoenberg's system reflects a new systematization of the world itself, of which the so-called totalitarian political regimes are themselves only a symptom."[24] The latter referent should remind us that the situation in which Adorno writes is that of the darkest moments of the Cold War, when a possible nightmarish climax to human destiny then only recently illuminated by Auschwitz and the nuclear terror appeared as a real possibility, if not indeed an inevitability.

Such narratives of the "fall" require an earlier idealized moment against which the present can be judged, and, for Adorno, the time of Beethoven serves this figural role, a period when the revolutionary dissolution of the older feudal order was reaching its crescendo. Hegel's formulation of the modern dialectic also occurs in this situation. At this point, Jameson advances a conclusion whose significance in terms of the structure of his own narrative will soon become evident: "Historical freedom, indeed, expanding and contracting as it does with the objective conditions themselves, never seems greater than in such transitional periods, where the life-style has not yet taken on the rigidity of a period manner, and when there is sudden release from the old without any corresponding obligation to that which will come to take its place."[25] However, such a moment is no longer his, and so the only options available to the critic, Adorno's work suggests, are to remain "resolutely unsystematic," as in the fragmentary essays and deferred theses of *Notes on Literature;* and deploy an unrelenting critical stringency, such as that on display in *Negative Dialectics.* In this way, we might keep faith with what remains in the present at least an unimaginable future; or as Adorno himself had earlier put it, "What is suspect today is not, of course, the depiction of reality as hell but the routine invitation to break out of it. If that invitation can be addressed to anyone today, it is neither to the so-called masses nor to the individual, who is powerless, but to an imaginary witness, to whom we bequeath it so that it is not entirely lost with us."[26]

Taking this as its initial starting point, wherein Adorno's work stands in for that of his contemporary Sartre in Jameson's earlier discussion of this historical moment (the formal reasons for this substitution too will become clear shortly), the subsequent narrative of *Marxism and Form* might be understood to give a new content to this "imaginary witness," as it labors to occupy what remains for Adorno the impossible exterior perspective on this total system, the objective pole in this dialectical narrative gradually turning over once more to the subjective. The next step takes us through three linked versions of a Marxist hermeneutic recoverable in the work of Walter Benjamin, Herbert Marcuse, and Ernst Bloch. Each offers a powerful dialectical rejoinder to Adorno, as they recover horizons of possibility not made available in Adorno's project.

In Benjamin's work, this takes the form of an obsession with memory and nostalgia, both serving as intimations of a psychic wholeness unavailable in the present. It is in this section as well that we witness Jameson's own initial engagement with the four-fold medieval allegorical schema that will play such an important role in *The Political Unconscious*. Allegory is, Jameson maintains, "the privileged mode of our own life in time, a clumsy deciphering of meaning from moment to moment, the painful attempt to restore a continuity to heterogeneous, disconnected instances."[27] Over and against this stands Benjamin's notion of "aura," a utopian "plenitude of existence in the world of things . . . available to the thinker only in a simpler cultural past," a past embodied in cultural forms such as storytelling.[28] Such forms are "a mode of contact with a vanished form of social and historical existence," a reminder of radically other ways of doing and being in the world; and in this way, Benjamin's work recovers for us some of the radical political potentiality of nostalgia and memory.[29]

Jameson opens his discussion of Marcuse, at this time his colleague at the University of California, San Diego, with an important reminder of the political function of hermeneutics, as it "provides the means for contact with the very sources of revolutionary energy during a stagnant time, of preserving the concept of freedom itself, underground, during geological ages of repression."[30] It is exactly this operation that Jameson argues is at work earlier in Friedrich Schiller's *Letters on the Aesthetic Education of Mankind,* with its notion of "nature"; and in the twentieth century, in Surrealism, with its deployment of the commodity icons of an earlier stage of twentieth-century capitalism. In a prefiguration of his well-known formulation in *Postmodernism,* Jameson also notes that today "the objects of Surrealism are gone without a trace. Henceforth, in what we may call postindustrial capitalism, the products with which we are furnished are utterly without depth."[31] Marcuse's work then offers us one of the first and most fully elaborated "explorations of the psychological and socio-economic infrastructure" of an entirely new moment in the history of capitalism, and thereby stands as a complement to the project of Adorno.[32] What disappears in such a situation, for both Adorno and Marcuse, is "any effective possibility of negating the system in general." However, here Marcuse takes a new turn, and formulates the fundamental task of the philosopher in such a situation as "the revival of the very idea of the negation," a revival, in short, of "the Utopian impulse" itself.[33] This takes the form of a double hermeneutic, a reading of the "life-style" freedoms of the present as "*figures* of Freedom in general"; and an unveiling of the foundations of such Utopian longings in a primeval memory of "a plenitude of psychic gratification . . . a time before all repression . . . prehistoric paradise."[34] If Adorno orients us toward the apparent immobility of the present, and Benjamin toward the otherness of the past, it is in Marcuse's work, as well as in that of his predecessors, that we see a "stubborn rebirth of the idea of freedom" as a potentiality of the future.[35]

The fullest expression of such a hermeneutics of the future is then found for Jameson in the thinking of Ernst Bloch.[36] Bloch's work fulfills the reorientation toward the future whose intimations we have already seen in Marcuse. Jameson claims that while Bloch's hermeneutic engages with an astonishing range of objects, his conceptual content remains at the core quite consistent: "everything in the world becomes a version of some primal figure, a manifestation of that primordial movement toward the future and toward ultimate identity with a transfigured world which is Utopia."[37] For Bloch, this horizon, available in every human cultural creation, takes the form of "the *novum,* the utterly and unexpectedly new, the new which astonished by its absolute and intrinsic unpredictability;" the future then is "always something *other* than what we sought to find there."[38] Moreover, in Bloch's thinking we see the dialectical sublation not only of the "anxiety" evident in Adorno's work, but of the doctrine of memory central for Benjamin, and whose traces are still present in Marcuse: in Bloch, the "no-longer consciousness," ultimately Freudian at base, is replaced by the "not-yet-consciousness, an ontological pull of the future, of a tidal influence exerted upon us by that which lies out of sight below the horizon, an unconscious of what is yet to come."[39]

The force of the work of all three thinkers, Jameson concludes, lies in the way they restore to any truly Marxist interpretation of cultural texts "a genuine political dimension . . . reading the very content and the formal impulse of the texts themselves as figures—whether of psychic wholeness, of freedom, or of the drive toward Utopian transfiguration—of the irrepressible revolutionary wish."[40] We have thus come full circle from the thesis of the negative dialectic of Adorno to the antithesis of the positive utopian dialectic of these three thinkers. (We can see another dialectical tripartite schema formed within the context of this individual chapter as well.) However, the story is not nearly over, for this "revolutionary wish" becomes concrete only in the realm of history. It is here that the next step in Jameson's narrative necessarily brings us, as only now we turn our attention to the work of Lukács. At this point, Jameson suggests a fundamental narrative unity in Lukács's project, one that mirrors the unity of the story he tells throughout this book: "a set of solutions and problems developing out of one another according to their own inner logic and momentum."[41] In addition to the concrete exploration of realist narrative we touched on above, what also re-emerges at this point is a vision of a collective agency, the subject of history, that is absent in each of the versions of the dialectic Jameson has examined thus far.

And yet, agency too turns out to be fundamentally linked to questions of epistemology, of each group's specific perspective on the world. The elaboration of the differences between bourgeois and working class epistemologies becomes the project of Lukács's major work of the early 1920s, *History and Class Consciousness*. What defines bourgeois philosophy, for Lukács, is "its incapacity or unwillingness to come to terms with the category of *totality* itself."[42] Most significantly, this means an inability to recognize the sheer and complete historicity of their world and its values. The working class, on the other hand, because of their location within the productive process, understand that any apparently finished "thing," including society itself, is "little more than a moment in the process of production."[43] The fundamental knowledge to be gained from whoever occupies the standpoint of the consciousness of the proletariat—a collective class perspective, of course, not necessarily embodied in any particular individual's existential experience—is "a sense of forces at work within the present, a dissolving of the reified surface of the present into a coexistence of various and conflicting historical tendencies, a translation of immobile objects into acts and potential acts and into the consequences of acts."[44] From such a perspective, ontology itself is understood to be thoroughly historical and social in nature, an application of the Giambattista Vico's "*verum-factum* principle" that Jay contends is central to Lukács's work and Western Marxism more generally.[45] Such a "true" picture of world cannot be rendered in terms of scientific taxonomies as successfully as in the elaboration of plot, and so it is no surprise, Jameson suggests, that so much of Lukács's intellectual attention turns to the realist narrative.

At this point, the thing, the social object of Adorno's negative dialectic, appears once again as a fluid historical process, the assumed perspective of the system of administered society giving way to that of the subject. While the climax of the story is hinted at in the Lukács discussion, it will be in the long penultimate chapter, "Sartre and History," where it achieves a full narrative figuration. It is the publication of the first volume of Sartre's monumental *Critique of Dialectical Reason* (1960), appearing shortly before Jameson's earlier *Sartre* study and only briefly alluded to in that text—"None of this holds true for Sartre's most recent work in the Marxist dialectic, which has another basis altogether"[46]—that now leads Jameson to approach his thought anew. The project Sartre engages in this work is akin to that of *Marxism and Form* itself: if "Marxism is a way of understanding the objective dimension of history from the outside," and "existentialism a way of understanding subjective, individual experience," then the project will be to bring the two together in "a kind of unified field theory in which two wholly different ontological phenomena can share a common set of equations and be expressed in a single linguistic or terminological system."[47] Sartre's fundamental target, Jameson ultimately demonstrates, is the economism of certain forms of "classical or orthodox Marxism": these have the singular "disadvantage of drawing attention to the separation and relatively autonomous development of each class, rather than to their constant interaction in the form of class struggle."[48]

The point here, however, Jameson maintains, is not simply to move from one pole to the other; to do so would still leave us trapped within the same antinomy of the object and subject, materialism and idealism, synchrony and diachrony, with which we began. Rather, Jameson argues that Sartre reinvents for a new historical moment the fundamental solution of Marx himself as he works to "strike at the very category of the specialized discipline as such, and to restore the unity of knowledge."[49] The genius of Marxism is that

[It] has at its disposal two alternate languages (or codes, to use the structuralist term) in which any given phenomenon can be described. Thus, history can be written either subjectively, as the history of class struggle, or objectively, as the development of the economic modes of production and their evolution from their own internal contradictions: these two formulae are the same, and any statement in one can without loss of meaning be translated into the other.[50]

In this too Jameson implicitly critiques the Althusserian notion of an "epistemological break" (*coupture*) in Marx's intellectual project. Drawing these two registers together is the notion of class, and it is to this interaction and conflict of these collectives that the narrative of *Marxism and Form* has finally led us.

Jameson's path to this dialectical resolution follows the same narrative structure that it has in the earlier chapters, and in the book as a whole. Thus, for example, while the issue of the "attraction at a distance" that the mass of workers represented for Sartre is raised in the first paragraphs of the chapter, it will not be until its final pages, after the careful and painstaking narrative working through of Sartre's intellectual project, that we might begin to "evaluate" this concept.[51] Suddenly, the entire project of Sartre's *Critique* can be cast "in a new light: it is Sartre's own attempt to see *himself,* to see his own class from the outside, to recuperate that external objectivity of both which is granted only through the judgment and look of the other upon them, or in other words through the concrete class antagonisms of history itself."[52] It is only at this conjuncture that Sartre and the narrative of *Marxism and Form* itself "attain the ultimate and determining reality of social being itself" in the social conflict and material praxis of classes and groups.[53]

The question that naturally arises here is what makes such an unveiling of totality possible at this particular historical conjuncture? Jameson offers the following answer:

Sartre's *Critique,* at the beginning of the 1960's, written during the Algerian revolution and appearing simultaneously with the Cuban revolution, the radicalization of the civil rights movement in the United States, the intensification of the war in Vietnam, and the worldwide development of the student movement, therefore corresponds to a new period of revolutionary ferment, and in the spirit of Marx himself offers a reworking of the economistic model in that terminology of praxis and of overt class conflict which seem now most consistent with the day-to-day lived experience of this period: it is a little like having the sound turned back on.[54]

With this rousing climax, we too are finally in a position from which we can effectively evaluate the historical situation to which the symbolic act that is *Marxism and Form* must be understood as a response. (In the later Afterword to *Sartre,* Jameson notes, "even writing books—especially writing books—can become an 'ideological interest' that inflects and commits your future, so that if you have to write them, it may be preferable to leave them incomplete, as Sartre was wont to do his whole life long.")[55] If, as Jameson suggests, "realism is dependent on the possibility of access to the forces of change in a given moment of history," then it is the social and cultural, political and intellectual ferment of the 1960s that makes his own "realist" narrative possible: "The simplest yet most universal formulation surely remains the widely shared feeling that in the 60s, for a time, everything was possible; that this period, in other words, was a moment of universal liberation, a global unbinding of energies."[56] The realism of *Marxism and Form* is thus both very much a product of this historical conjuncture, its plot rewriteable as a story about the fundamental intellectual transformations *within* the United States that occur as we move from the Cold War 1950s—with their despairing sense of total social closure and historical immobility—to the enthusiasm and sense of utopian potentiality characteristic of the 1960s. Indeed, of his own views of Adorno in this early work, which might also be extended to the Sartre presented in his first book, Jameson will later write, "In the age of wars of national liberation, Adorno's sense of Apocalypse seemed very retrogressive indeed, focused as it was on the moment of Auschwitz, and obsessed with the doom and baleful enchantment of a 'total system' that few enough—in a 'pre-revolutionary' moment defined notoriously by the sense that *'tout est possible!'*—sensed impending in our own future in the middle distance."[57]

However, as this passage intimates, such a horizon proves to be a short-lived one. In a later reassessment of the period of the 1960s, Jameson offers this very different characterization of this historical moment: "Yet this sense of freedom and possibility—which is for the course of the 60s a momentarily objective reality, as well as (from the hindsight of the 80s) a historical illusion—can perhaps best be explained in terms of the superstructural movement and play enabled by the transition from one infrastructural or systemic stage of capitalism to another."[58] That is, rather than heralding a fundamental break with capitalism, the 1960s later comes to be understood as a moment of the latter's reorganization, culminating in the early 1970s with the emergence of a full-blown postmodern "late capitalism."

A similar institutional restructuration can also be understood to have been under way within American intellectual life, a transformation in which *Marxism and Form* plays a vital role. A few years after the publication of *Marxism and Form*, Jameson explicitly addresses the role of realist narratives in such moments of historical transition. Deploying the conceptual tools made available by Gilles Deleuze and Félix Guattari's *Anti-Oedipus* (1972), Jameson now describes the work of realism less in terms of its mapping of an open and fluid social totality and more as a critical "decoding" operation, "a demystification of some preceding ideal or illusion."[59] *Marxism and Form* too engages in an operation of "decoding" of ideals and illusions at work within the American intellectual community.

This occurs on two distinct and yet linked levels. The first level at which this decoding is aimed is made explicit in the opening paragraph of the book:

> When the American reader thinks of Marxist literary criticism, I imagine that it is still the atmosphere of the 1930s which comes to mind. The burning issues of those days . . . no longer correspond to the conditions of the world today. The criticism practiced then was of a relatively untheoretical, essentially didactic nature, destined more for use in the night school than in the graduate seminar, if I may put it that way; and has been relegated to the status of an intellectual and historical curiosity.[60]

If work by Barbara Foley, Michael Denning, William J. Maxwell, and Caren Irr, among others, subsequently led to a more nuanced understanding of the Marxist intellectual labor of the 1930s, Jameson here responds to the dominant characterization of the limitations of Marxist cultural criticism in that moment still largely taken for granted in the U.S. academy.[61] This is the assumption at work, for example, in one of the most influential anthologies of literary criticism contemporary with *Marxism and Form*, Hazard Adams's *Critical Theory Since Plato* (1971)—the volume from which I, nearly fifteen years after its initial publication, and many others in my generation, were first introduced to literary theory. Adams's selections from twentieth-century Marxist cultural criticism are limited to Leon Trotsky's assault on the Russian Formalist method—of which Adams's prefatory note confidently asserts, "Though Trotsky's interpretations of his opponents' arguments are superficial, his essay is a fair reflection of assumptions that tend to guide materialist theories"—and fellow-traveler Edmund Wilson's critical overview of American Marxist literary criticism of the 1930s.[62] It is this common-sense version of Marxist cultural criticism to which *Marxism and Form* directs its decoding energies, clearing the space that will soon be inhabited by a much richer variety of species.

Moreover, the very characterization of "criticism" Jameson offers here points toward an even more general target: "of a relatively untheoretical, essentially didactic nature, destined more for use in the night school than in the graduate seminar": such a description can also readily be applied to what has by the late 1960s become the ossified strategies of the then still reigning New Critical formalism.[63] *Marxism and Form* thus participates in the widespread assault on these hegemonies—a series of very different interventions that ultimately will come to be assembled under the common flag of "theory." Jameson suggests such a link late in *Marxism and Form,* arguing that the fundamental operations of "much in modern thought" takes the form of a critical estrangement, "an assault on our conventionalized life patterns, a whole battery of shocks administered to our routine vision of things, an implicit critique and restructuration of our habitual perceptions."[64] Of course, it will be French models—first, briefly, structuralism and phenomenology, and then deconstruction and the various "poststructuralisms"—that will throughout the coming decades play a leading role in this decoding project, and it is no coincidence that Jameson's very next book, *The Prison-House of Language,* takes up the project of exploring the potentialities and limitations of these various critical practices. Even here, Jameson suggests that the ultimate advantage of dialectal thought over these other practices lies in its attention to the historical situation that calls forth such strategies in the first place: "the inability of a viewpoint for which history is but one possible type of discourse among others to deal historically with its material; and that even more symptomatic tendency of form to veer around into content, of a formalism to supply its historical absence of content by a hypostasis of its own method."[65]

However, this does not mean that the encounter with structuralism that takes place in this short book is not without a fundamental importance in the coming decade for Jameson's project. In the third and final section of *The Prison-House of Language*, "The Structuralist Projection"—preceded by "The Linguistic Model," a discussion of the revolution unleashed by the 1916 publication of transcripts of the late lectures of the Swiss linguist Ferdinand de Saussure, and "The Formalist Projection," an engagement with Russian Formalism (the real impact of which will be felt a few years later when Jameson begins to take up in earnest the genre of science fiction)[66]—Jameson points out, "Our approach to Structuralism as a coherent system, for instance, does not so much involve the testing of theories and hypotheses as it does the learning of a new language, which we measure as we go along by the amount of translation we are able to effect out of the older terminology into the new."[67] It is a new language Jameson learns extraordinarily well, and which he will employ to highly original ends in his next major work.

A few years later, in his 1975 essay on realism as a decoding practice, Jameson argues that ultimately a palpable sense of "fatigue" sets in with any realism's critical project, as the very objects of "such semiotic purification" begin to be exhausted: "This is, of course, the moment of modernism, or rather of the various modernisms," the effort to recode, to build a new language.[68] This will be the project of *The Political Unconscious*: if *Marxism and Form* is understood as a work that "unsticks" both U.S. Marxism in particular, and contemporary literary criticism more generally, *The Political Unconscious* will offer a highly original method—a recoding, rebuilding, and new language—for both Marxism and literary theory.

CHAPTER 2

Theoretical Modernisms (1970s)

Marxism and Form concludes with an extended meditation entitled "Towards Dialectical Criticism." Jameson opens it by stating that his goal is to develop a "phenomenological description of dialectical criticism," one that does not "tell" what such a criticism is—and again the resonances of Lukács's critique of naturalism are evident here—"so much as what it feels like."[1] If the dialectic is "thought to the second power: an intensification of the normal thought processes such that a renewal of light washes over the object of exasperation, as though in the midst of its immediate perplexities the mind had attempted, by willpower, by fiat, to lift itself mightily up by its own bootstraps," then its fundamental experience will be the deeply modernist one of *shock:* "The shock indeed is basic, and constitutive of the dialectic as such: without this transformational moment, without this initial conscious transcendence of an older, more naïve position, there can be no question of any genuinely dialectical coming to consciousness."[2] This description of shock is not unlike the important Russian Formalist concept of *defamiliarization*—"a making strange (*ostranenie*) of objects, a renewal of perception, takes the form of a psychological law with profound ethical implications"[3]—and it is no coincidence that in *The Prison-House of Language,* Jameson will also find in Russian Formalism, as well as in the later structuralisms, the intimations of a dialectical mode of thought.

The rest of the final chapter in *Marxism and Form* goes on to articulate some other features of a dialectical mode of criticism, features that were no doubt shocking to many of their first readers. These include, most centrally, the dialectical reversal, "that paradoxical turning around of a phenomenon into its opposite of which the transformation of quantity into quality is only one of the better known manifestations."[4] In order to initiate this narrative mode of analysis, the critic must first "isolate" the particular object of study, before placing it within a larger historical "succession of alternative structural realizations."[5] This latter structure is fundamentally differential in nature, such that Flaubert's novelistic practices, for example, are first and foremost defined by the fact that they are "no longer Balzac" and "not yet Zola."[6] Here too we see the first articulations of the strategies of periodizing analysis that will occupy much of Jameson's attention in the coming decades.

At the same time, a dialectical criticism would refuse "that sterile and static opposition between formalism and a sociological or historical use of literature between which we have so often been asked to choose," as "the essence of dialectical thinking lay in the inseparability of thought from content or from the object itself."[7] Such an approach thus attempts to think simultaneously on two levels, "about a given object on one level, and at the same time to observe our own thought processes as we do so."[8] This operation is not unlike what, in an award-winning essay first published in *PMLA* the same year as *Marxism and Form,* he defines as *metacommentary:* "every individual interpretation must include an interpretation of its own existence, must show its own credentials and justify itself."[9] The goal of such an approach then is not to "distinguish between the true and false elements" in a particular mode of analysis, the kind of ethical approach that I suggested earlier that Jameson consistently resists, but rather "to identify that concrete historical experience or situation" to which it "corresponds."[10]

This claim transforms utterly our perception not only of philosophical systems and interpretive strategies but of the literary and cultural text itself: rather than a finished object or thing, it is dissolved again into process, "as a complex, contradictory, polyvalent historical act."[11] In a formulation that he will return to a decade later, Jameson notes that according to Sartre, "Flaubert's work can be said to reflect the social contradictions of his period, but on condition that we understand it to do so on the mode of attempting to resolve, in the imaginary, what is socially irreconcilable."[12] If such an approach represents Jameson's re-vitalized version of ideological critique, he proceeds to complicate the question even further, arguing that "if there exist social contradictions which are structurally insoluble, at the same time we must remember the fact of successful revolutions as well, and make a place for an art which might be prophetic rather than fantasy-oriented, one which might portend genuine solutions underway rather than projecting formal substitutes for impossible ones."[13] Such a de-reifying, estranging mode of analysis restores the work to its original freshness as a form of cultural praxis, oriented not only toward its present but to possible other futures. "Thus the process of criticism," he concludes, needs to be understood, "not so much an interpretation of content as it is a revealing of it, a laying bare, a restoration of the original message, the original experience, beneath the distortions of the various kinds of censorship that have been at work upon it."[14]

What I want to emphasize is the provisional, working nature of the presentation of dialectical criticism offered at this juncture. "It is not the task of the present book," Jameson notes, "to bring such a synthesis to ordered, philosophical, *systematic* exposition."[15] Indeed, the problem and concerns articulated here are those to which he returns repeatedly throughout his intellectual career. Jameson will, however, attempt such a full blown "systematic exposition" a decade later in his next major intervention, *The Political Unconscious: Narrative as a Socially Symbolic Act* (1981). We might thus say that if *Marxism and Form* represents Jameson's equivalent to Hegel's already challenging "introduction" to dialectical thought, *Phenomenology of Spirit, The Political Unconscious* is his version of Hegel's far more imposing *Science of Logic*. Such a comparison becomes productive for another reason. The dialectic of the *Phenomenology* is one that is fundamentally narrative in structure: "the story of an ascent and a development, a description of the successive stages through which consciousness enriches and solidifies itself, and from its most individualistic and subjectively limited moments gradually arrives at the condition of Absolute Spirit, in which it learns that it ultimately includes within itself all the abundance and multiplicity of the external and objective universe."[16] Such a narrative movement is, as we noted in the previous chapter, the hallmark of realism, and hence we might say the narrative form of the *Phenomenology,* like *Marxism and Form,* is equally realist.

From our later vantage point, however, such a form is an impossible one, a veritable Benjaminian ruin: "Thus, even though one can reread Hegel, we are never able to reach the vantage point of that last chapter which would finally permit us to catch a glimpse of the work as a whole. The synthesis remains imperfect, a mere imperative to unity, a dead letter: and this imperfect focus holds true even down to the reading and rendering of the individual sentences."[17] The reasons for such failure are historical, and hence "a judgment on us and on the moment of history in which we live."[18] Such a changed historical situation requires a new set of representational strategies, as much in Hegel's moment as our own; and hence, the realist form of *Marxism and Form* will be displaced in *The Political Unconscious* by a *modernist* one.

"All modernist works are," Jameson argues, "essentially simply cancelled realistic ones . . . they are, in other words, not apprehended directly, in terms of their own symbolic meanings . . . but rather indirectly only, by way of the relay of an imaginary realistic narrative of which the symbolic and modernistic one is then seen as a kind of stylization."[19] Modernism as a topic is encountered in a similar indirect fashion within the narrative structure of *The Political Unconscious*. In the final paragraph of the climactic chapter of the book—followed by a brief denouement on "the dialectic of utopia and ideology," which I will return to in chapter 4—Jameson writes,

> After the peculiar heterogeneity of the moment of Conrad, a high modernism is set in place which it is not the object of this book to consider. The perfected poetic apparatus of high modernism represses History just as successfully as the perfected narrative apparatus of high realism did the random heterogeneity of the as yet uncentered subject. At that point, however, the political, no longer visible in the high modernist texts, any more than in the everyday world of appearance of bourgeois life, and relentlessly driven underground by accumulated reification, has at last become a genuine Unconscious.[20]

Interestingly, this statement suggests that the very object of the book's narration, embedded as it is in the title itself, likewise remains outside the frame of direct analysis—as with History, in the Lacanian and Althusserian formulations that play such a central role in this text, the political unconscious is "an absent cause . . . inaccessible to us except in textual form." We can thus approach it only indirectly "through its prior textualization, its narrativization."[21]

Something similar might be said about the place of modernism at this juncture in Jameson's intellectual project: both the central object and the very condition of possibility of his research agenda, it vanishes when we attempt to bring it to the center of our intellectual attention.

Thus, we can approach it only in an asymptotic, indirect fashion. This too accounts for the peculiar nature of the "modernist" texts he examines. For example, in the long penultimate chapter of *The Political Unconscious,* Jameson argues that the work of Joseph Conrad does not yet represent a true modernism, but rather "a strategic fault line in the emergence of contemporary narrative, a place from which the structure of twentieth-century literary and cultural *institutions* become visible," as the machinery of the older realism breaks down into the two dialectically interrelated phenomena of "high" modernist literature and a new mass culture.[22]

Similarly, in his previous book, *Fables of Aggression: Wyndham Lewis, the Modernist as Fascist* (1979), Jameson argues that what makes this disgraced and largely forgotten British writer and artist so interesting is his vexed relationship to the more celebrated and canonical modernisms: "A consistent perversity made of him at one and the same time the exemplary practitioner of one of the most powerful of all modernistic styles and an aggressive ideological critic and adversary of modernism in all its forms."[23] Indeed, Jameson suggests that Lewis's work in many ways prefigures "the contemporary poststructuralist aesthetic, which signals the dissolution of the modernist paradigm."[24] And finally, while much of James Joyce's work is referred to in the Lewis book as the "hegemonic modernist realization" against which Lewis's texts stand in contrast, Jameson will subsequently confess of one of his later direct engagements with *Ulysses* that in it he "tried to invoke a Third world and anti-imperialist Joyce more consistent with a contemporary than with a modernistic aesthetic."[25]

A similar indirect approach is required to map out the modernist form of *The Political Unconscious.* We can begin to do so by first substituting a number of "imaginary realistic narratives" for the plot of *The Political Unconscious,* of which the form itself is now understood as a kind of "stylization." The book might then first be read, for example, as a demonstration of the periodizing hypothesis in relation to narrative practice. Jameson presents us with four different moments—romance, realism, naturalism, and modernism—each at the center of attention in chapters 2 through 5. Or, we might approach it as a history of the modern novel: the novel emerges from the very different practices of the chivalric romance, passes through the utopian realism of Balzac and the asphyxiating naturalism of George Gissing, and finally reaches its outermost horizon with the protomodernist narratives of Conrad (thus, giving a new spin to T. S. Eliot's famous dictum that truly modernist texts like *Ulysses* and Lewis's later works are not novels).[26] Or again, we might recode the text as the story of the modern bourgeois subject, from its consolidation in the moment of Balzac (and to show its historicity, Jameson first demonstrates that there is nothing like it in the classical romance, the earlier form much more concerned with the mapping of space) to its decentering coinciding with the emergence of modernism. Or again, we might understand the work as narrating a spatial history of modernity, as first, the "social and spatial isolation" characteristic of the feudal period is overcome.[27] This inaugurates a process of spatial consolidation passing through the moment of the nation-state and on into a truly global imperial network.

Finally, there is a purely formal narrative at work, where chapters 3, 4, and 5 serve as concrete illustrations of the "three concentric frameworks" within which any particular literary text is to be interpreted (a "tripartite" schema that Jameson more recently points out is adapted from the three *durées* of Fernand Braudel's *The Mediterranean and the Mediterranean World in the Age of Philip II*):[28]

> first, of political history, in the narrow sense of punctual event and a chroniclelike sequence of happenings in time; then of society, in the now already less diachronic and time-bound sense of a constitutive tension and struggle between social classes; and, ultimately, of history now conceived in its vastest sense of the sequence of modes of productions and the succession and destiny of the various human social formations, from prehistoric life to whatever far future history has in store for us.[29]

Every text is thus to be understood as a *libidinal apparatus,* a concept Jameson adopts from Jean-François Lyotard and develops in his own fashion in *Fables of Aggression,* where he argues that "the theory of the libidinal apparatus marks an advance over psychologizing approaches in the way in which it endows a private fantasy-structure with a quasi-material inertness, with all the resistance of an object which can lead a life of its own and has its own inner logic and specific dynamics."[30] As such a libidinal apparatus, he later notes, any text "can be invested by a number of forces and meanings," and interpretation should be sensitive to "this possibility of multiple investments."[31] He then enacts such a reading strategy in *The Political Unconscious* through this three-leveled Marxist hermeneutic, which, he argues, must "be defended as something like an ultimate *semantic* precondition for the intelligibility of literary and cultural texts."[32]

On the initial level, "the individual work is grasped essentially as a *symbolic act*," a formalization of the notion of text as praxis first articulated in *Marxism and Form*'s concluding chapter. Jameson illustrates the notion of symbolic action through an engagement with Balzac's novels, where the narrative's plot is read, through a combination of Claude Lévi-Strauss's model of myth and A. J. Greimas's semiotic square, as an allegory of "the imaginary resolution of a real contradiction:" "The underlying ideological contradiction" of these novels "can evidently be expressed in the form of a meditation on history: Balzac as a royalist and an apologist for the essentially organic and decentered *ancien régime* must nonetheless confront the latter's palpable military failures and administrative insufficiencies."[33]

On the second level, the "object of study will prove to be the *ideologeme*, that is, the smallest intelligible unit of the essentially antagonistic collective discourses of social classes."[34] In his chapter on Gissing's naturalist fiction, Jameson follows Mikhail Bakhtin's lead, and maintains that ideologemes function as "the raw material, the inherited narrative paradigms, upon which the novel as a process works and which it transforms into texts of a different order."[35] In a prefiguration of the argument advanced by Nancy Armstrong in *Desire and Domestic Fiction: A Political History of the Novel* (1987), Jameson argues:

> Two strategic displacements were necessary to convert the earlier narrative machinery which has been described here into that of Gissing's greatest novels: the alienated intellectual becomes more locally specified as the writer, so that the problems of *déclassement* raised above are immediately linked to the issue of earning money. Meanwhile, the class conflict evoked in the earlier works is here largely rewritten in terms of sexual differentiation and the "woman question": this allows the "experimental" situation we described to be staged within the more conventional novelistic framework of marriage, which thereby gains an unaccustomed class resonance.[36]

Finally, Jameson's third horizon of interpretation becomes the most expansive of all, where the text is interpreted as "*the ideology of form . . .* formal processes as sedimented content in their own right, as carrying ideological messages of their own, distinct from the ostensible or manifest content of the works."[37] Form and content are thus understood as inseparable, "at this level 'form' is apprehended as content," enabling Jameson in chapter 5 to read Conrad's style as a response to the "concrete situation . . . of rationalization and reification in the late nineteenth-century."[38]

The brilliance and originality of *The Political Unconscious* is that it too is a libidinal apparatus, all of these narrative strands unfolding simultaneously, making the text available for a wide range of interpretive "realist" decodings. Moreover, the very proliferation of these "cancelled realist narratives" also points toward one of the central features of the modernist form of *The Political Unconscious*. I argued in the previous chapter that the realist narrative is best characterized for Jameson as a unity, a figuration on the level of textual form of the larger social totality. In the modernist text, it is this unity that must be reconstituted in the process of interpretation, and thus which always remains at a distance from the text itself. And it is this development that tells us something crucial about the historical context within which any modernism comes to fruition.

In the Conrad chapter of *The Political Unconscious,* Jameson maintains that the situation of modernism is one of a dramatic increase in the tempo and extent of what Max Weber calls "rationalization" and Georg Lukács "reification" of all aspects of modern life. The power of Marxism, Jameson also notes here, lies in its ability to embrace simultaneously a number of different "mediatory codes" for connecting together different social and cultural phenomena: thus, rationalization or reification can "be described as the analytical dismantling of the various traditional or 'natural' [*naturwüchsige*] unities (social groups, institutions, human relationships, forms of authority, activities of a cultural and ideological as well as of a productive nature) into their component parts with a view to their 'Taylorization,' that is their reorganization into more efficient systems which function according to an instrumental, or binary, means/ends logic."[39] Nearly a decade later, Jameson will argue that among the supreme manifestations of such a logic is the tendency toward "*autonomy,*" at once on the level of "aesthetic experience," of "culture," and finally, "of the work itself."[40] Even more significantly for our concerns, Jameson then turns to the way that these "various kinds of 'autonomy' now inscribe themselves in the very structure of individual works."[41] He argues that this process of autonomization "can now be initially observed on two levels of the modernist work in general, or, if you prefer, from two distinct standpoints, two positions unequally distant from the work as a whole. One of these distances—the longer one—discloses the process at work in the becoming autonomous of the episodes; while the more proximate one tracks it down into the very dynamic of the individual sentences themselves (or the equivalent ultimate 'autonomous' unit of formal syntax)."[42]

Jameson emphasizes, in both *Signatures of the Visible* and *The Political Unconscious*, that these aspects of the modernist work—at once evident in Conrad's fiction, *Ulysses* ("the Joycean chapter is virtually the archetypal emblem of the process of episodization in modernism"), and in Hitchcock's later "modernist" films—must be understood as "semi-autonomies":

> There is here, however, a constitutive tension between the episode and the totality not necessarily present on the level of the sentence itself. . . . It is this tension, or even contradiction, which probably accounts for the tenacious stereotype of the "plotlessness" of the modernist novel: as though there were any non-narrative moments in *Ulysses* (or in Virginia Woolf, for that matter)! But their narrativity is that of the episode and not of the work "as a whole," by which we probably mean the *idea* of the work, its "concept," what the single-word title of Joyce's book is supposed, for example, to convey. Autonomy—or, if you like, semi-autonomy—reemerges with a vengeance here, where the chapters run with their pretext, each setting its own rules in a certain independence, which is itself then authorized by the perfunctory allusion of the chapter as a whole to some corresponding section of the *Odyssey.*[43]

This recognition is indispensable for any periodizing description of the formal structure of the modernist text, "since when these two poles split definitively asunder (when semi-autonomy, in other words, breaks into autonomy *tout court*, and a sheerly random play of heterogeneities), we are in the postmodern."[44]

Such semi-autonomy is, as suggested in my various decodings offered above of the cancelled realist narratives of the text, characteristic of the form of *The Political Unconscious* as well, each chapter "setting its own rules in a certain independence from the others." Indeed, this text is marked by what Jameson names "generic discontinuity"—"not so much an organic unity as a symbolic act that must reunite or harmonize heterogeneous narrative paradigms"⁴⁵—a concept akin to the description of the dialogism, heteroglossia, and polyphony of the novel offered by Bakhtin (Bakhtin's concepts themselves also now being understood as most accurately designating the modernist text in the light of which Bakhtin, deploying a "regressive-progressive" dialectic akin to that of Marx's analysis of production, rewrites the entire history of the novel form).⁴⁶ This accounts too for the "tenacious stereotype of the 'plotlessness' " of this Jamesonian text (often read as being composed of a long synthetic program essay, "On Interpretation: Literature as a Socially Symbolic Act," followed by independent discussions, or at best demonstrations of the approaches outlined in the introduction, of the romance form, and Balzac's, Gissing's, and Conrad's fictions), "as though there were any non-narrative moments" in it. Rather, the book's "narrativity is that of the episode and not of the work 'as a whole,' by which we probably mean the *idea* of the work, its 'concept,' " what the title, *The Political Unconscious: Narrative as a Socially Symbolic Act,* is meant to convey.⁴⁷ That such a concept cannot be encountered directly, and indeed determines at a mediated distance the contents of any particular text, is suggestive of its thoroughgoing modernism as well.

This formal structure is then echoed on the level of the book's content in the centrality for Jameson's thinking at this point of the work of Louis Althusser, whose formulation of the "semi-autonomy" of the various features (culture, ideology, law, the economy and so forth) of the mode of production,⁴⁸ and of the absent presence of the totality of the Real (which Jameson, again following Lacan's lead, elsewhere describes as another term for "simply History itself")⁴⁹ are crucial to both Jameson's text as a whole and his theorizations, here and elsewhere, of modernism. Indeed, within the specific histories of Marxism, Althusser's structuralism might best be grasped as the moment of modernism: it will only be with the complete autonomization of the post-Marxism (more accurately Post-Althusserianism) of Ernesto Laclau and Chantal Mouffe that we enter into a postmodernism proper.⁵⁰

There is another significant modernist element of this text: the full-blown emergence of, or at least a new critical awareness about, Jameson's own signatory "style." Terry Eagleton acknowledges as much when he entitles his review of *The Political Unconscious* "Fredric Jameson: The Politics of Style," and opens with a paragraph-long parody of Jameson's prose.⁵¹ Interestingly, three years later, in the essay "Postmodernism, or, The Cultural Logic of Late Capitalism," Jameson will suggest that such a practice of parody is itself a particularly modernist phenomenon: "To be sure, parody found a fertile area in the idiosyncrasies of the moderns and their 'inimitable styles.'" All such parodies depend upon "a norm which then reasserts itself, in a not necessarily unfriendly way, by a systematic mimicry of their willful eccentricities," the norms here being generated by the individual writer rather than larger institutions (genre, academy, culture) she inhabits.[52] I would contend that just as such parodies as those found in "Bad Hemingway" or "Bad Faulkner" competitions are simply not available, except by way of a retrospective projection, for writers like Charles Dickens or Balzac, so too the kind of parody offered by Eagleton would not have been conceivable, except again retroactively from the fully modernist style of *The Political Unconscious,* for Jameson's earlier *Sartre, Marxism and Form,* or *Prison-House* books.

In this way, style becomes a stand-in for the monadic subject of the individual creative genius. However, Jameson argues that such modernist figures themselves need to be understood

> non- and anti-anthropomorphically . . . as *careers,* that is to say as objective situations in which an ambitious young artist around the turn of the century could see the objective possibility of turning himself into the "greatest painter" (or poet or novelist or composer) "of the age." That objective possibility is now given, not in subjective talent as such or some inner richness or inspiration, but rather in strategies of a well-nigh military character, based on superiority of technique and terrain, assessment of the counterforces, a shrewd maximization of one's own specific and idiosyncratic resources.[53]

His description here can be readily transferred from the general situation of high modernism to the more particular nonsynchronous institutional context out of which *The Political Unconscious* emerges. For this is the apex of "high theory," a movement that both Andreas Huyssen and Jameson will subsequently describe as the final stage in the long history of cultural modernism.[54] And like the earlier moment of "artistic" modernism (the distinction between artistic and other forms of modernism being one Jameson refuses), this too is an "objective situation" in which the possibility is available of becoming the "greatest" theorist "of the age"—or more precisely, in the appellation awarded to Jameson with the publication of this book, to become "the best Marxist critic writing today, possibly the best social-historically oriented critic of our time" (Hayden White). With the publication of *The Political Unconscious,* Jameson becomes one of the first Americans to join a largely European pantheon of theoretical giants, including Claude Lévi-Strauss, Jacques Lacan, Roland Barthes, Michel Foucault, Jacques Derrida, Hélène Cixous, Luce Irigaray, and Julia Kristeva, as well as the earlier generation of Frankfurt School theorists he had helped make famous with *Marxism and Form.* Jameson's leap in fame is signaled by a special issue of *Diacritics* devoted to *The Political Unconscious,* with the first published interview with him (an event too that marks the emergence of interest in Jameson as an intellectual "personality"), and the publication of the first systematic guide to any of his works.[55]

Jameson goes on to argue that the emphasis on such individual style in the moment of high modernism stands as a protest against the standardization and homogenization of modern life, and thus draws "its power and its possibilities from being a backwater and an archaic holdover within a modernizing economy." Modernism, he maintains, must "be seen as uniquely corresponding to an uneven moment of social development, or to what Ernst Bloch called the 'simultaneity of the nonsimultaneous,' the 'synchronicity of the nonsynchronous' (*Gleichzeitigkeit des Ungleichzeitigen*): the coexistence of realities from radically different moments of history—handicrafts alongside the great cartels, peasant fields with the Krupp factories or the Ford plant in the distance."[56] Thus, the "keen sense of the New in the modern period was only possible because of the mixed, uneven, transitory nature of that period, in which the old coexisted with the new."[57]

Within the academic context of *The Political Unconscious,* we see a similar "unevenness," as the then dominant disciplinary structures confront the new work advanced under the aegis of theory. Indeed, I would argue that it is specifically the interdisciplinarity of theory—the dramatic and dislocating encounter for literary scholars, for example, with work not only from such "foreign" disciplines as philosophy, linguistics, anthropology, and history, but also from very different national traditions—that strikes its readers in this moment with all the shock of the New, or Bloch's *Novum.* This is the moment both of the monumental figures and the great named avant-gardes—deconstruction, reader-response criticism, feminism, post-colonial criticism, New Historicism, queer theory, to note only a few of the more celebrated examples. The expressions of shock, outrage, and disgust on the part of the defenders of disciplinary practices and standards too are quite akin to the response of the artistic academies to the work of the high modernists. Indeed, Richard Aldington's infamous dismissal of *Ulysses* as an anarchic work, and, like the Dadaism he claims it most nearly resembled, an "invitation to chaos,"[58] is echoed in many of the more critical responses to the new theory. It is in this context then that Jameson's work will come to play an increasingly central and influential role.

However, there is a distinct price to be paid for the proliferation of these movements and unique voices:

> One did not simply read D. H. Lawrence or Rilke, see Jean Renoir or Hitchcock, or listen to Stravinsky, as distinct manifestations of what we now term modernism. Rather one read all the works of a particular writer, learned a style and a phenomenological world. D. H. Lawrence became an absolute, a complete and systematic world view, to which one converted. This meant, however, that the experience of one form of modernism was incompatible with another, so that one entered one world only at the price of abandoning another (when we tired of Pound, for example, we converted to Faulkner, or when Thomas Mann became predictable, we turned to Proust). The crisis of modernism as such came, then, when suddenly it became clear that "D. H. Lawrence" was not an absolute after all, not the final achieved figuration of the truth of the world, but only one art-language among others, only one shelf of works in a whole dizzying library. Hence the shame and guilt of cultural intellectuals, the renewed appeal of the Hegelian goal, the "end of art," and the abandonment of culture altogether for immediate political activity.[59]

Here we arrive at a central contradiction of a modernist aesthetic. Each particular practice, style, or movement declares itself to be the new universal; however, the very proliferation of such declarations signals the impossibility of any such unification. Such a development, Jameson elsewhere suggests, finds its roots in the "breakdown of a homogeneous public, with the social fragmentation and anomie of the bourgeoisie itself, and also its refraction among the various national situations."[60] This would include "not least those relatively homogeneous reading publics to whom, in the writer's contract, certain relatively stable signals can be sent."[61] Each modernist practice, style, or movement "demands an organic community which it cannot, however, bring into being by itself but can only express."[62] That *The Political Unconscious* advances similar ambitions is evident in its opening paragraph: "This book will argue the priority of the political interpretation of literary texts. It conceives of the political perspective not as some supplementary method, not as an optional auxiliary to other interpretive methods current today—the psychoanalytical or the myth-critical, the stylistic, the ethical, the structural—but rather as the absolute horizon of all reading and all interpretation."[63] Similar claims will be made by all of the modernist theoretical works and movements of this moment, and the conflicts and incommensurabilities between them echo through the pages of the proliferating journals of the 1970s and 80s, publications akin to the little magazines of an earlier artistic modernism.

What I am suggesting here is that this "theoretical modernism," exemplified for us in Jameson's central achievement of this moment, replays many of the same issues, anxieties, and concerns of high modernism proper—the difference here lying in the fact that theory's modernist period already had the earlier history of the rise and fall of modernism behind it, so that the central positions in the debate had already been set into place.[64] Thus, it should come as no surprise that the response to modernist theory's failure to constitute itself as an absolute, the "shame and guilt of cultural intellectuals" and the call for "the abandonment of culture (read here, Theory) altogether for immediate political activity," should also soon re-emerge.

Indeed, these are the terms of one of the first important commentaries on Jameson's book, that found in Edward Said's 1982 synoptic overview of cultural criticism in the "Age of Ronald Reagan."[65] Said finds in Jameson's book "an unadmitted dichotomy between two kinds of 'Politics': (1) the politics defined by political theory from Hegel to Louis Althusser and Ernst Bloch; (2) the politics of struggle and power in the everyday world, which in the United States at least has been won, so to speak, by Reagan."[66] Not only does Jameson privilege the first, Said maintains, the latter appears at only one place in the entire book, in a long footnote arguing for "alliance politics" as "the only realistic perspective in which a genuine Left could come into being in this country."[67] The relationship between these two forms of politics is never made clear, and this is because Jameson's "assumed constituency is an audience of cultural-literary critics."[68] In this, he is like many of the major theoretical thinkers and writers of the moment, located "in cloistral seclusion from the inhospitable world of real politics."[69] The "autonomy" of theoretical writing has been secured through a disengagement from the world, an increasingly reified technical specialization and what Said calls an agreement of *"noninterference* in the affairs of the everyday world."[70] In short, the political is "no longer visible" in these theoretical texts, "and relentlessly driven underground by accumulated reification, has at last become a genuine Unconscious."[71] Said's reformed scholarship, on the other hand, would take up the politically activist stance of *"interference,* crossing of borders and obstacles, a determined attempt to generalize exactly at those points where generalizations seem impossible to make."[72]

As a description of the status of humanist intellectual work among a larger readership in the United States in the early 1980s, Said's characterization is depressingly apt. However, in it, Said elides two of the concerns that are in fact central to all of Jameson's thought: that of genre and—what we have been focusing upon throughout this book—periodization. First, what Said is calling for here is not another kind of literary scholarship, but rather *another* kind of public critical engagement altogether—it is as if he were criticizing Marx for taking the time to write *Capital* ("There is no royal road to science") instead of committing himself exclusively to radical journalism. These are in fact very different tasks, each with its own value in our world, and each sites of "real" engagement and struggle.

My innvocation of Marx's text takes on additional resonance in the light of the "scandalous" argument of Jameson's recent book *Representing* Capital: *A Reading of Volume One* (2011). In this text, Jameson claims that many readers of *Capital* similarly misapprehend the generic nature of Marx's text: "*Capital* is not a political book and has very little to do with politics. Marx was certainly himself a profoundly political being, with a keen sense of the strategy and tactics of power to which any number of his other writings will testify. But in *Capital* the word 'revolution' always means a technological revolution in the introduction of new and more productive and destructive kinds of machinery. At best the occasional aside takes note of the enhanced power of political resistance which workers' associations are likely to enable."[73] Similarly, despite its title, we might advance the equally "scandalous opinion" that *The Political Unconscious* is *not* a political book, at least in the precise and circumscribed sense that Said means, and it is simply a categorical or generic mistake to read it as such.

With this kind of generic specification in place, the question shifts to what is possible for any particular practice of writing in its specific historical situation? With this inquiry, we return in fact to the long-standing debate between voluntarism and determinism: is the disengagement from the everyday a matter of free "moral choice" (Said's phrase) on the part of these theoretical writers, or a consequence of the specific "situation" in which they are working?[74] That *The Political Unconscious* has apparently turned from the immediacy of collective praxis glimpsed in the climax of *Marxism and Form,* and toward a more patient examination of the long *durée* of capitalist modernity tells us a great deal about the very different political situations in which each work appears.

Moreover, Said's discussion can be productively read as symptomatic of its historical moment in its abandonment of the dialectical view of modernism that Jameson offers in *The Political Unconscious.* There, Jameson writes,

> That modernism is itself an ideological expression of capitalism, and in particular, of the latter's reification of daily life, may be granted a local validity. . . . Viewed in this way, then, modernism can be seen as a late stage in the bourgeois cultural revolution, as a final and extremely specialized phase of that immense process of superstructural transformation whereby the inhabitants of older social formations are culturally and psychologically retrained for life in the market system.[75]

Clearly, the same claim can be made of the theoretical modernism that we have been discussing, as it "retrains" us for the very different forms of intellectual and academic life that begin to emerge in the later 1970s. "Yet," Jameson continues,

> modernism can at one and the same time be read as a Utopian compensation for everything reification brings with it . . . . The increasing abstraction of visual art thus proves not only to express the abstraction of daily life and to presuppose fragmentation and reification; it also constitutes a Utopian compensation for everything lost in the process of the development of capitalism—the place of quality in an increasingly quantified world, the place of the archaic and of feeling amid the desacralization of the market system, the place of sheer color and intensity within the grayness of measurable extension and geometrical abstraction.[76]

Such a characterization fits, to my mind, *The Political Unconscious* as well as the other theoretical modernisms of its moment. Moreover, the fact that this insight represents one of the most important lessons of *The Political Unconscious* is borne out in the short concluding chapter, wherein, as we shall see, this dialectic is expanded into a fundamental axiom of all Marxist cultural criticism.

In his review of Tafuri's *Architecture and Utopia,* Jameson advances this exchange one step further, and helps us place Said's essay in its context as well. Jameson argues that the two positions that result from the fission of this modernist dialectic—a rigorous "pessimism" about the possibilities of cultural work, something we can see in Said's evaluation of contemporary theoretical discourses, and a "complacent free play" that abandons the modernist projects of cultural and social transformation—are in fact "two intolerable options of a single double-bind."[77] Such a predicament then becomes one of the symptoms of *postmodernism*. And with this insight, we shift suddenly and even unexpectedly to the next period in Jameson's project.

CHAPTER 3

Symptomologies and Intimations of the Global (1980s–1990s)

The same landmark volume, *The Anti-Aesthetic: Essays on Postmodern Culture* (1983), that reprints Said's essay also first publishes a work that signals a dramatic turn in Jameson's intellectual program. Entitled "Postmodernism and Consumer Society," this short essay, originally presented in 1982 as a Whitney Museum Lecture, represents Jameson's first explicit foray into issues and questions that he had touched on in passing for more than a decade previously but would only now come to the center of his attention.[1] The labors begun here come to full fruition two years later in what is likely still his most well-known and influential essay, "Postmodernism, or, The Cultural Logic of Late Capitalism," an essay that will then serve seven years hence as the first chapter of a book-length study of the same name.[2] In his illuminating discussion of the context, origins, and subsequent adventures of Jameson's theorizations of the postmodern, Perry Anderson notes that the 1984 essay "redrew the whole map of the postmodern at one stroke—a prodigious inaugural gesture that has commanded the field ever since."[3]

In "Postmodernism and Consumer Society," Jameson investigates two features of an emergent postmodern culture: "pastiche and schizophrenia," characteristic of "the postmodernist experience of space and time respectively."[4] He finds the former exemplified by popular "nostalgia films"—*Chinatown, American Graffiti, Star Wars,* and *Body Heat* (a discussion that has its roots in an essay more than a decade earlier, "On Raymond Chandler")[5]—and the latter in the experimental work "China" by the Language Poet Bob Perelman. His concluding observations on Perelman's text are especially interesting in that they offer some of the earliest clues as to what will become the original formal structure of Jameson's 1991 book length study of postmodernism:

> In the present case, the represented object is not really China after all: what happened was that Perelman came across a book of photographs in a stationery store in Chinatown, a book whose captions and characters obviously remained dead letters (or should one say material signifiers?) to him. The sentences of the poem are *his* captions to those pictures. Their referents are other images, another text, and the "unity" of the poem is not *in* the text at all but outside it in the bound unity of an absent book.[6]

Similarly, I want to argue that the unity of Jameson's own analysis of postmodernism will not reside in the text, but rather outside it, in the absent totality of the reigning global cultural condition. As a consequence, what disappears in the full *Postmodernism* study are the narrative rhythms that structured the two earlier texts we have already examined: even the "cancelled realisms" of *The Political Unconscious* are no longer evident in a work that moves from object to object and text to text with no immediately discernible narrative logic. We can read in the pastiche aesthetic of nostalgia films—which Jameson characterizes as "an elaborated symptom of the waning of our historicity, of our lived possibility of experiencing history in some active way"[7]—the "schizophrenic fragmentation" of Perelman's poem—"if we are unable to unify the past present, and future of the sentence, then we are similarly unable to unify the past, present, and future of our own biographical experience or psychic life"[8]—and finally in the formal structure of Jameson's *Postmodernism* book, powerful figurations of one of the central dilemmas of the postmodern condition: our inability to tell the stories that would enable us to position ourselves within and hence act in our new world. The political task of this phase of Jameson's project will thus rest in the search for the forms of narrative, and hence an experience of history, that will aid us in moving beyond such a situation.

The form of this book also reflects Jameson's central contention that postmodernism is a cultural situation "increasingly dominated by space and spatial logic."[9] Indeed, while following the lead of the French social theorist Henri Lefebvre, and acknowledging that all social organizations are defined by distinctive productions of space, Jameson argues that "ours has been spatialized in a unique sense, such that space is for us an existential and cultural dominant, a thematized and foregrounded feature or structural principle standing in striking contrast to its relatively subordinate and secondary (though no doubt no less symptomatic) role in earlier modes of production."[10] In order to begin to bring into focus such a radically new situation, a new form of presentation, or a new *Darstellung,* is necessary, and Jameson will find the intimations of such a form in Walter Benjamin's neo-Platonist notion of the *constellation,* as well as in its further refinement in the late work of Theodor Adorno. Jameson develops his thoughts about these modes of presentation most directly in his 1990 book *Late Marxism: Adorno, or the Persistence of the Dialectic,* and thus *Late Marxism*—along with the discussion of periodization in *Signatures of the Visible* (also from 1990) that we touched on in the Introduction—should be understood to serve, among its diverse other projects, as an "epistemo-critical" prologue to *Postmodernism.*[11]

Jameson begins his discussion of the constellation form by meditating on the nature of Benjamin's influence on Adorno:

> "Influence" in this new sense would then describe the ways in which the pedagogical figure, by his own praxis, shows the disciple what else you can think and how much further you can go with the thoughts you already have; or—to put it another way, which for us is the same—what else you can *write* and the possibility of forms of writing and *Darstellung* that unexpectedly free you from the taboos and constraints of forms learnt by rote and assumed to be inscribed in the nature of things. This, at any rate, is the way in which I want to grasp Benjamin's "influence" on Adorno, as just such a liberation by mimesis and as the practical demonstration of another kind of writing—which is eventually to say: another kind of thinking.[12]

Benjamin and Adorno will exert a similar "influence" on Jameson in his composition of his postmodernism study, enabling him to break with engrained habits and practices of writing and thinking, even those particular to his project up to this point, and develop a form of presentation appropriate to the historical originalities of postmodernism.

The strategy that Adorno "mimics" is outlined in Benjamin's *Erkennt-niskritische Vorrede* to his 1928 publication of his unsuccessful (at least in terms of securing him an academic placement) *Habilitationsschrift*, *Ursprung des deutschen Trauerspiels* (translated as *The Origin of German Tragic Drama*) (1928). At the center of Benjamin's attention is the relationship between the Platonic notion of the "Idea" and theoretical presentation:

> The Idea is therefore simply the "system" of concepts, the relationship between a group of concepts: as such it has no content in its own right, is not a quasi-object (as the concept is) nor the representation of one: "ideas are not present in the world of phenomena" (OGT 215/35), any more than constellations "really exist" in the sky. Meanwhile, it becomes clear that philosophical writing or *Darstellung* will consist in tracing the constellation, in somehow drawing the lines between the empirical concepts thus "configured" together. But the concepts represent *aspects* of empirical reality, while the Idea (and its philosophical notation) represents the *relationships* between them.[13]

It is through the act of naming—an activity also fundamental in Alain Badiou's similarly Platonic conception of the instantiation of an event through a process of truth—that the Idea takes on a concrete form:

> "[T]ragedy" is just such a "name" and an "Idea", and will here become the object of a properly philosophical *Darstellung,* the tracing of an enormous constellation out of "empirical" concepts. In hindsight, we also know that a similar name, a similar idea, is somehow inherent in the notion of the "arcade" in the later project. Suddenly, the traditional Platonic repertoire of abstractions—whatever their social and historical content may have been in Plato's day—is radically transformed into a flood of modern "ideas" of a far more concrete and historical type, such as *capital* itself, or bureaucracy, or dictatorship, or even Nature or History, in their modern senses, or finally "Paris—Capital of the Nineteenth Century"![14]

Adorno then gives all of this a final turn with his musical figure of the *model:* "What we must retain, however, is the implication that 'twelve-tone' philosophy will do its work differently from the classical text: the concept or problem will not be independent of the *Darstellung* but already at one with it; there will be no conceptual events, no 'arguments' of the traditional kind that will lead to truth climaxes; the text will become one infinite variation in which everything is recapitulated at every moment; closure, finally, will be achieved only when all the possible variations have been exhausted."[15]

The passages cited above effectively outline the experimental form of the *Darstellung* Jameson develops in *Postmodernism*. "Postmodernism" operates for Jameson as just such the name of an Idea. The importance of this radical sense of naming is emphasized in the often cited final paragraph of the book:

> The rhetorical strategy of the preceding pages has involved an experiment, namely, the attempt to see whether by systematizing something that is resolutely unsystematic, and historicizing something that is resolutely ahistorical, one couldn't outflank it and force a historical way at least of thinking about that. "We have to name the system": this high point of the sixties finds an unexpected revival in the postmodernism debate.[16]

Jameson's task in writing this book will be to draw the constellation that holds together an immense and, at first glance, seemingly unrelated variety of concepts. The names of these concepts first appear in *Postmodernism*'s Table of Contents: Culture, Ideology, Video, Architecture, Sentences, Space, Theory, Economics, Film, and Conclusion.[17] These names function in a way akin to the titles of the convolutes in Benjamin's massive and unfinished *Arcades Project*: "Fashion," "Iron Construction," "The Flaneur," "Marx," and so forth.[18] Their significance is further born out in the fact that these concept-names, and not the particular titles, run in the headers above each chapter. The chapters then develop a new and original substance for each of these concepts— not culture, ideology, sentences, or space understood in some abstract universal fashion, but rather as themselves networks taking on a specific concrete content in the current world system. These are then ultimately drawn together into a constellated—and necessarily incomplete—totality by the Idea, the name, "postmodernism."

As for the study's empirical raw material, *Postmodernism* takes up a breathtaking range of different cultural forms and practices: the architecture of John Portman's Bonaventure Hotel and Frank Gehry's Santa Monica home; video productions by Nam June Paik; the late *nouvelle roman* of Claude Simon; paintings by Vincent Van Gogh and Andy Warhol (the latter gracing the book's cover); sculpture by Duane Hanson; conceptual and installation art by Hans Haacke and Robert Gober; punk rock and John Cage's avant-garde performances; science fiction by J. G. Ballard and Philip K. Dick; New Historicism and the theoretical nominalism of Paul de Man; market ideology; popular film in David Lynch's *Blue Velvet* (1986) and Jonathan Demme's *Something Wild* (1986); as well as an equally diverse set of issues and objects in the long concluding chapter, "Secondary Elaborations." Although Jameson's first forays into forms and practices other than those of literature or critical theory had in fact begun in the 1970s, it is with the publication of *Postmodernism* and the work surrounding it that visual and spatial forms such as film, painting, photography, installation art, and, most significantly of all, architecture, come to occupy a central place in his thinking.[19] Indeed, in an early defense of his arguments published in *New Left Review* and reworked as part of the concluding section of *Postmodernism,* Jameson notes that it was "the experience of new kinds of artistic production (particularly in the architectural area) that roused me from the canonical 'dogmatic slumbers'."[20]

This proliferation of objects in turn reflects some of Jameson's most important claims concerning the nature of postmodernism. First, Jameson contends that within a full-blown postmodernism the semi-autonomy of the aesthetic in relationship to other areas of social life—the famous Kantian spheres whose distinct operational logics someone like Jürgen Habermas so desperately battles to retain—as well as the hierarchies within culture itself, all begin to dissolve away. "Yet," Jameson notes,

> to argue that culture is today no longer endowed with the relative autonomy it once enjoyed as one level among others in earlier moments of capitalism (let alone in precapitalist societies) is not necessarily to imply its disappearance or extinction. Quite the contrary; we must go on to affirm that the dissolution of an autonomous sphere of culture is rather to be imagined in terms of an explosion: a prodigious expansion of culture throughout the social realm, to the point at which everything in our social life—from economic value and state power to practices and to the very structure of the

psyche itself—can be said to have become "cultural" in some original and yet untheorized way.[21]

Moreover, Jameson argues that forms and practices such as architecture and "political power" have become in the original situation of the postmodern increasingly "textualized," and hence made more readily available to scholars trained in strategies of literary and philosophical reading (a claim Catherine Gallagher and Stephen Greenblatt will then reconfirm a decade later in their "retroactive manifesto" for New Historicist practice).[22] Thus, in a significant way, the disciplinary boundaries that had been so effectively blurred in his earlier work now all but vanish: the entire expanded cultural and textual realm become grist for Jameson's voracious analytical mill, giving new resonance to Colin MacCabe's observation I referred to in the opening pages of this book, "nothing cultural is alien to him." Moreover, this work marks Jameson's own increasing influence in disciplines beyond literary scholarship—something too that also occurs in terms of the work of the other great theorists (think, for example, of Derrida's 1980s writings on architecture and his collaborations with Peter Eisenman, or of the diverse range of theorists brought together in the *Any* series of architectural conferences in the 1990s). And this expansion also means that the stakes in these discussions have been raised, as Jameson argues: "This is surely the most crucial terrain of ideological struggle today, which has migrated from concepts to representations."[23]

However, often overlooked in discussions of Jameson's work on postmodernism is the fact that in both the 1984 essay and the later book he approaches these diverse cultural "texts" through what are in fact two very distinct optics. First, some of his engagements are aimed at developing what he calls a "symptomology" of various dimensions of the original experience of the postmodern. "Art therefore," he maintains, and which we might expand to cultural and textual production more generally, "yields social information primarily as symptom. Its specialized machinery (itself obviously symptomatic of social specialization more generally) is capable of registering and recording data with a precision unavailable in other modes of modern experience . . . its configurations allow us to take the temperature of the current situation."[24] The "data" that he uncovers in this fashion are the central characteristics of the postmodern, the list of which has now become, in a large part thanks to his investigations, a familiar one: the collapse of critical distance, the waning of affect, the weakening of historicity, the dissolution of the centered subject, the disappearance of the referent, and the new centrality of the image and information technologies.[25]

The conception of the postmodern that Jameson offers here is thus "a historical rather than a merely stylistic one," as he attempts to grasp the postmodern as "the cultural dominant of the logic of late capitalism."[26] And indeed, in this study, Jameson will draw extensively upon Ernest Mandel's major work of political economy, *Late Capitalism,* for an explanation of the material transformations that lie at the root of postmodern cultural productions. Mandel's book, Jameson notes, "sets out not merely to anatomize the historic originality of this new society (which he sees as a third stage or moment in the evolution of capital) but also to demonstrate that it is, if anything, a purer stage of capitalism than any of the moments that preceded it."[27] Each of these two approaches to the postmodern, he goes on to argue, generates very different ways of conceptualizing this material: if the stylistic approach, wherein the postmodern becomes one optional practice among other, results in "moral judgments (about which it is indifferent whether they are positive or negative)," the historical offers "a genuinely dialectical attempt to think our present of time in history."[28]

Such a symptomological historical investigation is made both necessary and more difficult by another mutation that occurs in the postmodern: the shift from the older conceptual category of the "work" to that of the "text." This shift, Jameson contends,

> throws the chicken coops of criticism into commotion fully as much as it stirs those of "creation": the fundamental disparity and incommensurability between *text* and *work* means that to select sample texts and, by analysis, to make them bear the universalizing weight of a representative particular, turns them imperceptibly back into that older thing, the work, which is not supposed to exist in the postmodern. This is, as it were, the Heisenberg principle of postmodernism, and the most difficult representational problem for any commentator to come to terms with, save via the endless slide show, "total flow" prolonged into the infinite.[29]

It is this kind of "total flow prolonged into the infinite," or what Hegel calls "bad infinity," that we see in the proliferation of analyses in the

1980s and early 90s inspired by or imitating Jameson's discussion, as more and more objects and practices are read as symptoms of this new cultural system.

And yet, while he will claim a new global nature for culture within the postmodern, Jameson carefully demarcates the specific horizons of his analysis. First, he points out that his focus at this juncture remains almost exclusively on the particular cultural productions of the United States, "which is justified only to the degree that it was the brief 'American century' (1945–73) that constituted the hothouse, or forcing ground of the new system, while the development of the cultural forms of postmodernism may be said to be the first specifically North American global style."[30] Similarly, Jameson points out the particular class content of these forms, practices, and ideologies:

> For one can also plausibly assert that "postmodernism" in the more limited sense of an ethos and a "life-style" (truly a contemptible expression, that) is the expression of the "consciousness" of a whole new class fraction . . . a new petite bourgeoisie, a professional-managerial class, or more succinctly . . . "the yuppies". . . . This identification of the class content of postmodern culture does not at all imply that yuppies have become something like a new ruling class, merely that their cultural practices and values, their local ideologies, have articulated a useful dominant ideological and cultural paradigm for this stage of capitalism.[31]

There are two significant conclusions to be drawn from these comments. First, as Caren Irr points out in a superb reading of the dialectical and Hegelian roots of Jameson's theorization of postmodernism and globalization, we find in Jameson's work "a recurring treatment of national culture—especially American culture—as a dialectical ground, not as a cause in the Newtonian or simple mechanical fashion."[32] That is, operating in a way akin to the concept of production in Marx's theorization of the capitalist mode of production, American culture is in Jameson's theorization neither the "mechanical" cause nor even the inner logic "expressed" by postmodern culture, but rather the lonely hour of the last instance, or absent cause of postmodernism's global structure, the latter "nowhere empirically present as an element, it is not a part of the whole or one of the levels, but rather the entire system of *relationships* among those levels."[33] Second, on a more phenomenological level,

Jameson leaves open in these remarks the possibility that the postmodern will in fact be "lived" differently in other locations within the now unified global totality—exactly what, as we shall see momentarily, will become the focus of his intellectual work in the years following the publication of this book.

It is on the basis of this first dimension of his investigation that a number of critics have argued that Jameson's analysis of the postmodern is a despairing one, nostalgic for the critical distances and historicity of the modernist moment, and unable to see any way of challenging the terrible self-replicating stasis of the present.[34] However, this is to confuse only the first part of the story with the whole, and ignores the fact that Jameson goes on to conclude the 1984 essay with a call for the development, in terms of the original situation of the postmodern, of a new "pedagogical political culture"—the aesthetic practice he names *cognitive mapping*. Jameson opens his earlier essay entitled "Cognitive Mapping" with a confession: cognitive mapping is "a subject about which I know nothing, whatsoever, except for the fact that it does not exist." He goes on to note, echoing a classic Althusserian formulation, that the essay that follows will involve nothing less than an attempt "to produce the concept of something we cannot imagine."[35] The project he begins here thus offers less a fully articulated vision of this political aesthetic practice than an allegory, or a pre-figuration, of something only the earliest intimations of which might now be glimpsed. Jameson does, however, go on in this inaugural discussion to outline some of the fundamental coordinates of this type of cultural work: its pedagogical function, as it teaches us something about what would be involved in positioning ourselves in the world; its thoroughly spatial and collective orientation; and finally, its totalizing movement: "The project of cognitive mapping obviously stands or falls with the conception of some (unrepresentable, imaginary) global social totality that was to have been mapped."[36] This last aspect in particular is what makes cognitive mapping such an untimely endeavor in the postmodern present: "what I have called cognitive mapping may be identified as a more modernist strategy, which retains an impossible concept of totality whose representational failure seemed for the moment as useful and productive as its (inconceivable) success."[37]

Cognitive mapping fills in the absent place of the Symbolic in Althusser's idiosyncratic adaptation of the Lacanian tripartite schema of the Imaginary, the Symbolic, and the Real. In fact, what we have here are three forms of the symbolic, three different modes of presentation, or three different languages—a language of the Imaginary, of the Real, and with Jameson's addition of cognitive mapping, of the Symbolic itself. Cognitive mapping has the effect of coordinating these other two poles, the existential and phenomenological *experience* of people in their daily lives and the *abstract* global economic, political, and social totalities we always already inhabit. The former is most effectively presented through literary and aesthetic practices, while the latter is the focus of "theory" or what Althusser himself calls "science."[38] It is for this reason that cognitive mapping is *not* to be identified with other tools Jameson deploys, such as the Greimasian semiotic square: the latter as a formalization is a part of an Althusserian repertoire of science, a touching upon the real where the subject, individual or collective, is bracketed aside.

Thus, at once neither what we conventionally think of as art or theory/science, the cognitive mapping Jameson calls for here,

> will have to hold to the truth of postmodernism, that is to say, to its fundamental object—the world space of multinational capital—at the same time at which it achieves a breakthrough to some as yet unimaginable new mode of representing this last, in which we may again begin to grasp our positioning as individual and collective subjects and regain a capacity to act and struggle which is at present neutralized by our spatial as well as our social confusion. The political form of postmodernism, if there ever is any, will have as its vocation the invention and projection of a global cognitive mapping, on a social as well as a spatial scale.[39]

The rest of the book then moves between the two projects outlined in the inaugural essay, analyzing "symptomatic" texts—the experience of space in the Bonaventure Hotel, the experimental video *AlienNATION,* New Historicism, de Manian nominalism, and market rhetoric—to see what particular aspects of the postmodern condition they might illuminate; *and* exploring other allegories of the cognitive mapping process— for example, Gober's installation projects and the new genre Jameson names "allegorical encounter" films—for further lessons about what such a new political aesthetic might look like.

The practice of generating allegories of cognitive mappings is perhaps most effectively on display in Jameson's breathtaking analysis of the ways the architect Frank Gehry's home in Santa Monica, California, "tries to think through this spatial problem in spatial terms."[40] Jameson argues that Gehry's "wrapping" of a traditional suburban postwar ranch house in abstract high modernist forms produces an original third space: "It is essentially only this last type of space—the result of dialectical engagement between the two others—which can be characterized as postmodern: that is to say, some radically new spatiality beyond the traditional and the modern alike which seems to make some historical claim for radical difference and originality."[41] In this way, the problem that the structure "tries to think is the relationship between that abstract knowledge and conviction or belief about the superstate [i.e., the Real] and the existential daily life of people in their traditional rooms and tract homes [i.e., the Imaginary]. There must be a relationship between those two realms or dimensions of reality, or else we are altogether within science fiction without realizing it."[42] The thinking of this relationship is precisely the challenge of cognitive mapping more generally, and Gehry's house has the virtue not of solving this dilemma but of providing us with a figure of the problem that so urgently confronts us in the present.

There remains, however, a good deal of confusion surrounding Jameson's concept of cognitive mapping. For example, an essay on the science fiction film *The Matrix* (1999) opens with the claim that in the film "the new cognitive map of multinational capitalism has been drawn."[43] What occurs here is a slight but significant substitution—the concept of "map" in a sense that rarely (if ever) appears in Jameson's work for his preferred "mapping," or the full infinitive form, "to map." Jameson warns, in a early statement that foregrounds this distinction, "Since everyone knows what a map is, it would have been necessary to add that cognitive mapping cannot (at least in our time) involve anything so easy as a map; indeed, once you knew what 'cognitive mapping' was driving at, you were to dismiss all figures of maps and mapping from your mind and try to imagine something else."[44] To slip into the language of the map as an achieved thing is, Jameson argues, to give in to the hegemony of the image and the visual (marked, as we shall see, by a resurgence of traditional aesthetics and ethics) that is such a central dimension of postmodern ideology itself.

Moreover, this confusion of map and mapping is akin to the collapsing together of the concepts of totality and totalizing or totalization (and ultimately both into totalitarianism) that occurs in a good deal of the criticisms of Jameson's project in particular and Marxism more generally.[45] Cognitive mapping, like totalization, is always already, as the verb form suggests, a *process,* a way of *making* connections, of *drawing* networks, and of *situating* ourselves as both individual and collective subjects within a particular spatial system. Thus, I would argue that cognitive mapping needs to be understood as a way of producing *narratives,* mappings that unfold through time, rather than static images, formalizations, or maps—and it is in this affirmation of the power of narrative that we see most clearly Jameson's refusal to accept the apparent closures and ahistoricity of the postmodern that he so effectively outlines elsewhere. And, again as he stresses in his Foreword to Jean-François Lyotard's *The Postmodern Condition,* the "*insistence*" on narrative "in a situation in which the narratives themselves henceforth seem impossible" is a "declaration of intent to remain political and contestatory."[46]

Moreover, when he argues early on that cognitive mapping "does not exist" and needs to be invented, he is not calling for the development of the aesthetics of cognitive mapping per se, but rather for the production of a *new form of cognitive mapping,* one appropriate to the social, political, and economic realities we inhabit in this moment.[47] For as even his earliest discussions of this notion make apparent, cognitive mappings have occurred in the past, and continue to do so in the present, on a number of different spatial scales. In Kevin Lynch's original formulation in *The Image of the City,* from which Jameson draws this concept, cognitive mapping refers to the sense of place and location people actively construct in spaces such as those of the city: "Disalienation in the traditional city, then, involves the practical reconquest of a sense of place and the construction or reconstruction of an articulated ensemble which can be retained in memory and which the individual subject can map and remap along the moments of mobile, alternative trajectories."[48] Jameson then goes on to suggest that while Lynch's formulation "is limited by the deliberate restriction of his topic" to the spatial scale of the city form, "it becomes extraordinarily suggestive when projected outward" to new and emerging scales of the social totality.[49]

Such a movement across spatial scale is also, I would argue, a historical process. For it is the emergence of capitalist modernity that first gives rise to a new scale of cognitive mapping, one that successfully subsumes and supersedes older local ones—a cognitive mapping or narrative practice that will be called *nationalism.* It is what Benedict Anderson famously calls the "imagined community" of the nation that unifies and draws together into a coherent ensemble the lived everyday experience of individuals and the abstract economic and political realities of the newly emerging capitalist states. The fact that this cognitive mapping is a narrative operation is further borne out by Žižek, who notes that when we are asked to describe nationalism, we retreat to a form of story-telling: "All we can do is enumerate disconnected fragments of the way our community organizes its feasts, its rituals of mating, its initiation ceremonies, in short, all the details by which is made visible the unique way a community *organizes its enjoyment.*"[50] In the literary realm, the privileged aesthetic expression of this older form of cognitive mapping is the realist novel, especially in the form of what Bakhtin calls its "second stylistic trend."[51]

The achievement of this new scale of cognitive mapping—an achievement that represents a qualitative as much as a quantitative change—then creates the grounds for the emergence of a whole series of new forms of collective politics and struggle: the industrial union, the party, the national strike, decolonization, and ultimately, national revolution. Crucially, Jameson's underlying presupposition in calling for a new cognitive mapping is that these older political organizational forms are simply no longer sufficient for acting within the space and social totality we inhabit today. Indeed, Jameson, scandalously to many, argues:

> Politics works only when these two levels [the local and the global] can be coordinated; they otherwise drift apart into a disembodied and easily bureaucratized abstract struggle for and around the state, on the one hand, and a properly interminable series of neighborhood issues on the other, whose "bad infinity" comes, in postmodernism, where it is the only form of politics left, to be invested with something of Nietzsche's social Darwinism and with the willed euphoria of some metaphysical permanent revolution. I think myself that the euphoria is a compensation formation, in a situation in which, for a time, genuine (or "totalizing") politics is no longer possible; it is necessary to add that what is lost in its absence, the global dimension, is very precisely the dimension of economics itself, or of the system, of private enterprise and the profit motive, which cannot be challenged on a local level.[52]

In short, the production of new forms of cognitive mapping is imperative for a new and heretofore unimaginable politics to emerge. And it is in this shift in scale—from the national to the global—that also marks what may in fact be a new "period" in Jameson's thinking, or more precisely, the full flourishing of what has been put on the agenda by his earlier work on postmodernism.

Contemporaneous with his first major essays on postmodernism, Jameson also publishes what would become one of his most controversial essays, "Third World Literature in the Era of Multinational Capitalism."[53] Jameson defines third world literature in the following way: "Third-world texts, even those which are seemingly private and invested with a properly libidinal dynamic—necessarily project a political dimension in the form of national allegory: *the story of the private destiny is always an allegory of the embattled situation of the public third-world culture and society.*"[54] Jameson first develops the concept of national allegory in his book on Wyndham Lewis, through his reading of Lewis's novel *Tarr* (1918): "Such a juxtaposition reminds us that the use of national types projects an essentially allegorical mode of representation, in which the individual characters figure those more abstract national characteristics which are read as their inner essence."[55] The ways in which this concept prefigures that of cognitive mapping is made explicit a few pages later, where Jameson writes, "Thus, national allegory should be understood as a formal attempt to bridge the increasing gap between the existential data of everyday life within a given nation-state and the structural tendency of monopoly capital to develop on a worldwide, essentially transnational scale."[56] The events of the First World War, "with its demolition of the older diplomatic system of the nation states, put an end to national allegory," at least within the context of Europe, which then turns its attention to and develops new representational forms to grapple with "the great postnational ideologies of Communism and Fascism."[57] However, this essentially modernist practice finds a new lease on life in the emergent conditions of the decolonizing Third World, Jameson's case studies in the essay being Lu Xun's short story "Diary of a Madman" (1918), and the great Senegalese writer and "father of African film" Ousmane Sembène's novel and film *Xala* (1973 and 1975), the latter bearing out as well Perry Anderson's point about the way modernism experiences in the 1960s and in a number of different locations "a brief after-glow."[58] Within such a situation, where Western domination is a palpable fact of everyday life, Jameson concludes, "the telling of the individual story and the individual experience cannot but ultimately involve the laborious telling of the experience of the collectivity itself."[59]

I have argued elsewhere that one of the more under-appreciated dimensions of Jameson's argument is the degree to which it unfolds as an exercise in *generic thinking;* much of the debate surrounding Jameson's essay dissipates if we view it not as offering ontological claims about the nature of all cultural production in the "third world," but rather as a strategic intervention aimed, like all genre criticism, at constituting both a set of interpretive practices, pegged in fact to a particular spatial scale, and a corpus of texts upon which these will go to work.[60] The importance of this essay for our concerns here, however, lies in the way it marks a significant turning point in Jameson's intellectual project. In the essay's final footnote, Jameson observes that one of the fundamental philosophical underpinnings of his description of the genre is, along with Hegel's master-slave dialectic, Georg Lukács's model of class consciousness, or standpoint epistemology, wherein a "'mapping' or the grasping of the social totality is structurally available to the dominated rather than the dominating classes."[61] Moreover, he goes on to note that his concept of "national allegory" also represents a sub-genre of the larger aesthetic of cognitive mapping, this essay serving as "a pendant" to "Postmodernism, or, The Cultural Logic of Late Capitalism." Thus, when we read the two essays in conjunction in the ways Jameson suggests here, we suddenly realize that what is occurring is a gradual reconfiguration of the aesthetic category of cognitive mapping to incorporate different kinds of representational acts—acts, moreover, that originate in different locations within the global totality. Such a proliferation of perspectives continues in the collection of essays that make up the first part of *Signatures of the Visible*: the films that serve as the central objects of analysis here originate in the U.S. Hollywood system (*Jaws, The Godfather, Dog Day Afternoon, The Shining*); France (*Diva*); West Germany (Hans-Jürgen Syberberg's 1970s documentary trilogy); Poland (*Fever*); Venezuela (*La Casa de Agua*); and Colombia (*Condores ne entierran todos los dias*).

In *Signatures of the Visible* as much as in the diptych he suggests is composed of the "Third World Literature" and "Postmodernism" essays, the various perspectives offered on an emerging global reality remain largely detached from one another. However, in Jameson's next major film study, *The Geopolitical Aesthetic: Cinema and Space in the World System* (1992), we see a self-conscious effort to coordinate these various perspectives—there must be relationships between them or we already live in science fiction without knowing it—in order to produce a more systematic, and hence more totalizing, mapping of the present. Moreover, in the very form of this remarkable and original book we witness the re-emergence of the kinds of narrative energies that I suggested were in abeyance in the postmodernism studies.

Or to put this another way, the form of the presentation (*Darstellung*) of *The Geopolitical Aesthetic* stands as an allegorical figuration of what a truly global cognitive mapping might look like.[62] Jameson opens the book with a discussion of U.S. conspiracy films, expanding upon an observation in the "Postmodernism" essay that "conspiracy theory (and its garish narrative manifestations) must be seen as a degraded attempt—through the figuration of advanced technology—to think the impossible totality of the contemporary world system."[63] Clint Burnham usefully glosses this insight in this way: "The great philosophical 'tic' of the dialectician is to see connections everywhere; this is not quite the same thing as seeing conspiracies; the latter come about, like religion, when political impulses toward the collective cannot reach their fruition through an authentic means."[64] In short, conspiracy signals the desire for cognitive mapping in those situations where its realization seems most difficult to achieve. This impossible desire, a desire for narrative, reaches its most complete figuration in a scene from *All the President's Men* (1976) that Jameson recalls at the chapter's climax. There we see the film's "social detectives" at work in the Library of Congress, wherein unexpectedly the camera "literally rises from the very small (the reading-room call slips) to the social totality itself." Jameson comments,

> For it is the impossible vision of totality—here recovered in the moment in which the possibility of conspiracy confirms the possibility of the very unity of the social order itself— that is celebrated in this well-nigh paradisal moment. This is then the link between the phenomenal and the noumenal, or the ideological and the Utopian. This mounting image, underscored by the audible emergence, for the first time in the film, of the solemn music that so remarkably confirms the investigation's and the film's *telos,* in which the map of conspiracy itself, with its streets now radiating out through Washington from this ultimate center, unexpectedly suggests the possibility of cognitive mapping as a whole and stands as its substitute and yet its allegory all at once.[65]

However, the story does not end here, as Jameson then proceeds to read films from a set of sites all of which might be best characterized as transitional zones: the Soviet Union in its last hours (Alexander Sokurov's *Days of Eclipse*); Taiwan, or the "newly industrialized First-World tier of the Third World or Pacific Rim" (Edward Yang's *Terrorizer*)[66]; France, as it faces subsumption into the transnational entity of the European Union (Jean-Luc Godard's *Passion*); and the Philippines, presented as a privileged site for the recognition of a relentless modernization that affects a European First World as well (Kidlat Tahimik's *Perfumed Nightmare*). Not only do these various sites remind us of the insufficiency of the older national categories through which we continue to think, or narrate, the present, their multiple cartographic projections, when brought into the kind of coordination represented here by the narrative totality of Jameson's book itself, begin to illuminate the horizon of an emergent "geopolitical unconscious." Each chapter can be said to complement the visions offered in the others, such that none can be fully grasped without taking into account what unfolds in all of them considered as a collective. Jameson more recently has offered this characterization of such a process:

> These then begin to stake out the bounds of the Real, they approach it asymptotically in their very variety and in their contradictions, like the legendary blind men feeling the equally imaginary elephant's sensory properties—tail, trunk, hide, tusks, and so forth—and reporting back on their contradictory findings. This is then the triangulation of the Real, the identification of a heavy yet invisible body at the heart of space that moves all the counters and the pointers on all the dials of the universe in a barely perceptible yet inescapable way, a fluttering and a fluctuation through which the Real becomes as inescapable as it is unrepresentable.[67]

In *The Geopolitical Aesthetic*, Jameson argues that in just this way the earlier "national allegory" becomes refashioned "into a conceptual instrument for grasping our new being-in-the-world. It may henceforth be thought to be at least one of the fundamental allegorical referents or levels of all seemingly abstract philosophical thought: so that a fundamental hypothesis would pose the principle that all thinking today, is *also,* whatever else it is, an attempt to think the world system as such. All the more true will this be for narrative figurations."[68]

Equally importantly, the views from each of these locations are dramatically different, and thus offer the possibility of radically transforming and enriching our *collective* grasp of our shared global postmodern condition. In his concluding note to his engagement with *Passion,* Jameson writes,

A metaphor in the real: this peculiar object, calculated to mesmerize Lacanian theorization at its most hyperintellectual, is not without some structural similarity to the inner form of *Passion* itself—its love-work analogy projected onto the aesthetics of the visual, with gaps and distances for which, for the moment, we still only have the term "allegorical" as the sign of a theory yet to be constructed. This is now the task with which *Passion* confronts us, as a peculiar signifying artifact of a wholly new sort, which nonetheless, like a meteorite fallen from outer space, bears within it the promise and the suggestion that grasping its structure—were that really ever possible!—would also lead to grasping the structure of the modern age itself.[69]

Then in the book's subsequent and final chapter, Jameson argues that *Perfumed Nightmare* demonstrates that "What the First World thinks and dreams about the Third can have nothing whatsoever in common, formally or epistemologically, with what the Third World has to know every day about the First. Subalternity carries the possibility of knowledge with it, domination that of forgetfulness and repression."[70] Moreover, in his stirring conclusion to this chapter, Jameson argues that in both the form and content of this unique film we see the possibilities of new collective forms of life coming into being:

Unlike the "natural" or mythic appearances of traditional agricultural society, but equally unlike the disembodied machinic forces of late capitalist high technology, which seem, at the other end of time, equally innocent of any human agency or individual or collective praxis, the jeepney factory is a space of human labor which does not know the structural oppression of the assembly line or Taylorization, which is permanently provisional, thereby liberating its subjects from the tyrannies of form and of the pre-programmed. In it aesthetics and production are again at one, and painting the product is an integral part of its manufacture. Nor finally is this space in any bourgeois sense humanist or a golden mean, since spiritual or material proprietorship is excluded, and inventiveness has taken the place of genius, collective co-operation the place of managerial or demiurgic dictatorship.[71]

It is the lessons they hold for us about radically other ways of human being in the world that make so invaluable such spaces—again not outside, but rather located differently within the global totality (and in *Valences of the Dialectic,* Jameson notes "that these differences do not have to do with Difference so much as with where it is located or positioned").[72] For it is here that we see the re-emergence of the sense of historicity, or storytelling, so relentlessly driven out by the hegemonic postmodern. And what is history in this sense but our experience of our capacity to act in such a way as to (re)make our world?

It is the absolute and fundamental necessity of maintaining these multiple perspectives that also enables us to make sense of Jameson's subsequent interest in the political potentialities of Kenneth Frampton's "critical regionalism": "not a rural place that resists the nation and its power structures but rather a whole culturally coherent zone (which may also correspond to political autonomy) in tension with the standardizing world system as a whole." It is such a practice, Jameson goes on to suggest, that might contain lessons for any effort at "resisting the standardizations of a henceforth global late capitalism and corporatism."[73] Similarly, Jameson has investigated the struggles to maintain national film industries in the face of the onslaught of Hollywood:

> It should be understood that the triumph of Hollywood film (from which I won't here separate out television, which is today just as important or even more so) is not merely an economic triumph, it is a formal and also a political one. . . . This is of course in another sense a relatively final death of the modern, insofar as independent filmmakers all over the world could be seen to be guided by a certain modernism; but it is also the death of the political, and an allegory of the end of the possibility of imagining radically different social alternatives to this one we now live under.[74]

The maintenance of such zones of autonomy—which might include the university itself—thus provides exactly the perspectival positions from which aspects of the world order of global capitalism can begin to be glimpsed; however, it is only in their collective unification and coordination then that any kind of cognitive mapping of such a globality will commence.

It is this emphasis on the multiplication of perspectives, as well as their necessary coordination, in an effort to think the contemporary geopolitical framework that I want to argue stands as one of the most significant lessons of Jameson's work for the collective project of cognitively mapping our emerging global cultural and social reality. However, as Jameson has stressed all along, cognitive mapping must be understood as only a first step; and the issue that I would like to end this discussion with is the way Jameson's own geopolitical aesthetic might serve as another kind of allegory—an allegory, or perhaps a pre-figuration, of the political formations that we will need to produce in order to regain the "possibility of imagining," and in imagining begin to produce "radically different social alternatives to this one we now live under." Eschewing any singular privileged perspective and stressing the importance of maintaining the particularity of every local intervention, while also always emphasizing the necessity of linking local struggles and thinking through them the economic horizons of the world system as a whole—whatever collective formations emerge that take up such an "impossible" task will be the global equivalent of the older national parties and political movements. Indeed, it may be exactly these new collective formations whose first stirrings can be seen in the alter-globalization practices that emerged in the latter part of the 1990s, such as the WTO protests, José Bové and François Dufour's French Farmers Confederation, and the Porto Allegre meetings. These are all expressions of what Hardt and Negri will then theorize as the creative "singularity of the multitude" in a truly postmodern global present. It will be to similar efforts in Jameson's project to think such collectivities that I will turn my attention in the remaining chapters of this book.

From the Symbolic to the Real

In this section I explore the implications for a materialist dialectics of A. J. Greimas's semiotics, and in particular what Jameson has described as its "supreme achievement," Greimas's "semiotic square."[1] My approach challenges what has become a commonplace—advanced, for example, in both Paul de Man's classic essay "The Resistance to Theory" (1982) and Paul Ricoeur's three-volume opus *Time and Narrative* (1983–85)—that Greimas's work and the tools he elaborates represent the quintessence of a structuralist drive to abstraction, marked by totalizing/totalitarian tendencies and a rejection of indeterminacy, historicity, and the diachronic. In de Man's terms, this drive to abstraction is the result of Greimas's absolute privileging of the deep grammatical level of a text over its surface rhetorical scheme. Ricoeur similarly concludes, "The whole strategy thus amounts to a vast attempt to do away with diachrony."[2]

While such a reading may be accurate in certain orthodox uses of these tools, a different set of possibilities emerges when in an imaginative leap the semiotic square is read in conjunction with the work of Greimas's contemporary Jacques Lacan, and in particular, "the fundamental classification system around which all his theorizing turns," the three orders of the Symbolic, Imaginary, and Real.[3] In this chapter, I use the rich semiotic resources of the Greimasian square to tell a number of interrelated stories: about the history of the novel; developments in the last few decades in theory more generally and in the work of Jameson in

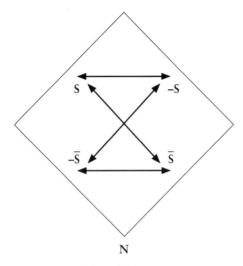

Figure 2. The semiotic square of A. J. Greimas.

particular; and the value of dialectical thinking for our present moment of globalization.

My gesture of reading Greimas with Lacan takes its lead from Lacan's work, by way of his essay "Kant avec Sade." In a footnote to a discussion of the essay, Slavoj Žižek suggests that "far from being restricted to Lacan, this procedure of reading 'X with Y' has a long Marxist lineage"; indeed, Žižek argues, "is not the main point of Marx's critique of Hegel's speculative idealism precisely to read 'Hegel with political economy,' that is, to discern in the speculative circular movement of Capital the 'obscene secret' of the circular movement of the Hegelian Notion?"[4] Furthermore, Žižek maintains that we misread this relationship if we see the latter figure in the couple as "the truth" of the former: "on the contrary, the Sadeian perversion emerges as the result of the Kantian compromise, of Kant's avoiding the consequences of his breakthrough. Sade is the *symptom* of Kant: . . . the space for the figure of Sade is opened up by this compromise of Kant, by his unwillingness to go to the end, to retain the full fidelity to his philosophical breakthrough."[5] Something similar occurs, I want to argue, when we read Greimas with Lacan. The latter shows us something new about the nature of the former's breakthrough: the always already existent symptom haunting the illusory closure of the structuralist schemas, a materializing horizon of dialectical possibilities implicit within the Greimasian mapping as well as the very structures they represent.[6]

The value for any dialectical criticism of Greimas's work—as well as that of Lacan—has been explored in great detail by Jameson, one of Greimas's most influential proponents in the English-language context, and it will be by way of the changes that occur in Jameson's original and creative deployment of Greimas's semiotic square that the device's full dialectical power becomes clear.[7] Eschewing any orthodox or disciplined application of the semiotic square, Jameson effects its Brechtian refunctioning (*Umfunktionierung*), acting in a way much like the workers in the Jeepney factory figured in Kidlat Tahmik's *Perfumed Nightmare:* both display a "kind of Brechtian delight with the bad new things that anybody can hammer together for their pleasure or utility if they have a mind to."[8] Jameson wrote the Foreword to *On Meaning* (1987), the first English-language collection of Greimas's writings, and one of the 88 books in the University of Minnesota Press Theory and History of Literature (THL) series (1981–1998), which also published the original two volumes of *The Ideologies of Theory* as well as a host of other landmark theoretical texts and translations, all of which contributed inestimably to the education of my generation of students and scholars. In his Foreword, Jameson notes, "my own testimony is that of a fellow traveler of Greimassian semiotics, with a deplorable nonchalance toward its orthodoxies, but also a passionate interest in the ongoing development and dynamic of this new 'discipline,' whose capacity to produce fresh problems, and urgent, exciting problems at that, is not the least sign of the deeper truth and rightness of its starting point."[9] In this context too, Jameson emphasizes the materiality, the labor of dialectical thought and writing, enacted in the semiotic square: "As for its heuristic value, however, experience testifies that you must blacken many pages before you get it right and that a number of key decisions intervene in the process."[10]

In short, Jameson "betrays," in the specific sense I discussed in my Introduction, the letter of Greimas "in order to remain faithful to (and repeat) the 'spirit' of his thought . . . the creative impulse underlying it."[11] The Utopian drive of such an approach, not only to Greimas but any theoretical legacy, is indicated in the opening of *Archaeologies of the Future,* where Jameson notes, "There is here some affinity with children's games; but also with the outsider's gift for seeing over-familiar realities in a fresh and unaccustomed way."[12] It is in this spirit of the creative play of the child and outsider that I continue the project Jameson inaugurates, by reading his most recent use of Greimas's semiotic square "with" Lacan's three orders. I do so in the hope of seeing both formalizations in fresh and unaccustomed ways.

For those less familiar with the workings of the square, or semiotic rectangle as he on occasion refers to it, Jameson's concise characterization in *The Political Unconscious* is still helpful:

> Briefly the semiotic rectangle or "elementary structure of signification" is the representation of a binary opposition or of two contraries (S and –S), along with the simple negations or contradictories of both terms (the so-called subcontraries –S̄ and S̄): significant slots are constituted by the various possible combinations of these terms, most notably the "complex" term (or ideal synthesis of the two contraries) and the "neutral" term (or ideal synthesis of the two subcontraries).[13]

From an initial binary opposition, or indeed from any single concept term, which always already presupposes a binary other, eight different slots become available (as well as two additional implicit ones in terms of the transversal axes, which Jameson notes, "map the place of tensions distinct from the principal or binary one").[14] The last two terms Jameson touches on in his description above, the *complex* and the *neutral*, will have especially significant roles to play in the development of his intellectual project more generally.

A few years later, Jameson further elaborates on what he takes to be the three "operative decisions" the critic must make in order most productively to use the device. First, there "is the inaugural decision, not merely about the terms of the binary opposition to be expanded and articulated in the square as a whole, but also, and above all, the very order in which those terms are arranged." It matters, in other words, how one presents the two terms of the initial binary, or even, as we shall see later, what constitutes the primary and secondary binaries. Secondly, he stresses, "the four primary terms [S, –S, S̄, –S̄] need to be conceived polysemically, each one carrying within it its own range of synonyms, and of the synonyms of its synonyms—none of them exactly coterminous with each other, such that large areas of relatively new or at least skewed conceptuality are thereby registered." It is such a polysemy that enables the construction of multiple overlapping schemas, often out of a single text (something Greimas himself suggested was necessary when dealing with complex narrative structures such as the novel). Finally, Jameson notes "the peculiar nature of the fourth term, the negation of the negation: [–S̄]. This must be (when the operation is successful) the place of novelty and of paradoxical emergence: it is always the most critical position and the one that remains open or empty for the longest time, for its identification completes the process and in that sense constitutes the most creative act of the construction."[15]

Jameson advances a similar claim in his inaugural discussion of Greimasian semiotics in his 1972 book on Russian Formalism and its structuralist descendants, *The Prison-House of Language*. At this early juncture, Jameson's focus remains primarily on the four internal "S" terms, and the dialectical movement he notes between them. Here, Jameson suggests that the fourth term, the $-\bar{S}$ that would be located in the bottom left slot in figure 2, may be identified

> as none other than the "negation of a negation" familiar from dialectical philosophy. It is, indeed, because the negation of a negation is such a decisive leap, such a production or generation of new meaning, that we so frequently come upon a system in the incomplete state shown [in figure 3] (only three terms out of four given). Under such circumstances the negation of the negation then becomes the primary work which the mechanism is called upon to accomplish.[16]

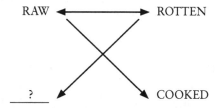

Figure 3. Fredric Jameson, *The Prison-House of Language*, 166.

Jameson goes on to demonstrate how this generative machinery operates through a brief discussion of Charles Dickens's *Hard Times* (1854), a novel in which "we witness the confrontation of what amounts to two intellectual systems: Mr. Gradgrind's utilitarianism ('Facts! Facts!') and the world of anti-facts symbolized by Sissy Jupe and the circus, or in other words, imagination."[17] Jameson argues that the narrative's plot is to be understood as "nothing but an attempt to give" the absent fourth term "imaginative being, to work through faulty solutions and unacceptable hypotheses until an adequate embodiment has been realized in terms of the narrative material. With this discovery (Mr. Gradgrind's education, Louisa's belated experience of family love), the semiotic rectangle is completed and the novel comes to an end."[18]

It is worth underscoring that even at this early stage Jameson already conceptualizes the Greimasian schema in decidedly dynamic terms, as a presentation (*Darstellung*) of the labor of narrative, "the all informing process of *narrative*," he will later claim, being "the central function or *instance* of the human mind."[19] The Greimasian semiotic square thus provides an effective answer to a question that he raises earlier in *The Prison-House of Language* during his discussion of Russian Formalism and Vicktor Shklovsky's *Theory of Prose:*

> The problem of plot is thus not solved by the above enumeration of techniques or devices. There remains the second and more difficult question of their organization, the ultimate question, in short, of the totality of the work: "What is necessary in order for a story to strike us as *complete?*" To put it another way, one of the basic requirements for any theory of plot must be that it contain some means of distinguishing that which is not plot, that which is incomplete, that which does not work.[20]

Greimas helps us grasp something like a "structuralist aesthetic," wherein effective narrative closure occurs only when "all the bases in some underlying semiotic system" have been touched, all of the possible permutations of the original conceptual problem worked through and given figurative expression.[21]

With his next deployments of the semiotic square, in his essays on Max Weber (1973), Philip K. Dick (1975), and Lacan (1977), and then, even more spectacularly, in the Balzac and Conrad chapters of *The Political Unconscious,* Jameson's attention shifts to the four outer poles of the schema, and especially the position at its summit, the "complex" term (C).[22] Greimas's semiotic square becomes an ideal means of illustrating the fundamental narrative operation that Jameson is now in a position to fully theorize as "a symbolic act, whereby real social contradictions, insurmountable in their own terms, find a purely formal resolution in the aesthetic realm."[23] It is in this way, too, that the cultural text, conceived here fundamentally as allegory, makes available to its later readers its historical context, encountered by us, he famously maintains, only in this mediated textual form.

Rather than summarizing one of Jameson's discussions, I will illustrate this first full deployment of the resources of the Greimasian semiotic square through a brief reading of my own. My case study is one of the most well known English novels of the early nineteenth century, and one of the ur-texts of the modern genre of science fiction, Mary Shelley's

Frankenstein; or, The Modern Prometheus (1818). The dilemma this gothic fantasy confronts, as numerous commentators have pointed out in different ways, is that of the modern intellectual and, more specifically, scientific labor. At the root of the problem in the novel is the education, or culture, that Victor Frankenstein receives at his modern (i.e., German) university.

Early on, Mary Shelley develops a character schema that enables her to divide human knowledge in a proto-Kantian fashion into the spheres of science, ethics, and aesthetics, each personified by one of the primary characters. Thus, Victor observes,

> Elizabeth was of a calmer and more concentrated disposition; but, with all my ardour, I was capable of a more intense application and was more deeply smitten with the thirst for knowledge. She busied herself with following the aerial creations of the poets; and in the majestic and wondrous scenes that surrounded our Swiss home. . . . It was the secrets of heaven and earth that I desired to learn . . . my inquiries were directed to the metaphysical, or in its highest sense, the physical secrets of the world. Meanwhile, Clerval occupied himself with the moral relations of things. The busy stage of life, the virtues of heroes, and the actions of men were his theme.[24]

As long as a balance among the three is maintained, trouble is averted. However, when Victor leaves the companionship of Clerval and Elizabeth, he embarks on a much more dangerous path: "From this day natural philosophy, and particularly chemistry, in the most comprehensive sense of the term, became my sole occupation."[25] This sunders the older "natural" unity ("Our meddling intellect / Mis-shapes the beauteous forms of things:— / We murder to dissect") championed by Shelley's circle of Romantic intellectuals.[26]

However, Victor's culpability lies less in his giving life to his "unnatural" creature—an aesthetically horrifying reanimated assemblage of different bodies—than in his subsequent abandonment of that to which his labor had given rise. That is, Victor's real failure, and his responsibility for the subsequent terror and innocent deaths, lies, as the creature itself notes, in his unwillingness to offer it the guidance found in a proper enculturation: "Unfeeling, heartless creator! You had endowed me with perceptions and passions and then cast me abroad an object for the scorn and horror of mankind."[27]

The contradiction with which this novel deals with is actually the same as in Greimas's original demonstration, that of culture and nature.[28] I have already touched on two of the resolutions found in Shelley's work, that on the left-hand side of the schema, and that on the bottom, or what Greimas labels the "neutral term" (N): first, the combination of culture, or bourgeois education, and the "unnatural"—intellectual overspecialization, or instrumentalization as Max Horkheimer and Theodor Adorno will later describe it—represented by the figure of Victor; and second, the destructive and improperly educated force of the creature itself. This mapping makes clear the double structure of "monstrosity" at work in the novel, at once meant to include the modern intellectual and his creations (figure 4).[29] The parallels between the two become increasingly evident as the novel progresses: both are isolated from intercourse with other humans, and, in the end, "revenge" becomes each being's "devouring and only passion."[30]

The resolution directly opposite Victor also suggests the classed nature of the crisis being dealt with here: for this is figured in the novel by the peasantry, those who may be connected to older natural or agricultural rhythms ("The untaught peasant beheld the elements around him and was acquainted with their practical uses"), but who lack the proper ethical education to respond with anything but animal fear and revul-

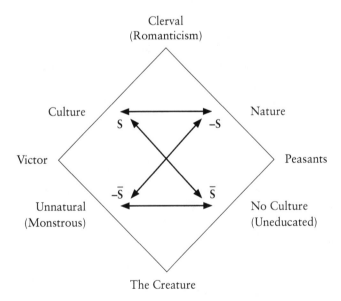

Figure 4. Mary Shelley, *Frankenstein; or, The Modern Prometheus* (1818).

sion when confronted with the radical otherness of the creature: "The whole village was roused; some fled, some attacked me."[31] Of course, these very lumpen bodies compose the flesh of the monster and they thus encounter in him their own denaturalized state, what Sartre would call their "practico-inert" form. In this way, the monster takes on an additional allegorical resonance, becoming a figure of a now alienated peasantry recently removed to the new urban environs—or, as Franco Moretti suggests, a figure already of the emergent industrial proletariat, the novel expressing the "elementary scheme" described by Marx "of simplification and splitting ('The whole of society must split into the two classes. . .')."[32]

And what then of the final space, the complex term, "the ideal synthesis which would 'resolve' the initial binary opposition by subsuming it under a single unity"?[33] It is filled by Victor's childhood companion, Henry Clerval, a figure we are told who stands in the text for Mary Shelley's husband, the Romantic poet Percy Bysshe Shelley:[34]

> Clerval! Beloved friend! Even now it delights me to record your words and to dwell on the praise of which you are so eminently deserving. He was a being formed in the "very poetry of nature." His wild and enthusiastic imagination was chastened by the sensibility of his heart. His soul overflowed with ardent affections, and his friendship was of that devoted and wondrous nature that the world-minded teach us to look for only in the imagination. But even human sympathies were not sufficient to satisfy his eager mind. The scenery of external nature, which others regard only with admiration, he loved with ardour.[35]

However, here the realism of Mary Shelley's work comes to the fore, for this ideal creature can find no place in the world, and he perishes (as Shelley himself would do a few years after the book's original publication), leaving us at the narrative's conclusion with the apocalyptic scenario of Victor and the creature tormenting each other in a pursuit across a frozen landscape, a desperate quest that ends only with their mutual destruction—a terrible object lesson aimed at both the story's narrator, the ambitious young explorer Robert Walton, and the reader.[36]

The story that Mary Shelley relates here is thus one of a failed cultural revolution, the inability of the Romantic intellectuals to take up a position of cultural and social leadership, to become, in other words, the *acknowledged* "legislators of the world" (a fantasy brought to fruition in the science-fiction alternate history of William Gibson and Bruce Sterling's *The Difference Engine* [1990]).[37] The consequence of this failure is immense, for it has left other kinds of irresponsible intellectuals, driven by "mad enthusiasm," who mold "nature"—literally in this case the uneducated masses of the people—into something monstrous.[38] And with this turn, the full allegorical significance of both Victor and his monster becomes evident: "Victor Frankenstein and his startling creation are a scientific cipher for an overhasty radical intellectual at the time of the French Revolution animating (like the Ingolstadt Illuminati, so well known to the Shelleys) the '[hardly adequate] materials' (chap. 4) of the broad popular forces."[39]

That such a fear was prominent for English intellectuals more generally in this moment is borne out by Greimasian mappings of the narrative schemas in two of *Frankenstein*'s contemporaries, Walter Scott's *The Heart of Midlothian* (1818) and Jane Austen's *Emma* (1815) (figures 5 and 6). The strategies for confronting this crisis differ in each case: if Mary Shelley gives us the precursor to the twentieth-century dystopian narrative (her utopian mentality, like George Orwell's, a form of what Karl Mannheim names a "conservative" one), Scott, on the other hand, tries to assure his readers that the resolution to the crisis has already occurred with the establishment of the new legal structures of Great Britain nearly a century earlier, structures that the British people have freely chosen.[40] Conflicts in the novel's conclusion are then exported "out there," into the rapidly expanding field of the second British Empire.[41]

However, Austen's solution is the most ingenious of all. In a classic reading of the novel, Wayne Booth notes,

> "Jane Austen," like "Henry Fielding," is a paragon of wit, wisdom, and virtue. She does not talk about her qualities; unlike Fielding she does not in *Emma* call direct attention to her artistic skills. But we are seldom allowed to forget about her for all that. When we read this novel we accept her as representing everything we admire most. She is as generous and wise as Knightley; in fact, she is a shade more penetrating in her judgment. She is as subtle and witty as Emma would like to think herself. Without being sentimental she is in favor of tenderness. She is able to put an adequate but not excessive value on wealth and rank. She recognizes a fool when she sees one, but unlike Emma she knows that it is

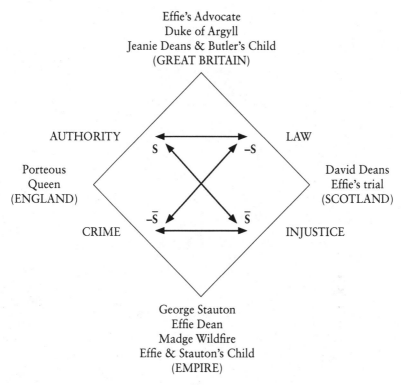

Figure 5. Walter Scott, *The Heart of Midlothian* (1818).

both immoral and foolish to be rude to fools. She is, in short, a perfect human being, within the concept of perfection established by the book she writes; she even recognizes that human perfection of the kind *she* exemplifies is not quite attainable in real life.[42]

In other words, it is not the character Emma who produces what Austen recognizes to be a necessary and proper (i.e., gradual and reformist) reordering of the social field, but rather the ghost who stands behind her, the novelist Austen herself, who orchestrates the various marriages that enable the conflicts of the novel to be dispelled and a new kind of national imaginary to be set into place. (The spatial movements in the plot that this entails have been effectively mapped by Moretti.)[43] In this way, the domestic novel becomes, as Nancy Armstrong has taught us, the preeminent political and pedagogical tool—so effective precisely

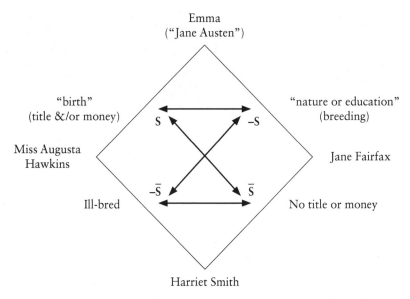

Figure 6. Jane Austen, *Emma* (1816). "Emma, your infatuation about that girl blinds you. What are Harriet Smith's claims, either of birth, nature or education. . . ?"

because it presents itself as feminine, domestic, and apolitical—in a properly British middle-class cultural revolution.[44]

It is this deployment of the Greimasian semiotic square as an effective way of mapping ideological closure that becomes over the next few decades such a significant and influential aspect of Jameson's work. However, in the very years that he is finishing work on *The Political Unconscious,* Jameson begins to experiment with another, even more original refunctioning of the tools made available by Greimas. This first occurs in a long review essay, published in a 1977 issue of *Diacritics,* on Louis Marin's *Utopiques: jeux d'espace* (1973) (figure 7).[45] Jameson shows that in Marin's development of his concept of Utopian neutralization—the figure of the Other Utopian order emerging as a point-by-point cancellation of the historical situation from which it emerges—it is the bottom term in the Greimasian schema that becomes the most significant one. Utopian narration serves in Marin's hands as

> the structural inversion of myth in the following sense: where as the narrative operation of myth undertakes to mediate between the two primary terms of the opposition S and –S, and

to produce a complex term that would be their resolution, Utopian narrative is constituted by the union of the twin contradictories of the initial opposition, the combination of $-\overline{S}$ and $\overline{S}$, a combination which, virtually a double cancellation of the initial contradiction itself, may be said to effect the latter's *neutralization* and to produce a new term, the so-called neuter or neutral term N.[46]

Jameson demonstrates this new use of the Greimasian schema through a reading of the Utopian figuration that takes place in the work of composer and architect Iannis Xenakis: "Xenakis' cosmic city is *both* decentralized and concentrated all at once, and designates, as a figure, that place in which some future urban conceptuality, the categories of some concrete collective and city life as yet inconceivable to us, remain to be invented."[47] However, Jameson goes on to point out that what is at one moment the corrosive clearing away and historical opening that is Utopian neutralization becomes, at another moment, simply ideology itself:

So the Utopian neutralization of the old ideology ends up making a contribution to the production of that new communicational one whose variants may be found in McLuhanism,

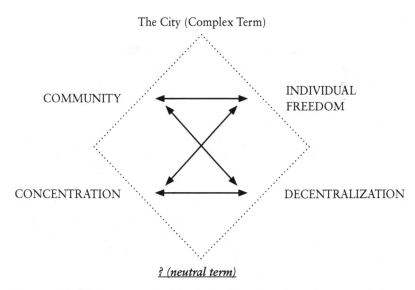

Figure 7. Fredric Jameson, "Of Islands and Trenches: Neutralization and the Production of Utopian Discourse," in *The Ideologies of Theory,* volume 2, 91.

systems theory, Habermas' "communications theory of society," and structuralism, to the degree to which each of these,
above and beyond its value as an instrument of analysis,
projects a more properly ideological anthropology or theory
of "human nature" according to which it is proposed that
society be organized.[48]

In this latter claim we also see some of the first indications of the line
of thought that will culminate a few years later in Jameson's original
and influential theory of postmodernism as the cultural logic of late
capitalism.

However, Jameson would not truly begin to explore this other deployment of the Greimasian schema until his later postmodernism study,
The Seeds of Time (1994). In this book, Jameson suggests that each of
the three essays, originally presented as the 1991 Wellek Library Lectures at the University of California, Irvine, "attempts a diagnosis of the
cultural present with a view toward opening a perspective onto a future
which they are clearly incapable of forecasting in any prophetic sense."[49]
The first essay offers a mapping of the central conceptual antinomies of
the postmodern; the second, by way of a reading of *Chevengur,* the "rediscovered" 1920s Soviet Utopia by Andrei Platonov, a confrontation
"with what has vanished from the postmodern scene;"[50] and the third,
of most interest to us here, a Greimasian permutational mapping of the
various architectural styles that have emerged in the present moment.

While Jameson claims that only the first chapter is "dialectical" in
its representational form (the third properly structural, and the second
"probably best characterized in more Freudian or depth psychological
terms"), I would suggest that there is a larger dialectical *Darstellung* at
work in the book as a whole.[51] Indeed, *The Seeds of Time* has a narrative structure whose unity and drama approach that of *Marxism and
Form.* The first section of the book begins by offering a provisional
mapping of some of the antinomies that structure the contemporary
situation: constant change and absolute stasis, spatial heterogeneity and
global homogeneity, a hostility to nature and a renewed sense of nature
as limits to human energy, and utopia and anti-utopia. These provide
an ideological shape to the lived experience of the particular historical
order, or "arrested dialectic," named the postmodern. The second section begins opening up this imaginary closure by marking the absences
haunting this situation—Utopia, modernism, and, at this moment, the
quite recent and unexpected disappearance of the Soviet Union and the

end of the Cold War. In this regard, Jameson's project here is not unlike that taking place in Jacques Derrida's *Specters of Marx: The State of Debt, the Work of Mourning, and the New International* (1993), a book that shortly thereafter will be the occasion of Jameson's most extended engagement with Derrida's work since *The Prison-House of Language.*[52]

In the third, final section of *The Seeds of Time,* Jameson presents and then elaborates upon the following two Greimasian mappings of contemporary architectural practice (figures 8 and 9). In the discussion that follows, Jameson turns his attention away from the complex term that had been at the center of his earlier uses of Greimas. In the first schema, he is primarily concerned with the two side resolutions and the ways that the architectural practices of Rem Koolhaas and Peter Eisenman offer partial, residual (or is it reemergent?) modernist architectural practices. Then in his final study, he explores the ways in which what Kenneth Frampton names Critical Regionalism emerges as a neutralization of the dominant practices of a "stylistic postmodernism," the latter represented by the canonical work of Michael Graves.

There are two very suggestive consequences of this new deployment of Greimas's semiotic square. First, Jameson's reading points toward an autonomy (but, as I will show shortly, really a semi-autonomy) of the three horizontal planes created by the exterior poles of the schema. Second, and even more importantly, the final or neutral position takes

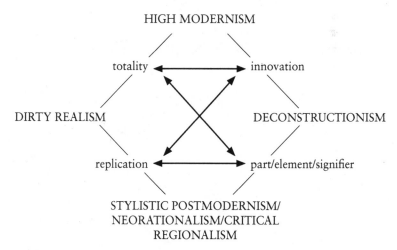

Figure 8. Fredric Jameson, *The Seeds of Time,* 133.

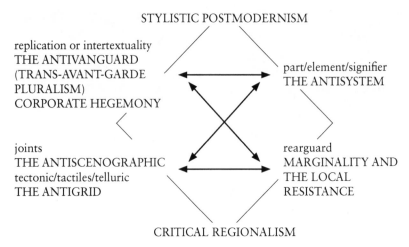

Figure 9. Fredric Jameson, *The Seeds of Time*, 195.

on a new centrality as the site of potential emergence within the spatial closure of the Greimasian mapping. The full dialectical force of this discovery is made evident in the following passage:

> For while it can be said that Critical Regionalism shares with them a systematic repudiation of certain essential traits of high modernism, it distinguishes itself by attempting at one and the same time to negate a whole series of postmodern negations of modernism as well, and can in some respects be seen as antimodern and antipostmodern simultaneously, in a "negation of the negation" that is far from returning us to our starting point or from making Critical Regionalism over into a belated form of modernism.[53]

Jameson is quite careful not to overvalue the achievements of this movement as it currently exists: rather, in his reading it stands as the formal allegorical placeholder for concrete potentialities, "the possibility of inventing some new relationship to the technological beyond nostalgic repudiation or mindless corporate celebration."[54] He subsequently notes,

> Frampton's conceptual proposal, however, is not an internal but rather a geopolitical one: it seeks to mobilize a pluralism of "regional" styles (a term selected, no doubt, in order to forestall the unwanted connotations of the terms *national*

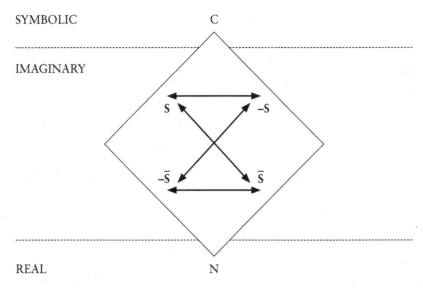

SYMBOLIC

IMAGINARY

REAL

Figure 10. Greimas's semiotic square with Lacan's three orders.

square, as they name the two poles of a historical contradiction whose logical matrix is composed by the four internal terms of the square.

Finally, the neutral term is homologous to the Lacanian Real, which Lacan describes in his first seminar as "*ce qui résiste absolument à la symbolization*" ("what resists symbolization absolutely"), and which in Jameson's earliest characterization becomes another name for "simply History itself."[62] Or, as Lorenzo Chiesa more precisely frames the issue in his insightful study, *Subjectivity and Otherness: A Philosophical Reading of Lacan* (2007), "there is something real in it which escapes the Symbolic, something which renders the symbolic Other 'not-all' and, for the same reason, makes it possible precisely as a differential symbolic structure."[63] Crucially, in a way whose significance will become clear in a moment, it is this resistance to symbolization, or to incorporation into the reigning order, that both accounts for the traumatic experience of any encounter with such a Real (hence, the monstrous figuration of the Real of revolution in Mary Shelley's fiction) and, even more significantly, assures the nonclosure or suturability of any reality, here represented by the other two planes of the Greimasian square.

The deeply dialectical nature of both Lacan's conceptualization of the three orders and Greimas's semiotic square lies in their emphasis on the inseparability of these multiple levels. Indeed, there is in this light an interesting figural resonance between the full Greimasian schema and Lacan's late typology of the Borromean knot. Moreover, the outer rectangle formed by the four terms of interest to us here may be productively understood as a figuration of the fourth ring Lacan describes in his final seminars as the sinthome.[64] At the same time, there is a heretofore unremarked upon correspondence between Greimas's figure and Lacan's earlier schema L, if the latter is rotated as shown in figure 11.[65] A dialectical criticism conceived in this fashion thus reveals its kinship with the work of analysis as Lacan presents it in his early work: intervening from the position of the Symbolic order, analysis attempts to cut through the deadlock, or disabling antinomies of the Imaginary, and enable an encounter with the traumatic Real.[66]

This emphasis on the Real also represents a significant shift within Lacan's own project, a shift that occurs, Chiesa argues, around the time of the 1959–60 seminar on *The Ethics of Psychoanalysis*. This takes the form a movement away from the earlier dominant formula, "There is an Other of the Other." Chiesa unpacks this formula in the following way: "the fact that there is a (symbolic) Other of the (symbolic) Other indicates that the Other as the order of signifiers is guaranteed by another transcendent Other, namely the paternal Law."[67] In this moment in Lacan's project, what Chiesa identifies as Lacan's structuralist phase,

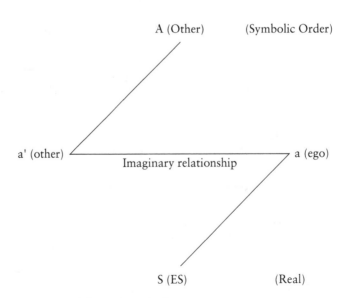

Figure 11. Lacan's Schema L, revised.

"the order of the Real is entirely separated from the Symbolic. The Real can be defined only negatively as that which the Symbolic is not" (i.e. as what resists symbolization absolutely).[68]

However, beginning with his 1960 essay "The Subversion of the Subject and the Dialectic of Desire in the Freudian Unconscious"—an essay that engages directly and critically with the "schema Hegel gave us of History" in *The Phenomenology of Spirit*—Lacan begins to turn his attention to the consequences of the new formula, "There is no Other of the Other."[69] Chiesa summarizes this development in the following way:

> Consequently, the most important effect of the passage from "there is an Other of the Other" (A) to "there is no Other of the Other" (A barred) is that the lack in the Other—the fact that, because of the differential logic of the signifying structure, a signifier is always missing from the battery of signifiers—is no longer intrasymbolic but should be considered as *real,* as a presence of the Real in the open structure of the Symbolic.[70]

It is precisely this opening up of the structure of the Greimasian schema that, I want to argue here, Jameson effects when he shifts his attention from the complex term (a structuralist deployment of the semiotic square) to the neutral, the latter best understood as a hole in the whole of the Greimasian figure—and indeed, there is a striking resonance between Chiesa's figure for the formula "There is no Other of the Other" and the Greimasian semiotic square as I refunction it here—something that becomes fully apparent only when we read Greimas with Lacan. The ultimate conclusion Chiesa draws from this reconceptualization is worth citing here as well, as it has important implications for the questions I will take up in the final section of this chapter:

> It goes without saying that such a direct politicization of *jouissance* is compatible with Lacanian psychoanalysis only if the fundamental fantasy it sets up is radically *new:* in other words, a Master-Signifier is progressive and consequently worth fighting for only if it closely follows the temporary assumption of the real lack in the Symbolic, *jouis-sans.* At the risk of oversimplifying an intricate issue which is only introduced here, I would go so far as to suggest that any possible political elaboration of the extreme ethics of the *ex*

nihilo should rely on the equation between what is new and what is good.[71]

My hypothesis would be that the Greimasian schema reconceived in this way offers us a representation of the very movement of dialectical thinking and writing. Most immediately, this claim enables us to read in a new way the labor taking place in some of Jameson's own earlier schemas. For example, in his Foreword to *On Meaning,* Jameson develops a mapping of Hayden White's masterpiece, *Metahistory: The Historical Imagination in Nineteenth Century Europe* (1973), that places the resolutions represented by the figures of Nietzsche and Hegel/Marx opposite each other on the plane of the Greimasian schema that I have suggested corresponds to the Lacanian Imaginary.

However, Jameson also notes that White ultimately gives a "tentative priority of Nietzsche over the other two positions insofar as Nietzsche 'includes' their moments of Tragedy and Comedy and then projects further new and original possibilities, Metaphor and Irony (properly linguistic or reflexive moments), out of the earlier pair."[72] Nietzsche "begins with an identification of Tragedy and Comedy, which luminously eclipse each other and in their indistinction give rise to something else, which will be an Ironic sense of the powers of language that now once again releases the great Metaphoric energies."[73] This privileging of the Nietzschean view over the classical Marxist Hegelian one takes all the force in White's moment of the early 1970s of a conceptual breakthrough, suggesting that we rotate Jameson's graph so that Nietzsche now occupies the neutral position we have identified with the Lacanian Real. This in turn makes clear the degree to which White's book also serves in Jameson's presentation as a symptom of an emergent postmodernism: *Metahistory* represents another example of the "communicational ideology" that we already have seen at work in Jameson's discussion of Xenakis, while also offering the intimations of some radically new and currently unimaginable way of being in the world (as with the Nietzsche of Derrida or of Deleuzian affirmation).

For a second example, I turn to Jameson's ingenious reading in *Postmodernism* of Jonathan Demme's *Something Wild* (1986) and David Lynch's *Blue Velvet* (1986), both understood as examples of what he names *allegorical encounter* films, an original postmodern form that unexpectedly emerges "from a kind of cross, if not synthesis, between the two filmic modes we had until now been imagining as antithetical: namely, the high elegance of nostalgia films, on the one hand, and the grade-B

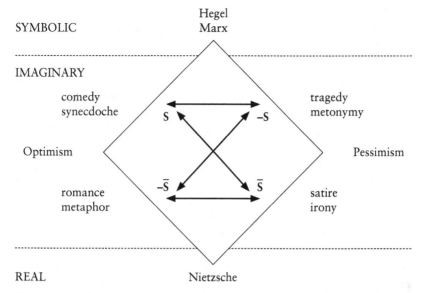

Figure 12. Fredric Jameson, Foreword to *On Meaning: Selected Writings in Semiotic Theory,* by A. J. Greimas (1987), revised.

simulations of iconoclastic punk film, on the other."[74] Jameson finds in these two films an allegorical staging of encounters with different cultural figurations of the 1950s, a settling of accounts with outmoded masculine identities, and a clearing of the space for the emergence of something new. In his discussion of Demme's film, Jameson develops a Greimasian presentation of the film's characterological system that emphasizes both the central encounter taking place between Charley Driggs (Jeff Daniels) and Ray Sinclair (played in a bravura breakthrough performance by Ray Liotta), and the mediatory role of the pair's common love interest, Audrey "Lulu" Hankel (Melanie Griffith). Jameson's presentation offers another illustration of the heuristic value of Greimas's schema, as it not only heightens our awareness of the deep ambivalence surrounding the character of Ray, who as an allegorical embodiment of 1950s rebellion is both a dangerous force that must be neutralized and an object of attraction—"The fifties stands for genuine rebellion, with genuine violence and genuine consequences, but also for the romantic representations of such rebellion, in the films of Brando and James Dean"[75]—it forces us to acknowledge the centrality for the film's cognitive work of two minor characters in the action, a high school classmate of Ray and Audrey, Peggy (played, in her only credited screen appearance, by Sue "Su Tissue" McLane, the lead singer of the California post-punk band Suburban Lawns, whose 1980 video, "Gidget Goes to Hell," was also directed by Demme) and the now noticeably pregnant wife of Charley's colleague, Larry Dillman (Jack Gilpin). The last couple, Jameson maintains, "occupy the semic slot of the 'squares,' but without any social basis or content any longer (they can scarcely be read as embodiments of the Protestant ethic, for example, or of puritanism or white racism or patriarchy). But they at least help us to identify the deeper ideological purpose of this film, which is to differentiate Charley from his fellow yuppies by making him over into a hero or protagonist of a different generic type than Ray."[76]

While Jameson's presentation effectively illustrates the film's ideological framework, its narrative labors and proto-cognitive mapping efforts become even more apparent when we rotate the square so that Ray becomes the "name" for the soon to be revealed obsolete Symbolic order the characters inhabit at the outset. My revised version of Jameson's Greimasian square would thus appear as follows (figure 13). This revision further makes explicit the double nature of the neutralization taking place in the film's "exclusively male" framework: for not only does Charley in the film's climax overcome Ray, he also, Jameson points out, "sheds his corporate job," breaking from the world he inhabited with his colleague Larry—indeed, the film highlights this break with a brief closing scene of Charley cleaning out his desk and bidding farewell to Larry.[77] Earlier in the essay, Jameson suggests an awareness in the film of a point of identification between Ray and Larry: "even Charley's illicit use of company credit cards is scarcely commensurable with the genuine criminality his corporation can be expected, virtually by definition, to imply."[78] Both Ray and Larry then, I would suggest, are figures of an older "1950s" masculinity from which Charley must break—the rebel and the corporate "organization man," the latter again becoming a site of complex investments only later with the cultural phenomenon of the television series Mad Men (2007 on). But this is not only a break with the period of the 1950s (a period that extends as Mad Men bears out into the first years of the 1960s, really coming to its end, perhaps, with the assassination of John F. Kennedy), but with the particular nostalgic reprise of the period that occurred in Reagan's 1980s America: Charley is thus an early figuration of what Susan Jeffords describes as Hollywood's "New Man, the one who can transform himself from the hardened, muscle-bound, domineering man [an effective characterization of Liotta's Ray] of the eighties into the considerate, loving, and self-sacrificing man of the nineties."[79]

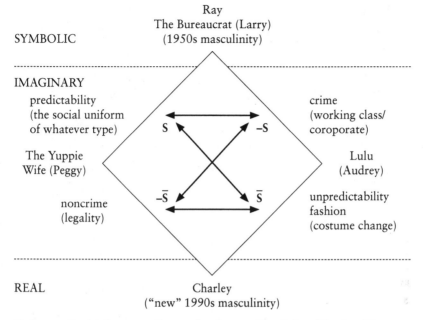

SYMBOLIC

Ray
The Bureaucrat (Larry)
(1950s masculinity)

IMAGINARY

predictability
(the social uniform
of whatever type)

The Yuppie
Wife (Peggy)

noncrime
(legality)

crime
(working class/
coroporate)

Lulu
(Audrey)

unpredictability
fashion
(costume change)

REAL

Charley
("new" 1990s masculinity)

Figure 13. Fredric Jameson, *Postmodernism, or, The Cultural Logic of Late Capitalism*, 293, revised.

To test more fully the effectiveness of this retooling of the Greimasian schema, I would like to show how it unfolds in two of the most significant achievements in dialectical criticism produced in the last few decades: Michael McKeon's *The Origins of the English Novel, 1600–1740* (1987) and Slavoj Žižek's *Tarrying with the Negative: Kant, Hegel, and the Critique of Ideology* (1993). On the most general plane, McKeon sets for himself the task of explaining "how categories, whether 'literary' or 'social,' exist in history: how they first coalesce by being understood in terms of—as transformations of—other forms that have thus far been taken to define the field of possibility."[80] Taking his lead from the dialectical analysis of the concept of production found in Marx's *Grundrisse* (1857–61), McKeon shows how the "simple abstraction" of the novel comes into being as the culmination of a centuries-long debate over the two intertwined sets of epistemological and social concerns that McKeon names, respectively, questions of Truth and questions of Virtue. What ultimately occurs is a neutralization of both the older sense of the authority of established texts as the final epistemological court of appeals and an aristocratic romance idealism found manifest in the great chivalric romances—a neutralization that ultimately will be named "the novel."

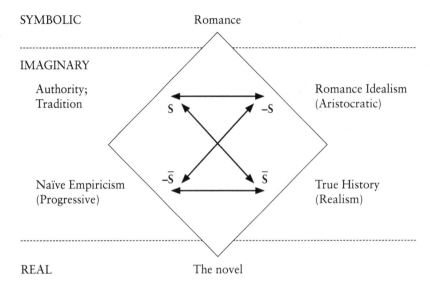

SYMBOLIC   Romance

IMAGINARY

Authority;   Romance Idealism
Tradition   S   -S   (Aristocratic)

Naïve Empiricism   -S   S   True History
(Progressive)   (Realism)

REAL   The novel

Figure 14. Michael McKeon, *The Origins of the English Novel, 1600–1740*.

While McKeon's study offers a rich and exemplary model of a dialectical literary criticism throughout, one whose very breadth of historical scholarship and demonstration makes it an imposing achievement, it is the climax to his narrative that is of most interest to me here. McKeon challenges two lines of inquiry that would privilege as the first true novel either Samuel Richardson's work (a move exemplified by Ian Watt's classic study) or that of Henry Fielding. McKeon argues that "within the present account of the origins of the English novel—as a long-term historical process that consists both in the experimental conflation of epistemological and social concerns and in the experimental opposition of narrative strategies—there is little sense in seeking the identity of 'the first novelist.' "[81]

Rather, McKeon maintains, "the novel is constituted as a dialectical unity of opposed parts."[82] That is, the novel as a simple abstraction, or what I am referring to as the name or Idea of a Symbolic order, encompasses the strategies of both of the "two stylistic lines of development" in the novel identified by Mikhail M. Bakhtin: those of Richardson— what McKeon describes as a naïve empiricism and a progressive ideology, originally imagined as a negation of a preexisting romance idealism and aristocratic ideology, combined with a moralizing focus on the internal and the subjective (the latter becoming fully evident only with Fielding's later rejoinder)—and those of Fielding—the combination of radical skepticism and conservative ideology, a negation of Richardson's intervention, and the disavowal of Richardson's artifice that Fielding names "nature" or "true history," and that will shortly simply be referred to as realism (which, McKeon reminds us, "is only art by another name") (figures 14 and 15).[83]

The public controversy between the two is thus properly an Imaginary one, the two authors employing "antithetical methods of writing what is nonetheless recognized as the same species of narrative"; indeed, each adopts the strategies of the other in their later works, works that now occupy the fully established institution of the novel.[84] One of the real values of mapping McKeon's narrative in this way is that it helps us to see more clearly how the plane of the Imaginary at once *precedes* historically and yet is *constituted by* the totality named by the Symbolic. This also offers a rigorous Lacanian formulation of what Raymond Williams aims at in his key concept of *structures of feeling,* "a kind of feeling and thinking which is indeed social and material, but each in an embryonic phase before it can become fully articulate and defined exchange. . . . [A]lthough they are emergent or pre-emergent, they do not have to await definition, classification, or rationalization before they exert palpable pressures and set effective limits on experience and on action."[85]

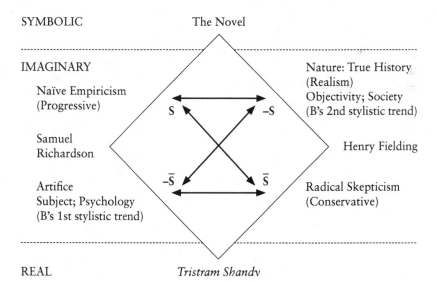

Figure 15. Michael McKeon, *The Origins of the English Novel, 1600–1740.*

However, this is not quite the end of McKeon's story. In a final note whose implications for the future study of the development of any genre call for much further exploration, McKeon writes,

> Of course the claim to historicity continues to be serviceable, in various ways, to future generations of novelists. But in a more general sense, both the claim and its subversion end in the triumph of the creative human mind, a triumph already prefigured at the moment of the novel's emergence: in Richardson the triumphant mind is that of the protagonist; in Fielding it is that of the author. The implications of the formal breakthrough of the 1740s are pursued with such feverish intensity over the next two decades that after *Tristram Shandy* [1759–67], it may be said, the young genre settles down to a more deliberate and studied recapitulation of the same ground, this time for the next two centuries.[86]

In short, McKeon argues that we see already prefigured in the uncategorizable masterpiece of Laurence Sterne the "end of the novel" that will not occur until much later in a practice that brings together under the name of *modernism* the skepticism about the representational possibilities of realism with an emphasis on psychological interiority (keep in mind T. S. Eliot's dictum that whatever else it may be, *Ulysses* is "not a novel").[87] It is no coincidence then that Sterne's work is "rediscovered" in the moment of modernism, by Shklovsky, Walter Benjamin, James Joyce, and others: writing of Shklovsky in particular, Jameson similarly observes, "*Tristram Shandy* thus takes its place, for the Formalists, as a predecessor of modern or avant-garde literature in general."[88]

This also points toward a kinship of Greimas's notion of the neutral, at least as it has been being refunctioned in the preceding discussion, and Badiou's concept of the *inexistent*: to adapt Bruno Bosteels's comments on the Paris Commune, despite the fact that *Tristram Shandy* becomes in the eighteenth century a dead end in the novel's early development, the work's appearance means that—for a brief moment at least—the novelistic order that legitimates modernism's aesthetic "inexistence" is destroyed. Sterne's production, like the Commune in the political realm, thereby becomes the trace of "what is here called historically impossible."[89] The example of *Tristram Shandy* also helps make clear another fundamental distinction in Badiou's project itself, between the site of an event and its actualization: "It is not at all the same thing to say that there is a site of an event and to say that there is an event. It is not at all the same thing to say that every situation contains a point of excess, a blank space, a blind spot, or an unrepresented point, and to say that this already amounts to the event's effectuation properly speaking."[90] In short, whereas the Greimasian schema can map such a void in such a situation, it is only possible to do so after it has been effectuated, or *forced,* by a particular concrete and sustained intervention, be it the Commune or a work such as *Tristram Shandy.*

There is a further insight to be gained from this mapping of McKeon's narrative. If we read in conjunction the two Greimasian schemas I have produced (modeled on the double mapping Jameson generates in *The Seeds of Time*), such that the concept of the novel in each—occupying the neutral or Real position in the first presentation and that of the complex or the Symbolic in the second—becomes the point of overlap, an interesting historical bifocality emerges, what Žižek, following the lead of Kojin Karantani, calls the "parallax view," a "constantly shifting perspective between two points between which no synthesis or mediation is possible."[91] On the one hand, the novel serves as the name for a particular Symbolic order, or what we would conventionally refer to as a "period" within literary history. On the other hand, as our perspective shifts to the two end points of the larger mapping, the novel becomes the name of a transitional phase—what Jameson calls a "vanishing mediator" and Lacan the "space between two deaths"—between the orders of the romance and that of modernism.[92] Such a dialectical parallax is characteristic, Jameson suggests in *A Singular Modernity,* of every periodizing narrative.

The case I would like to look at from Žižek's *Tarrying with the Negative* also comes from the book's final chapter, "Enjoy Your Nation as Yourself!" However, whereas McKeon's discussion remains centered on the eighteenth century, Žižek takes us directly into the contested and unstable field of the final decade of the twentieth century. Thus, while McKeon's work opens up onto an historical question—why does it take a century and a half for the breakthrough figured by Sterne to become actualized on a larger social institutional scale?—Žižek's analysis focuses on what he takes to be the fundamental political question of the post–Cold War moment (and in this, *Tarrying with the Negative* is also a contemporary of *The Seeds of Time* and *Specters of Marx*): How do we begin to break through the closures of the Symbolic order of late capitalism—or what we now call, to use the term whose rapid ascent to prominence is just beginning in the years of the publication of Žižek's book, *globalization*?[93]

On the level of the geo-political Imaginary, this closure takes the form of the global deadlock of "today's liberal democracy." Žižek offers this description of his contemporary situation:

> The problem with liberal democracy is that a priori, for structural reasons, it cannot be universalized. Hegel said that the moment of victory of a political force is the very moment of its splitting: the triumphant liberal-democratic "new world order" is more and more marked by a frontier separating its "inside" from its "outside"—a frontier between those who manage to remain "within" (the "developed," those to whom the rules of human rights, social security, etc., apply) and the others, the excluded (the main concern of the "developed" apropos of them is to contain their explosive potential, even if the price to be paid for such containment is the neglect of elementary democratic principles).[94]

Žižek argues that the then-recent and unexpected disappearance of the socialist bloc's third way—"a desperate attempt at modernization outside the constraints of capitalism"—has set into place a new fundamental opposition between, on the one hand, the corporate and state sponsors of neoliberalism, advocating the violent dissolution of all traditional and preexisting social and cultural formations through processes David Harvey calls "accumulation by dispossession" and Naomi Klein names "shock therapy;" and, on the other, the various fundamentalisms, which includes for Žižek both religious fundamentalisms and neo-ethnic nationalisms, which, under the mantle of the maintenance of (invented) traditions, resist these transformations.[95] As Jameson stresses too in his contemporary reflections on globalization, "Since the discrediting of socialism by the collapse of Russian communism, only religious fundamentalism has seemed to offer an alternative way of life—let us not, heaven help us, call it a lifestyle—to American consumerism. . . . Neo-Confucianism or Islamic and Hindu fundamentalism themselves are new, are postmodern inventions, not survivals of ancient ways of life."[96] For both Žižek and Jameson, any full account of globalization must take into account both of these contradictory poles.

A similar vision of the antinomies of globalization is on display more recently in the critically and popularly acclaimed Danny Boyle film *Slumdog Millionaire* (2008). The allegorical staging of this binary opposition does not occur through the narrative of the film's central protagonist, the former Mumbai "slumdog" and ultimate *Who Wants to Be a Millionaire?* game-show champion, Jamal Malik (Dev Patel). Jamal's story unfolds according to the dictates of the narrative paradigm that Jameson has identified as that of the secularized providential and salvational plot: "The greatest modern version of this narrative cunningly marshals its two immense trajectories (the plights of each lover) to map the geographical and the class levels of a whole historical society."[97]

The film's naturalist plot, on the other hand—whose reigning ideological concept, Jameson suggests, is the "metaphysics of failure" that "still very much govern[s] our imagination of poverty and underdevelopment"[98]—is relegated to Jamal's older brother, Salim (Madhur Mittal). Salim is the figure who throughout most of the film readily adopts a neo-liberal ethics of self-interested individualism: neither tradition nor a sense of responsibility for the welfare of others, including at times his brother, trouble his relentless pursuit of a place for himself in the India modernizing all around them. When the brothers are reunited as young adults in their transforming childhood home, skyscraper construction dominating the skyline of their one-time slum residence, Salim, who has risen to the position of right-hand man of the leading local organized crime boss, tells Jamal, "India is at the center of the world now, bhai. And I . . . I am at the center . . . of the center." The organized crime syndicate to which he belongs thus serves in the film as the very embodiment of the truth of neo-liberal economic, political, and military violence.

What Jameson notes of the allegorical structure of an earlier classic film representation of collective criminality, *The Godfather*, holds here too, as long as we translate *The Godfather*'s national to *Slumdog Millionaire*'s global or geopolitical framework:

> When indeed we reflect on an organized conspiracy against the public, one which reaches into every corner of our daily lives and our political structures to exercise a wanton ecocidal and genocidal violence at the behest of distant decision-makers and in the name of an abstract conception of profit—surely it is not about the Mafia, but rather American business itself that we are thinking, American capitalism in its most systematized and computerized, dehumanized, "multinational" and corporate form.[99]

Unlike *The Godfather*'s Michael Corleone, however, Salim does in the end manage to break with the criminal culture in which he is enmeshed:

it is Salim's heroic self-sacrifice that ensures the happiness of Malik and his love, Latika (Frieda Pinto). And yet in this act of self-sacrifice, Salim swings to the opposite pole, apparently embracing a radical Muslim fundamentalism, committing suicide in lashing out against the criminal order of which he is a part: indeed, with his dying breath, he cries out, "God is great." His conversion is foreshadowed earlier when Jamal oversees him one morning at his prayer rug, intoning repeatedly, "Oh Lord forgive me. I know that I have sinned." Jamal's own rejection of religion is made clear early in the film when he tells the police officer interrogating him, "If it wasn't for Allah and Rama our mother would still be alive." (She was murdered during the communal violence that swept India in the same period that Žižek's book was first published.)

Thus, the film teaches us that neither of the stark options embraced by Salim are desirable ones. And yet, *Slumdog Millionaire*'s "happy ending"—Malik's fidelity pays off, as he wins the money and gets the girl, all in front of millions of television viewers throughout India (the only truly successful collective we get in the film is this serialized one)—complete with an elaborate Bollywood dance sequence during the final credits, suggests an equally critical or even cynical recognition, similar to that found in the conclusion of Boyle's earlier film adaptation *Trainspotting* (1996), that such an individualistic resolution to the very real contradictions of our present is, at best, an imaginary one (fortune and family, and virtue rewarded, but only for the lucky few).

However, in what we now should recognize as the indication of a dialectical thought process under way, Žižek's analysis differs from that of the film in that it does not stop here, and, indeed, moves into what was surely intended by Žižek and will be for many readers a far more scandalous terrain:

> This antagonistic splitting opens up the field for the Khmer Rouge, Sendero Luminoso, and other similar movements which seem to personify "radical Evil" in today's politics: if "fundamentalism" functions as a kind of "negative judgment" on liberal capitalism, as an inherent negation of the universalist claim of liberal capitalism, then movements such as Sendero Luminoso enact an "infinite judgment" on it.[100]

The full Greimasian mapping of Žižek's narrative would thus appear as in figure 16.

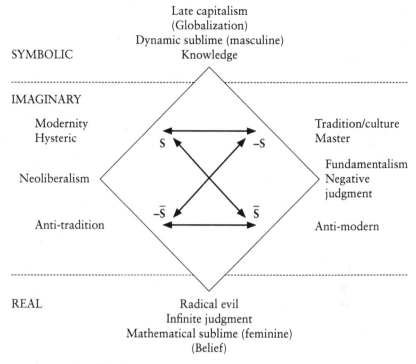

Figure 16. Slavoj Žižek, *Tarrying with the Negative*, 223–25.

Earlier in the book, Žižek defines the Kantian concept of radical Evil as a force "which disrupts the pattern of the organic substantial whole." The example he offers us of this is a fascinating one:

> Suffice it to recall Thomas More, the Catholic saint who resisted the pressure of Henry VIII to approve of his divorce.... From a "communitarian" point of view, his rectitude was an "irrational" self-destructive gesture which was "evil" in the sense that it cut into the texture of the social body, threatening the stability of the crown and thereby of the entire social order. So, although the motivations of Thomas More were undoubtedly "good," *the very formal structure of his act was "radically evil"*: his was an act of radical defiance which disregarded the Good of community.[101]

Radical Evil is thus the name the dominant order gives to any social agency that appears as a traumatic disruption. Moreover, Žižek is even more interested in the way ideology collapses the two quite distinct positions of the negative judgment and the infinite judgment—the original reference for this latter figure being, Žižek argues, the French Revolution itself—into the undifferentiated ethical figure of evil. Such an ethical gesture serves as a way of avoiding any encounter with the Real, both blinding us to the formal existence of radically other possibilities of collective resistance within our world and preventing us from any specific political discussion of the content, the value and limitations, of these other movements as they actually exist. Žižek then goes on to describe this other force in a way that brings us full circle back to Mary Shelley's novel:

> It seems that only today, with the advent of late capitalism, has this [Hegelian] notion of "rabble" achieved its adequate realization in social reality, through political forces which paradoxically unite the most radical indigenist antimodernism (the refusal of everything that defines modernity: market, money, individualism . . .) with the eminently modern project of effacing the entire symbolic tradition and beginning from a zero-point (in the case of Khmer Rouge, this meant abolishing the entire system of education and killing intellectuals). What, precisely, constitutes the "shining path" of the Senderistas if not the idea to reinscribe the construction of socialism within the frame of the return to the ancient Inca empire? The result of this desperate endeavor to surmount the antagonism between tradition and modernity is a double negation: a radically anti-capitalist movement (the refusal of integration into the world market) coupled with a systematic dissolution of all traditional hierarchical social links, beginning with the family. . . . The truth articulated in the paradox of this double negation is that capitalism cannot reproduce itself without the support of precapitalist forms of social links. In other words, far from presenting a case of exotic barbarism, the "radical Evil" of the Khmer Rouge and the Senderistas is conceivable only against the background of the constitutive antagonism of today's capitalism.[102]

Žižek concludes in a way that bears out how these forms of radical evil occupy the neutral position on our Greimasian mapping:

The Khmer Rouge and the Senderistas therefore function as a kind of "infinite judgment" on late capitalism in the precise Kantian sense of the term: they are to be located in a third domain beyond the inherent antagonism that defines the late-capitalist dynamic (the antagonism between the modernist drive and the fundamentalist backlash), since they radically reject both poles of the opposition. As such, they are—to put it in Hegelese—an integral part of the notion of late capitalism: if one wants to comprise capitalism as a world-system, one must take into account its inherent negation, the "fundamentalism," as well as its absolute negation, the infinite judgment on it.[103]

Lest my examples here lead one to conclude that such an approach is limited only to contemporary theoretical texts, I end this section by briefly outlining two additional examples drawn from earlier moments in the rich history of dialectical criticism. The first takes as its case study Benjamin's *Ursprung des deutschen Trauerspiels* (translated as *The Origin of German Tragic Drama*) (1928), a work, Benjamin would later note in a letter to Max Ryncher, that while not yet materialist, "was dialectical."[104] What becomes evident in a reading of Benjamin's narrative through the rigorously formalist lens of our enhanced Greimasian semiotic schema is that Benjamin's figurations of the German mourning play (*Trauerspiel*) and the device of allegory occur through a dialectical neutralization of the dominant institutional modes of tragedy and the symbol (figure 17). Moreover, in Benjamin's study, the *Trauerspiel* form becomes an allegory in its own right of modernism—not the least of which includes the modernist practice of Benjamin's *Habilitationsschrift*—and the means by which Benjamin is able to break through to his own radically original mode of historicism that he would then set to work in his unfinished masterpiece of the *Arcades Project*.

My final schema (figure 18) is the most far reaching, offering an open dialectical or totalizing presentation of the problematic of Marxism itself. Marxism is the science of the mode of production of capitalism, and its Imaginary unfolds, as Étienne Balibar suggests in *The Philosophy of Marx,* into the antinomies of hegemony and reification (and the homologous political opposition of voluntarism and determinism).[105] The only way to break through such a deadlock is by way of what Jameson describes as an "absolute formalism, in which the new content emerges

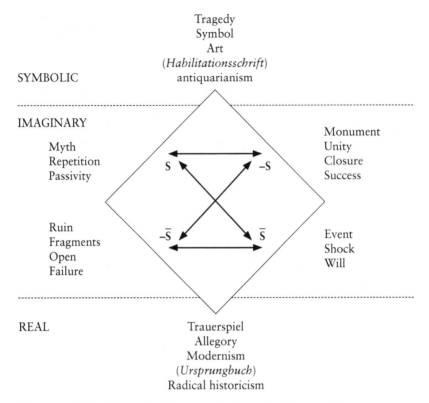

Tragedy
Symbol
Art
(*Habilitationsschrift*)
antiquarianism

SYMBOLIC

IMAGINARY

Myth
Repetition
Passivity

Monument
Unity
Closure
Success

Ruin
Fragments
Open
Failure

Event
Shock
Will

REAL

Trauerspiel
Allegory
Modernism
(*Ursprungbuch*)
Radical historicism

Figure 17. Walter Benjamin, *Ursprung des deutschen Trauerspiels.*

itself from the form and is a projection of it;" such an absolute formalism will enable a confrontation with the traumatic material—the consciousness of the proletariat, revolution, and communism itself—that is too often evaded in today's intellectual Marxisms, a situation of which Žižek, Jameson, and other contemporary dialectical thinkers offer a powerful analysis.[106] This is the Marxism Jameson invokes in the concluding lines of his stirring post–Cold War defense of the Marxist problematic, "Actually Existing Marxism":

> Marxism is the very science of capitalism; its epistemological vocation lies in its unmatched capacity to describe capitalism's historical originality; its fundamental structural contradictions endow it with its political and its prophetic vocation, which can scarcely be distinguished from the analytic ones. This is why, whatever its other vicissitudes, a postmodern

capitalism necessarily calls a postmodern Marxism into existence over against itself.[107]

The lesson of this last schema thus nicely sums up the real value of the model of dialectical criticism that I have been arguing for throughout this chapter, for it shows us, to adapt Oscar Wilde, that a map of Marxism today that does not include Utopia, or radical love, is not worth even glancing at—an argument that I will develop in more detail in the next chapter.

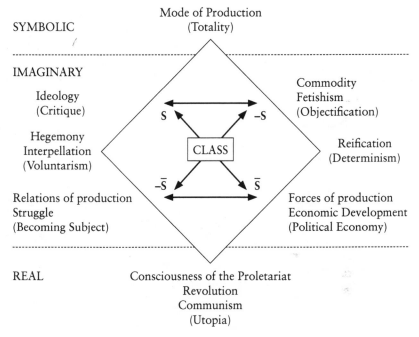

Figure 18. The problematic named Marxism.

PART II

Untimely Modernisms

CHAPTER 4

"The Point Is . . ."

On the Four Conditions of Marxist Cultural Studies

Die Philosophen haben die Welt nur verschieden *interpretiert;* es kommt drauf an, sie zu *verändern.* (The philosophers have only *interpreted* the world in various ways; what is necessary is to *change* it.)
—Karl Marx, "Thesen über Feuerbach," These XI (1845)

Ceux qui parlent de révolution et de lutte de classes sans se référer explicitement à la vie quotidienne, sans comprendre ce qu'il y a de subversif dans l'amour et de positif dans le refus des contraintes, ceux-là ont dans la bouche un cadavre. (Anyone who talks about revolution and class struggle without referring explicitly to everyday life, without understanding what is subversive about love and positive in the refusal of constraints, has in their mouths a corpse.)
—Raoul Vaneigem, *Traité de savoir-vivre à l'usage des jeunes generations* (1967)

I.

This chapter assesses the contribution that Jameson makes to the traditions of Marxist cultural studies by way of a mapping of the contours of the Marxist problematic more generally. I hope ultimately to show how Jameson's work, more through its examples than its incitements, makes an appeal for contemporary Marxist cultural criticism to "remove the corpse from its mouth" and renew its engagement with what Vaneigem and the Situationists refer to as the "subversiveness of love," or what I will name here more generally Marxism's *fourth* condition.[1]

The concept of the "conditions" of thought is taken from the work of perhaps the single most important living French philosopher—and, as Bruno Bosteels now so effectively bears out, one of the other most significant dialectical thinkers working today—Alain Badiou. In his collection of essays entitled *Conditions* (1992)—a follow-up to the monumental recasting that he undertakes in *Being and Event* (1988) of the problem of ontology according to axioms of mathematical set theory—Badiou writes, "Philosophy is prescribed by *conditions* that constitute types of truth- or generic-procedure."[2] Badiou names these four conditions science, art, politics, and love. Philosophy does not produce truths of its own, but rather articulates the particular truths produced by the subjects laboring in each of these procedures.

My aim here is not to reconcile the differences between Badiou and Jameson's projects—much could be said here in particular of the different status of narrative, philosophy, and theory in each of their agendas—but rather to underscore some of the continuities between the work of these two preeminent practitioners of dialectical materialist thinking and writing.[3] Moreover, Bosteels points out that Badiou too remains solidly within the "lineage of the eleventh of Marx's 'Theses on Feuerbach'": writing of Badiou's more recent *Logic of Worlds* (2006), Bosteels stresses that "ultimately the avowed goal even of this massive follow-up to *Being and Event* is not the doctrine of how a world appears, complete with its transcendental regime, its objects, its relations among objects, but rather the doctrine of how a world can become transformed as the result of a subjective intervention."[4] As a result, Bosteels concludes, Badiou "assigns to philosophy—in the ideological context of a new materialist dialectic—the task of formulating a systematic interpretation of the very possibility of transforming the world to begin with."[5]

In an essay that serves as a sequel to my last chapter, I show how the four discourses of Jacques Lacan, first articulated in his 1969–70 seminar XVII, published in 1991 under the title *L'Envers de la Psychanalyse* (*The Other Side of Psychoanalysis*), might be productively mapped along the lines of a reconfigured Greimasian semiotic square.[6] If, as we saw in the last chapter, reading "Greimas with Lacan" opens up the closure of the semiotic square to its full potentiality for thinking dialectical becoming, then reading "Lacan with Greimas" similarly helps us more effectively grasp the significance of Lacan's own shift from what Badiou describes as a structural dialectical of three (orders) to a historical dialectic of four (discourses) (more on this opposition in a moment). Badiou has long been engaged with Lacan's "anti-philosophical" thought—or more specifically, the species of anti-Platonism that Badiou sees as first emerging in Nietzsche and coming to increasing prominence during the course of the twentieth-century (and hence, which may very well be another name for the un-disciplinary or perhaps non-philosphical labors of theory).[7] Badiou even bases the structure of his earlier groundbreaking and untimely *Theory of the Subject* (1982) on that of Lacan's seminars.[8] I would like to go further here and advance the proposition that Badiou's four conditions be understood as themselves in part deriving from Lacan's four discourses, such that the correspondences between each of these four-fold schema appear as follows (figure 19).[9]

All of this suggests something very interesting about Badiou's odd fourth condition of love. Peter Hallward points out, "Badiou has had less to say, thus far, about love than about the other generic procedures."[10] Slavoj Žižek speculates on a possible reason for this reticence. Žižek maintains that "the first three truth-procedures . . . follow the classic logic of the triad True-Beautiful-Good" (science-art-politics), while the fourth condition "stick[s] out from the series, being somehow more

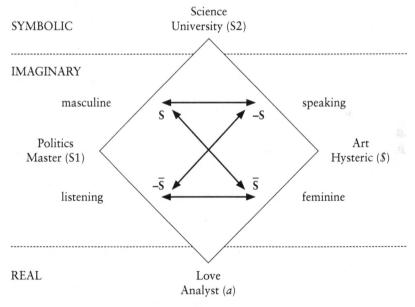

Figure 19. Badiou's four conditions, with the Greimasian presentation of Lacan's four discourses developed in Phillip E. Wegner, "Lacan avec Greimas: Formalization, Theory, and the 'Other Side' of the Study of Culture," *Minnesota Review* 77 (2011): 62–86.

fundamental and universal," and thus serves "as a kind of underlying formal principle or matrix of all procedures." As a result, Žižek suggests, Badiou's four-fold schema should really be understood as "*three plus one*."[11] Moreover, as in Lacan's case, it is the addition of this "plus one" that transforms the static transcendental Kantian triad into a dynamic open materialist and historical structure.

A similar logic of "three plus one" is also at work in the dialectical version of the Greimasian semiotic square I elaborated in the previous chapter. Of the four terms mapped in that discussion—the complex term, or Lacan's Symbolic; the middle opposition of the Imaginary; and the final Real of Greimas's neutral—it is this last, the "plus one," that takes on a singular significance, as it marks the place of an opening in the otherwise closed structuralist schema. It indicates what Badiou would call the void of the situation re-presented by the formalization of the semiotic square, and hence serves as the locus of the unfolding of Engels's dialectical law of the "transformation of quantity into quality and vice versa"[12]—the point of emergence, in other words, of the unexpectedly new that Badiou names the event.

Strictly speaking, however, in the Greimasian presentation the distribution would be more along the lines of $3(1[\text{Symbolic}] +2[\text{Imaginary}]) +1(\text{Real})$. Bosteels helps clarify the special status of the condition of science, the privileged expression of which for Badiou is mathematics: "In short, if we return to the title of Badiou's major work, mathematics is operative both on the side of being and on the side of the event. This double inscription is what gives mathematics a unique status, completely distinct from politics, art, or love, which operate only at the level of truth procedures as conditions for philosophy."[13] It is precisely because it unfolds as a rigorous formal or symbolic language that mathematics can be uniquely operative on the side of being as well as that of the event. The main thrust of Bosteels's argument in his book is to show that in Badiou's work, the truth procedure of "politics is by far the most consistent and elaborate. Even though Badiou has written extensively on art and literature, as well as on psychoanalysis as an immanent reflection on love as a truth procedure, there is no match for the depth and complexity of Badiou's intervention in the field of politics."[14] I have no reason to doubt this claim, and only add that I would wager that in second place would be the condition named art (indeed, it is worth recalling that in addition to being a philosopher and activist, Badiou is also an accomplished playwright, something at long last more evident to an English-speaking readership with the translation of his drama *The*

Incident at Antioch: A Tragedy in Three Acts).[15] This is because these two conditions unfold exclusively on the lived historical plane, or what Lacan calls the Imaginary, and hence are most readily represented by the imaginary or everyday language of philosophy. If science or mathematics, like the Greimasian semiotic square considered strictly as a symbolic presentation, offers a formalization of ontology, marking both its being and becoming, then the truth condition of love—in my Greimasian presentation, the real of the four generic procedures—gives expression to the sheer unrepresentability of all events. Love at once unveils the foundational subjective and interpersonal or collective dimension of the other conditions—the objective side being the situation or open multiplicity, codified by the axioms of set theory, into which the newly constituted subject of a truth intervenes—and serves as a placeholder for a radically other way of being in the world.

In some of his more recent work, beginning with the chapter of *Conditions* entitled "What Is Love?," Badiou elaborates more on the foundational "plus one" of the condition of love. This labor culminates in his July 14, 2008, exchange with Nicholas Truong, published under the title *Éloge de l'amour* (*In Praise of Love*). Badiou begins by noting, "In today's world, it is generally thought that individuals only pursue their own self-interest. Love is an antidote to that."[16] We need first, however, Badiou maintains (taking his lead in this regard from Rimbaud), to "reinvent" the concept of love, reframing it more rigorously in terms of the notions of "separation and disjuncture," and of the encounter or event, "namely of something that doesn't enter into the immediate order of things."[17] As Jameson notes of the preconceptions entangled with the concept of the "map" when he begins to articulate a narrative practice of cognitive mapping, Badiou here asks us to dismiss all figures of love and loving from our minds and try to imagine something else—a task made even more difficult in this case, as love remains, along with what Raymond Williams identifies as the "keywords" of "culture" and "nature," "one of the two or three most complicated," overly familiar, and ideologically laden of our concept terms.[18] Against any such a priori understanding, Badiou maintains that love needs to be understood, once again stressing the process or temporal dimension of and the labor involved in all truth procedures, as "a quest for truth . . . truth in relationship to something quite precise: what kind of world does one see when one experiences it from the point of view of two and not one? What is the world like when it is experienced, developed and lived from the point of view of difference and not identity?"[19] For this reason, the "two scene" of a "love that is real is always of interest to the whole of humanity, however humble, however hidden, that love might seem on the surface."[20]

It is the deeply material and affective dimensions of the evental encounter of love that marks its difference from friendship: "surrendering your body, taking your clothes off, being naked for the other, rehearsing those hallowed gestures, renouncing all embarrassment, shouting, all this involvement of the body is evidence of a surrender to love."[21] For Badiou then, there can be no "politics of friendship," as the stance of friendship is at its core an ethical one involved in maintaining the world as it currently exists; the point of love, as with all of the truth conditions, is, however, to change it. At the same time, while Badiou reasserts the value of maintaining a rigorous distinction between the truth procedures of politics and love, avoiding the suture of philosophy to any single one of them (as he sees repeatedly occurring in the twentieth century—Heidegger's phenomenology to art, analytic philosophy to science, or even in some of Badiou's own students whose "contagious enthusiasm for the Cantorian revolution frequently pushes them to the point of what we would have to call a complete suture of philosophy onto mathematics"),[22] he also notes a "secret resonance that is created, in the most intimate individual experience, between the intensities life acquires when a hundred per cent committed to a particular Idea and the qualitatively distinct intensity generated by the struggle with difference in love."[23] As with the commitment, or fidelity, involved in the unfolding of a truth of politics (or art or science), Badiou thus means here to develop an original "concept of love that is less miraculous and more hard work, namely a construction of eternity within time, of the experience of the Two, point by point."[24] This is possible because love—and again this is a fundamental axiom of all the truth procedures—is only realized in the world through repetition, by a constant re-enactment of a fidelity to the event by those whose subjectivity is constituted by it; and this is also why an especially effective figuration of this Utopian aspect of love is to be found in the heuristic genre Stanley Cavell names the "comedy of remarriage," whose characteristic feature is the repeated unions, break-ups, and reunions that characterize the practice.[25]

Finally, in a claim that has great significance for our discussion here, Badiou notes late in his exchange with Truong that he understands *communism* as "that which makes the held-in-common prevail over selfishness, the collective achievement over private self-interest. While we're about it, we can also say that love is communist in that sense, if one accepts, as I do, that the real subject of a love is the becoming of the couple and not the mere satisfaction of the individuals that are its component parts. *Yet another possible definition of love: minimal communism!*"[26] Communism is thus the name for and a figuration of an unrepresentable and radically other collective mode of being in the world, realized—in something of a reprise of the two-stage theory that Lenin develops in *State and Revolution*—through the particular generic procedure of politics, but arranged in accordance with Badiou's description of the universal condition of love.[27]

Badiou's formulation of love as minimal communism, and the corollary of communism as maximal love, offers a provocative framework for the reconsideration of a wide range of twentieth-century cultural interventions, from James Joyce's *Ulysses* (1922) to Andrei Tarkvosky's *Stalker* (1979). Here let me illustrate this potential by a brief reexamination of one of the populist Hollywood film classics of the mid-century, Frank Capra's *It's a Wonderful Life* (1946). If we view according to the condition of politics the film's narrative, with its embrace of reformism and its affirmation of the essential soundness of capitalist institutions (the problem the film's fundamentally ethical outlook maintains lies not in the system, but in a few malevolent individuals who operate in it), then its ideological horizons are readily apparent. However, things become far more interesting when the film is read instead in terms of the condition of love—that is, as an illustration of what it means to consistently experience the world through the perspective of difference. This is the case not only for the particular romantic couple of George Bailey (James Stewart) and Mary Hatch (Donna Reed), who must re-confirm their fidelity to the event of their encounter again and again, but also for the collective whole of Bedford Falls. The various crises George encounters and overcomes are now to be understood as opportunities for him to enact his consistent fidelity to this truth. One of the most memorable scenes in the film, that of the Depression era "run" on the Bailey Savings and Loan, enables George to articulate the nature of his fidelity. When one of its patrons demands that the Savings and Loan immediately turn over his cash, George replies, "You're thinking of this place all wrong, as if I had the money back in a safe. The money's not here. Well, your money's in Joe's house. That's right next to yours. And in the Kennedy house, and in Mrs. Macklin's house and in a hundred others. You're lending them the money to build and they're going to pay it back to you as best they can. What are you going to do, foreclose on them?" To the patron's response articulated exclusively in terms of private interest,

George struggles to persuade him, and even more pointedly the others around him, instead to encounter it, as he has done repeatedly throughout his life, in terms of a collective unfolding in time. Indeed, it is his fidelity to the held-in-common that has led George repeatedly to defer his long cherished dreams of traveling the world, attending college, and becoming an architect, in order to defend this truth against the pernicious reigning interests (*le service des biens,* a concept Badiou borrows from Lacan)[28] represented by the voracious local banker and landlord, Henry F. Potter (Lionel Barrymore).

A more global crisis occurs when the seemingly inexorable closure of circumstances leads George to renounce his life's project, and conclude that those around him would have been better off if he "had never been born." George's declaration at this point serves as a textbook illustration of the ethical failure, or evil, Badiou names *betrayal:*

> Betrayal is not mere renunciation. Unfortunately, one cannot simply "renounce" a truth. The denial of the Immortal in myself is something quite different from an abandonment, a cessation: I must always convince myself that the Immortal in question *never existed,* and thus rally to opinion's perception of this point—opinion, whose whole purpose, in the service of interests, is precisely this negation. For the Immortal, if I recognize its existence, calls on me to continue; it has the eternal power of the truths that induce it.[29]

This Immortal is externalized in the film in the allegorical figure of the angel Clarence (Henry Travers), who thrusts George into an alternate history where he was never born, and where, as a result, a corrosive selfishness has taken root. The town has even been renamed Pottersville, a name that recalls the American term "potter's field," a burial place for the unknown and indigent. In this way, George experiences fully the falseness of the opinion to which in his despair he has momentarily rallied. George learns well the lesson of this encounter, and his delirious joyful sprint through the snow-covered streets of Bedford Falls signals both his triumph over this "crisis of fidelity" and his recommitment to "the sole maxim of consistency (and thus of ethics): 'Keep going!' "[30] Although the film ends in classic Hollywood comedic fashion, with the restoration of the "green world" of the enclosed community, whose members rise to George's defense and provide without hesitation the funds needed to repay the amount he has falsely been accused of embezzling, a far more daring climax is suggested earlier when George expresses to the police who have arrived at his home, "Isn't it wonderful, I'm going to jail!" This claim makes clear that George now understands that in no way does the "opinion" of the community change the truth at the basis of his fidelity.

In a 1947 FBI memo on "The Communist Infiltration of the Motion Picture Industry," the writer notes that *It's a Wonderful Life* "deliberately maligned the upper class, attempting to show the people who had money were mean and despicable characters." Such a portrayal, he determines, is a "common trick used by Communists."[31] To describe the film's "politics" as communist is patently false, as is easily demonstrable; however, this FBI agent will become a far more perspicacious reader of the film if he, as we are doing here, instead views it as unfolding in the condition of love.

II.

I concluded the previous chapter by pointing toward the possibility of mapping along the coordinates of the semiotic square the totality of the *problematic* of Marxism. Jameson's description of the concept of the problematic remains a significant staring place for us here as well. Jameson argues that a problematic is "not a set of propositions about reality, but a set of categories in terms of which reality is analyzed and interrogated, and a set of 'contested' categories at that."[32] Only when one abandons the commitment to a particular set of categories does one break with a problematic. The Greimasian schema thus offers a way to set into coordination the outer horizons of the Marxist problematic, its core relationships and circulations of energy throughout becoming more evident as well. Beginning with two most important binary oppositions in Marx's work—those of ideology and commodity fetishism and of the subjective "relations" and objective "forces" of production—I elaborate on Marxism's four conditions. These take on a variety of names at different moments in Marxism's rich intellectual history, but I will refer to them here with the terms *hegemony, reification, the mode of production,* and *consciousness of the proletariat.* These four terms correspond to Badiou's four conditions in the following manner (figure 20).

In his valuable little book *The Philosophy of Marx,* Étienne Balibar argues that Marx's early unpublished work, what Balibar's teacher, Louis Althusser, dismissed as the product of Marx's humanist phase,

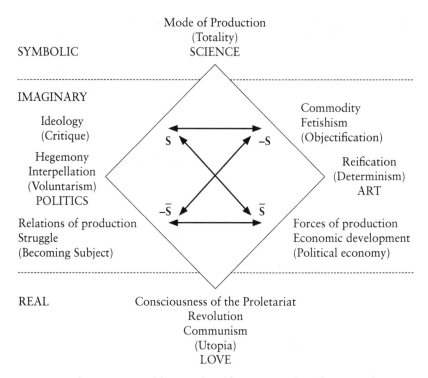

Figure 20. The Marxist problematic from figure 18, with Badiou's conditions.

explores in some detail the concept of ideology. The notion is influenced by the "Young Hegelian" Ludwig Feuerbach's description of religious alienation, especially as it is developed in Feuerbach's *Das Wesen des Christentums* (1841). Ideology is at the center of *The German Ideology* (1845–46; published 1932), the manuscript in which Marx and Engels argue for the necessity of "inverting" Feuerbach's idealism. In this manuscript—famously abandoned as Marx later put it to "the gnawing criticism of the mice" since with it they "had achieved [their] main purpose—self-clarification"—Marx and Engels first draw a distinction between how individuals "appear in their own or other people's imaginations" (*wie sie in der eignen oder fremden Vorstellung erscheinen mögen*) and how "they *really* are" (*wie sie* wirklich *sind*).[33] Thus, "If in all ideology men and their circumstances appear upside-down as in a *camera obscura,* this phenomenon arises just as much from their historical life-process as the inversion of objects on the retina does from their physical life-process." Furthermore, whereas idealist philosophy begins with "what men say, imagine, conceive," historical materialists "set out from real, active men, and on the basis of their real life-process we demonstrate the development of the ideological reflexes and echoes of this life-process. The phantoms formed in the human brain are also, necessarily, sublimates of their material life-process, which is empirically verifiable and bound to material premises. . . . Life is not determined by consciousness, but consciousness by life."[34]

Marx further expands this insight in *A Contribution to a Critique of Political Economy* (1859). There, he famously distinguishes between the base, the "totality of these relations of production [that] constitutes the economic structure of society, the real foundation" and the "legal and political superstructure and to which correspond definite forms of social consciousness. The mode of production of material life conditions the general process of social, political and intellectual life. It is not the consciousness of men that determines their existence, but their social existence that determines their consciousness."[35] Marx further observes, "The changes in the economic foundation lead sooner or later to the transformation of the whole immense superstructure. In studying such transformations, it is always necessary to distinguish between material transformation of the economic conditions of production, which can be studied with the precision of natural science, and the legal, political, religious, artistic or philosophic—in short, ideological forms in which men become conscious of this conflict and fight it out."[36]

However, by the late 1850s, Balibar notes, ideology becomes extremely rare in Marx's writing, and its problematic is instead "taken up again under the heading of fetishism," beginning with the opening section of *Capital,* volume 1 (1867).[37] Marx claims that the commodity "is a very strange thing, abounding in metaphysical subtleties and theological niceties."[38] Moreover, in the commodity form appears "the definite social relation between men themselves which assumes here, for them, the fantastic form of a relation between things." "In order, therefore," Marx further argues, "to find an analogy we must take flight into the misty realm of religion." At this point, the influence of Feuerbach's critique of religious alienation re-emerges. Marx goes on,

> There the products of the human brain appear as autonomous figures endowed with a life of their own, which enter into relations both with each other and with the human race. So it is in the world of commodities with the products of men's hands. I call this the fetishism which attaches itself to the products of labor as soon as they are produced as commodities, and is therefore inseparable from the production

of commodities. As the forgoing analysis has already demonstrated, this fetishism of the world of commodities arises from the peculiar social character of the labor which produces them.[39]

Balibar observes, "fetishism is not a subjective phenomenon or a false perception of reality, as an optical illusion or a superstitious belief would be. It constitutes, rather, the way in which reality (a certain form or social structure) cannot but appear," a point that Žižek then develops in some detail in his discussion of Marx's "invention of the symptom."[40] Such a formation is unique to capitalism, and its originality lies in its dispensing with the older "extra-economic" legitimations, ideological as well as coercive, to reproduce itself. Marx writes in the last pages of *Capital,* volume I, "The silent compulsion of economic relations sets the seal on the domination of the capitalist over the worker. Direct extra-economic force is still of course used, but only in exceptional cases. In the ordinary run of things, the worker can be left to the 'natural laws of production', i.e. it is possible to rely on his dependence on capital, which springs from the conditions of production themselves, and is guaranteed in perpetuity by them."[41]

This shift, or epistemological break (*coupture*), in Marx's work produces, Balibar argues, two distinct trends in later Marxist political and cultural theory. The first explores questions he calls "Hegelian in origin," including education, intellectuals, "symbolic violence," and the "mode of domination inherent in the state"—questions I am assembling here under the concept of "hegemony," and whose most significant later theorists would include Antonio Gramsci (who in his *Quaderni del carcere* (*Prison Notebooks*) first develops the modern Marxist notion of hegemony, "the 'spontaneous' consent given by the great masses of the population to the general direction imposed on social life by the dominant social group"),[42] Louis Althusser, and, in different ways, Bertolt Brecht, Roland Barthes, Michel Foucault, and Judith Butler. The second takes up problems raised by the economic, "the mode of subjection or constitution of the 'world' of subjects and objects inherent in the organization of society as a market and its domination by market forces."[43] Georg Lukács's concept of *reification* names this second line of investigation: "The transformation of the commodity relation into a thing of 'ghostly objectivity' cannot therefore content itself with the reduction of all objects for the gratification of human needs to commodities. It stamps its imprint upon the whole consciousness of man; his qualities and abilities are no longer an organic part of his personality, they are things which he can 'own' or 'dispose of' like the various objects of the external world."[44] Some of the other figures associated most prominently with this line of investigation include Theodor Adorno, Henri Lefebvre, and the Situationist Guy Debord, and their more distant descendants in later cultural studies and various historicist explorations of the literature and culture of consumer societies.

As my Greimasian mapping of these first two conditions of Marxism bears out, these lines of inquiry form the fundamental plane of the Imaginary, of self and other, in which many of the battles of Marxist cultural criticism subsequently take place. Moreover, when we think of this as a spatial mapping of the narrative of Marx's own arduous intellectual journey, something else very interesting emerges. What becomes apparent is the way in which this Imaginary opposition at once genetically precedes and constitutes the field in which the concrete abstraction named the mode of production is "lived." Only the mode of production is available for "scientific" analysis—that is, as long as science is understood along the lines of mathematical language, "whose most interesting structural peculiarity," Jameson observes, "lies in its . . . distance from the individual subject or speaker."[45] Science conceived in this way, or what we might better refer to as theoretical discourse, involves the elaboration of axioms. Hallward notes, "An axiom, in the modern sense, is indeed something we *make,* something artificial or postulated. It is simply a rigorous convention accepted on the basis of its utility and its compatibility with other similarly accepted conventions."[46] Hallward further argues that the mathematician Kurt Gödel saw the specific "axioms of set theory as self-evident and immediately accessible: they 'force themselves on us as being true,' he believed, in much the same way that physical objects force themselves upon sense perception."[47] It is in its forcing of a knowledge of the world that any axiom becomes most productive.

These axioms take the form of the "all" statements that appear throughout Jameson's and all the other great theorists' work. For example, in his 1979 essay "Reification and Utopia in Mass Culture," of which I will have more to say momentarily, Jameson writes, "all contemporary works of art—whether those of high culture and modernism or of mass culture and commercial culture—have as their underlying impulse—albeit in what is often distorted and repressed unconscious form—our deepest fantasies about the nature of social life, both as we live it now, and as we feel in our bones it ought rather to be lived."[48] In

"Science Versus Ideology," Jameson further distinguishes between these axioms and propositions:

> between a pregiven or constituted "axiomatic" and the various "enunciations" logically drawn form those axioms which are something like the individual "utterances" of mathematical language. The latter can be evaluated or "proven" or disproven; the former cannot be, and would seem to form a rough equivalent to those "absolute presuppositions" Collingwood felt able to discover at work within any philosophical or metaphysical statement or proposition.[49]

If axioms or absolute presuppositions correspond to the Symbolic dimension, enunciations, utterances, or propositions do so to the Imaginary. The mode of production is in effect the grammar, or to use the older metaphor, the base, to the superstructure of these various utterances, ideological and commodity formations as well as economic forces and relations of production, what Deleuze and Guattari call codes. Need I add here that, like the deep grammar so important for structuralists such as Greimas, the axiomatic system of a mode of production exists nowhere in the world in an empirical observable form? In short, it is *not,* as the figure of the base is sometimes understood, reducible to some kind of economic foundation of our experiences; rather, it is the name given to the concrete abstraction, Benjamin's Idea, that is the totality of contemporary life.

This distinction between the imaginary opposition of hegemony and reification and the Symbolic order named the capitalist mode of production also provides one answer to the often asked question of why Marx chose to begin *Capital* with the difficult discussion of commodity fetishism (in his preface to the French edition, Marx proclaims, echoing Hegel's observation from his preface to *The Phenomenology* that I cited in part I, "There is no royal road to science, and only those who do not dread the fatiguing climb of its steep paths have a chance of gaining its luminous summits").[50] Only when the dialectical other to his earlier work on the problems of ideology (read hegemony) was laid into place could the scientific analysis of capitalism as a particular and concrete mode of production commence.

Finally, and most significantly, we begin to see the absolute necessity for the immense theoretical labors that Marx dedicates the last decades of his life to in developing the project first outlined in the *Grundrisse* notebooks and then commenced in the never-completed seven volumes of *Capital*. In effect, with this totalizing project, Marx comes full circle and is able to confront with a new clarity and precision the passions of his earlier years—the revolutionary overturning of capitalism and the opening of a path toward the maximal or universal love called communism. In Lacan's terms, Marx endeavored to show how the Symbolic order of the capitalist mode of production generates its own particular void of the real, the proletariat—or as Marx and Engels more dramatically put it in *The Manifesto of the Communist Party*, "What the bourgeoisie therefore produces, above all, are its own grave-diggers."[51] However, what could only be a performative utterance in that early text would, Marx demonstrates, become a constative by the time the project of *Capital* was completed.

III.

This Greimasian presentation of Marx's project effectively highlights the incompleteness of much of the work today that proceeds under the name of Marxist cultural criticism. A good deal of these labors have been devoted to the first two conditions, those of hegemony and reification, offering rich and detailed critical readings of the manifestations of the imaginaries or lived experiences of capitalism at its various moments. Although less common, there have also been and continue to be luminous scientific or symbolic efforts to articulate a totalizing portrait of the current mode of production. Much of the earlier work in these directions took the form of what Raymond Williams describes as "epochal" rather than "historical" approaches: Marxist cultural criticism, Williams contends, "is usually very much better at distinguishing the large features of different epochs of society, as commonly between feudal and bourgeois, than at distinguishing between different phases of bourgeois society, and different moments within these phases."[52] Williams's own original efforts, such as his still vital *The Country and the City* (1973) as well as the periodizing analyses of Jameson ("Postmodernism as the cultural logic of late capitalism") and others have gone a long way toward refining our focus to more precise historical scales (this is also one of the goals in my book *Life Between Two Deaths, 1989–2001: U.S. Culture in the Long Nineties* [2009]).[53] In sum then, we could say that Marxist cultural criticism has been extraordinarily effective at interpreting our world, in various ways—however, hasn't the point always been, as Marx reminds us at the very outset of his project, to change it?

Badiou provides us in *Theory of the Subject*—a work Bosteels persuasively contends remains foundational for all of Badiou's subsequent project—with tools to think about this same problem in a manner especially applicable to the Greimasian schema at the center of our discussion. As I suggested a moment ago, much of Marxist cultural study unfolds in the field constituted by the top three terms of the schema. This results in what Badiou refers to as a *structural dialectic:*

> The structural dialectic has a tendency (that is its idealist side), first, to make the structural aspect of this dialectic prevail over its historical aspect, that is place over force; and, second, within this very same primacy of the structural foundation, to make the theory of the splace, on the basis of its regulated universe, predominate over the emergence of the outplace [our fourth condition or love]. . . . The structural dialectic immobilizes the position of the terms into a symmetry, or into an invariant asymmetry, rather than seizing the becoming-principle of the secondary, the rupture of any splace by the explosion of its rule and the loss of principle of the initial position.[54]

Badiou earlier in the book defines the concept of the "splace" in the following way: "if one opposes force to place, as I shall continually do, it will always be more homogeneous to say 'space of placement' to designate the action of the structure. It would be even better to forge the term *splace*."[55] To this Badiou opposes what he names a *historical dialectic:* the latter replaces the former's "logics of places" with the "logic of forces."[56] Later in *Theory of the Subject,* Badiou emphasizes, "If the *structural* concept of contradiction (the splitting)," the very motor of a structural dialectic, "points to the lack as its mainspring and to the law as its horizon, the *historical* concept of contradiction is forged on the basis of destruction whose sphere of action lies in the nonlaw."[57]

The sphere of action which lies in the nonlaw—how better to describe Marxism's foundational fourth condition highlighted for us by the full Greimasian schema? For it is in this fourth condition that Marxist cultural criticism encounters its own void of the real, that fourth or "plus one" condition, which at once remains generative of its entire project and yet unrepresentable within it.

What Lukács formulates in the other half of the dialectic he names reification *and* "the consciousness of the proletariat"—a dialectic that is too often sundered in Marxist cultural criticism—similarly serves as a placeholder for this impossible effort to present Marxism's *raison d'être,* the revolutionary break with the capitalist mode of production. Crucially for Lukács, bourgeois and proletariat—dominant and dominated— consciousnesses are not two different ideologies, but qualitatively different ways of occupying the world, emerging from radically different standpoints within the totality of the capitalist mode of production:

> For the proletariat, however, the "same" process means *its own emergence as a class.* In both cases a transformation from quantity to quality is involved. We need only consider the line of development leading from the medieval craft via simple co-operation and manufacture to the modern factory and we shall see the extent to which even for the bourgeoisie the qualitative changes stand out as milestones on the road. The *class meaning* of these changes lies precisely in the fact that the bourgeoisie regularly transforms each new qualitative gain back on to the quantitative level of yet another rational calculation. Whereas for the proletariat the "same" development has a different class meaning: it means the *abolition of the isolated individual,* it means that workers can become conscious of the social character of labour, it means that the abstract, universal form of the societal principle as it is manifested can be increasingly concretized and overcome.[58]

All of this elaborates further on Marx's insight that consciousness is determined by life, not life by consciousness. Reification is in this sense the perception and experience of reality from the perspective of the dominant standpoint, and expressed in the institutions, practices, and positivist science that Lukács describes in great detail in his essay; and to the degree that all individuals are subject to this domination it is also "the necessary, immediate reality of every person living in capitalist society." Lukács thus concludes, "the structure can be disrupted only if the immanent contradictions of the process are made conscious. Only when the consciousness of the proletariat is able to point out the road along which the dialectics of history is objectively impelled, but which it cannot travel unaided, will the consciousness of the proletariat awaken to a consciousness of the process, and only then will the proletariat become the identical subject-object of history whose praxis will change reality."[59]

It is this latter collective perspective that, in Badiou's terms, emerges from the void of the situation, and thereby forces its truth (i.e., the totality and mutability of capitalism): that is, the consciousness of the proletariat as a collective standpoint is the world "experienced, developed and lived from the point of view of difference and not identity." The proletarian in this sense is thus not to be identified with the industrial working class; nor, as Jameson now argues, should *Capital* be understood as a book about labor. Rather, "it is a book about unemployment."[60] Similarly, the proletariat in capitalism is what Jacques Rancière names the nonclass, those within capitalism's global structure but who have no identifiable place in it. Such a grasp of the world as that presented by the consciousness of the proletariat is strictly speaking "impossible" from within the splace of capitalism, and dismissed by those under its sway as paranoid, terroristic, or, at best, "utopian" in the dismissive sense of idealist daydream. Equally significantly, in its collective nature, abolishing the self-interested individualism that is the common sense of capitalist modernity, the proletariat consciousness already prefigures a radically other mode of being in the world.

The question I want to confront is in what ways might Marxist cultural criticism similarly think from the perspective of the permanent scandal of the consciousness of the proletariat and revolution, Utopia and love, or communism. To do so, however, requires another reorientation of how we go about our work as scholars of culture. Our labors we rightly assume deal largely with representations and practices, which are understood as reflections or embodiments or accretions of the lived experiences of contemporary or historical capitalism, its ideologies and subjective formations, or its "symptoms," to use another of Jameson's favorite terms. And as those whose political and existential situations incline us to recognize the devastating effects of this mode of production, our analyses tend to be "critical" in their ultimate evaluation of these representations and practices. Where our work becomes more hopeful in its outlook, as in the case of classic interventions of cultural studies such as Dick Hebdige's *Subculture: The Meaning of Style* (1979), is where we find cultural representations or practices that "resist" or even momentarily "subvert" (*detourn* as the Situationists would have it) what Williams calls the "dominant and effective" representations and practices of our present situation.[61]

Lest I be misunderstood, let me state unequivocally here my conviction that such labors of ideological, destructive, or deconstructive critique remain absolutely necessary as long as we live in the world we do. It is not possible to "get beyond" the work of ideological demystification, as some have understood Barthes to be suggesting in his 1971 essay "Change the Object Itself: Mythology Today."[62] Such labors remain, as long as we live within the symbolic order of capitalism, and perhaps beyond, interminable. However, alone these labors represent only part of the challenge facing us. A full Marxist cultural criticism would also need to confront head-on the challenge and risks of bringing into consciousness those representations and practices that are in effect unrepresentable—revolutionary events and forms of collective life that are radically other to our current predicament. If we accept Jameson's claims that critical Marxist criticism approaches texts as allegories, then what I am calling for here would be a hermeneutic attention to the *figurative* dimensions of these same cultural texts. Such a labor involves tremendous risk, as we move from the firm ground of what-is-though-shouldn't-be to what-should-be-but-isn't, and as we shift from a critical to a much more affirmative stance.

IV.

Perhaps the most significant advocate of this kind of Marxist cultural criticism also remains one of the tradition's most underappreciated figures: the preeminent philosopher of Utopia, whose career spanned the first eight decades of the twentieth century, Ernst Bloch. In the last pages of the first volume of his three-volume magnum opus, *The Principle of Hope* (1959), a work Jameson describes as "a vast and disorderly exploration of the manifestations of hope on all levels of reality," Bloch too acknowledges the dangers cultural critics face in pursuing this Utopian content: "From this point of view the New is most easily, even most heartily mocked."[63] And yet such a dismissive attitude risks reinforcing the pedagogy of pessimism, and its consequent inaction, and thus Bloch concludes, "the most dogged enemy of socialism is not only, as is understandable, great capital, but equally the load of indifference, hopelessness."[64] It is the responsibility of a committed cultural criticism to challenge such hopelessness wherever it emerges.

Bloch too finds support for such a project in Marx's earliest writings. In *The Principle of Hope,* Bloch offers a virtuoso re-reading of Marx's

"Theses on Feuerbach," with the aim of locating in Marx's work the conceptual break, or what he calls the "departure," much as Althusser more famously would do a few years hence: "Marx was a materialist at the latest from 1843 onwards; 'The Holy Family' gave birth to the materialist interpretation of history in 1844, and with it scientific socialism. And the 'Eleven Theses', *produced between 'The Holy Family' of 1844/45 and 'The German Ideology' of 1845/46,* thus represents the formulated departure from Feuerbach, together with a highly original entry into a new original inheritance. . . . The adopted standpoint of the *proletariat* allowed Marx to become causally and concretely, that is, truly (fundamentally) humanistic."[65]

Bloch begins by arguing that the "Theses"—a work meant for "private reference, not intended for publication"—need to be reorganized into four conceptual groups:

> firstly, the epistemological group dealing with *perception and activity* (Theses 5, 1, 3); secondly, the anthropological-historical group dealing with *self-alienation, its real cause and true materialism* (Theses 4, 6, 7, 9, 10); thirdly, the uniting or theory-practice group, dealing with *proof and probation* (Theses 2, 8). Finally there follows the most important thesis, the *password* that not only marks a final parting of the minds, but with whose use they cease to be nothing but minds (Thesis 11).[66]

While Feuerbach's "anthropological materialism" had a profound influence on Marx's intellectual development, enabling the "transition from mere mechanical to historical materialism," it remained trapped in a merely contemplative relationship to the world: this is because, as with all other materialisms preceding Marx, it "lacks *the constantly oscillating subject-object relation called work.*"[67] In the "Theses," Marx thus launches a two-front assault, at once "against mechanistic environmentalism, which ends in fatalism of being, and against the idealistic subject-theory, which ends in putschism, or at least in exaggerated activity-optimism."[68] Similarly, in the second set of theses Marx adopts "the new, proletarian standpoint," which "far from removing the value-concept of humanism, in practice allows it to come home for the very first time; and the more scientific the socialism, the more concretely it has the *care for man at its centre, the real removal of his self-alienation as its goal.*"[69]

This argument comes to its dramatic climax with the last two clusters, wherein Marx reconfigures truth not as "a theory relationship alone, but *a definite theory-practice relationship.* . . . Every confrontation in the history of philosophy confirms in this case the Novum of the theory-practice relationship as opposed to mere 'application' of theory."[70] Hegel comes closest to a "premonition" of this—"a transition occurs in Hegel's psychology from 'theoretical mind' (perception, imagination, thinking) to the antithesis 'practical mind' (feeling, driving will, bliss), out of which then, synthetically, 'free mind' was to result"—but pulls up short, "so that in the end, it is not practice which crowns truth, but 're-minding', 'science of appearing knowledge' and nothing more."[71] However, Bloch emphasizes that Marx's corrosive criticisms were not in any simple way "directed at Hegelian philosophy and other great philosophies in the past." Indeed, Marx's aim is susceptible to "an interested misinterpretation" that finds "in the highest triumph of philosophy—which takes place in Thesis 11—an abdication of philosophy, in fact a kind of non-bourgeois pragmatism."[72] Bloch heaps great disdain on the anti-theory stance of pragmatism and what he calls the "scorners of intelligence and practicists" among the socialists: "The practicists, with at best short-term credit for theory, especially complicated theory, create in the middle of the Marxist system of light the darkness of their own private ignorance and of the resentment which so easily goes with ignorance. . . . It must therefore be repeatedly emphasized: *in Marx a thought is not true because it is useful, but it is useful because it is true.*"[73] The dialectic Bloch traces here can be productively overlain on the schema we have been discussing throughout this chapter, and would appear as follows (figure 21).

Bloch maintains that in the climactic eleventh thesis, which served as one of the epigraphs of this chapter, Marx issues a challenge to reorient thinking in a dramatic fashion: "interpretation is related to contemplation and follows from it; *non*-contemplative knowledge is thus now distinguished as a new flag which truly carries us to victory."[74] If contemplative knowledge, idealist or materialist, was "related essentially to what is past," and pragmatist or practicist anti-knowledge stuck in an eternal present, then the historical materialism Marx inaugurates in the "Theses" opens up onto future horizons of concrete possibility: "Thus, the beginning philosophy of revolution, i.e. of changeability for the better, was ultimately revealed on and in the *horizon of the future;* with the science of the New and the power to guide."[75] Moreover, in an astonishing prefiguration of Vaneigem's claims with which I also opened

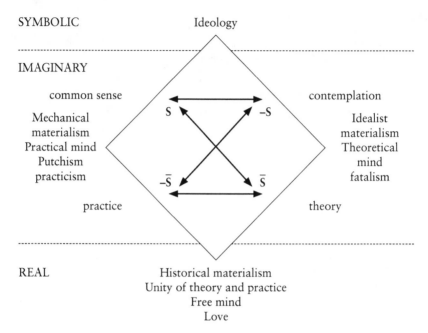

SYMBOLIC   Ideology

IMAGINARY

common sense   contemplation

Mechanical   Idealist
materialism   materialism
Practical mind   Theoretical
Putchism   mind
practicism   fatalism

practice   theory

REAL   Historical materialism
              Unity of theory and practice
                    Free mind
                      Love

Figure 21. Ernst Bloch on the "Theses on Feuerbach."

this chapter, Bloch argues that "warmth also definitely seeks to be inherent in thinking here, since it is helpful thinking. The warmth of wanting to help itself, of love for the victims, of hatred of the exploiters. Indeed these feelings bring partiality into play, without which no true knowledge combined with good action is at all possible in socialist terms."[76] This stance is truly universal, Bloch suggests, because it is interested, in stark opposition to any apparently disinterested contemplative outlook, "which, precisely because of its abstractly declamatory love of mankind, does not in the least seek to change the world today for the good, but to perpetuate it in the bad."[77] Indeed, Bloch concludes, "Without factions in love, with an equally concrete pole of hatred, there is no genuine love, without *partiality* of the revolutionary class standpoint there only remains backward idealism instead of forward practice."[78] More recently, Hardt and Negri similarly note, "the power of love must also be, second, a force to combat evil. Love now takes the form of indignation, disobedience, and antagonism. . . . It should be clear at this point that love always involves the use of force or, more precisely, that the actions of love are themselves deployments of force. Love may be an angel, but if so it is an angel armed."[79]

Bloch later develops a similarly charged vision of the revolutionary power of love in a moving explication of the *figure* of marriage:

> Marriage initiates and survives the fire-ordeal of truth in the life of the partners, of the steadfast befriending of gender in everyday life. Guest in the house, peaceful unity in fine, burning otherness, this therefore becomes the imago of marriage and the nimbus it undertakes to win. Often making the wrong choice, as is well-known, with resignation as the rule, with happiness as the exception, almost even as mere chance. And seldom does marriage become the outbidding truth of what was initially hoped for, therefore deeper, not merely more real than all the songs of the bride. Nevertheless it has its utopian nimbus with justification: only in this form does the by no means simple, the cryptic wishful symbol of the house work, is there any prospect at all of good surprise and ripeness. Just as the pain of love is a thousand times better than unhappy marriage, in which there only remains pain, fruitless pain, so too the landlocked adventures of love are diffuse compared with the great sea voyage which marriage can be, and which does not end with old age, not even with the death of one partner.[80]

The reading strategy that Bloch deploys here in regards to love and marriage is not unlike the operation Judith Butler later names "resignification" in her own masterpiece of a revitalized cultural criticism—and an essay that marks a significant turning point in her rich intellectual project as well—"Gender Is Burning: Questions of Appropriation and Subversion." At the center of the essay is the film *Paris Is Burning* (1990), a documentary exploring urban drag balls and the communities that surround them. In the course of the essay, Butler highlights the limitations of critical approaches to the film that would either denounce the ideological nature of the representations therein, or, conversely, celebrate the performative power to subvert reigning norms. While there are partial truths in both views, in the end they leave the dominant symbolic order, that of a patriarchal heteronormativity, unchallenged.

The celebratory outlook in particular, when absolutized as an end in itself—a strategy wrongly associated, Butler stresses, with her own work—represents the kind of bad infinity that Bloch associates with the undialectical stream of eternal becoming championed by certain strands of German Romanticism or, closer to his own moment, Bergsonian vitalists. In contrast, Bloch contends for the necessity of moments of concrete crystallization, a partial summing up and reinforcement of the gains made, in every movement forward:

> Even if a stationary halt in the On The Way is as bad or even worse than On The Way made absolute, every halt is still correct in which the utopian present moment of the final state itself is not forgotten, on the contrary, in which it is retained by the agreement of the will with the anticipated final moment (summum bonum). There are such moments in all concrete revolutionary work, in the realization of the proletariat as abolition of philosophy, in the abolition of the proletariat as realization of philosophy. They are in every articulation of unknown self-being through artistic pre-appearance and in the hearth of all articulations of the central question. They are even in the stupor of negative astonishment, and all the more so in the shiver of positive astonishment, as a landing announced by bells.[81]

Similarly, Butler argues that the real value of an engagement with the film *Paris Is Burning* lies in the partial summing up or concrete figuration it offers the viewer of radically new collectivities. This occurs, Butler argues, through the operation of resignification:

> The resignification of the family through these terms is not a vain or useless imitation, but the social and discursive building of community, a community that binds, cares, and teaches, that shelters and enables. This is doubtless a cultural elaboration of kinship that anyone outside of the privilege of heterosexual family (and those within those "privileges" who suffer there) needs to see, to know, and to learn from, a task that makes none of us who are outside of heterosexual "family" into absolute outsiders to this film. Significantly, it is in the elaboration of kinship forged through a resignification of the very terms which effect our exclusion and abjection that such a resignification creates the discursive and social space for community, that we see an appropriation of the terms of domination that turns them toward a more enabling future.[82]

As Bruce Robbins reminds us, Butler is another of the most significant contemporary dialectical thinkers, albeit working outside of the problematic of Marxism, and so the convergence of her contemporary work with that of Bloch's mid-century efforts is not without justification.[83] Moreover, the positions Butler articulates coincide in some productive ways with the Greimasian schema elaborated thus far (figure 22).

V.

Bloch's work has remained a vital resource for Jameson's project since at least the late 1960s. Indeed, it is through his engagement with Bloch's writings that Jameson first comes to acknowledge the indispensability for any full Marxist cultural criticism to take into account Marxism's fourth condition. In *Marxism and Form,* Jameson describes the unique hermeneutic principle driving Bloch's project: "The Utopian moment is indeed in one sense quite impossible for us to imagine, except as unimaginable; thus a kind of allegorical structure is built into the very forward movement of the Utopian impulse itself, which always points to

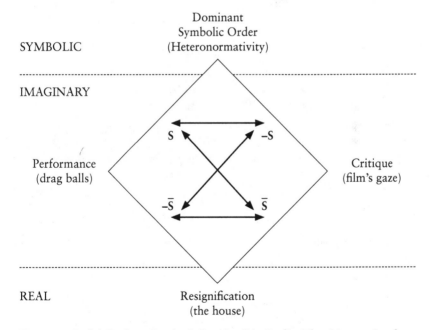

Figure 22. Judith Butler, "Gender Is Burning," in *Bodies That Matter: On the Discursive Limits of Sex.*

something other, which can never reveal itself directly but must always speak in figures, which always calls out structurally for completion and exegesis."[84] For Bloch, according to Jameson, this Utopian content is a fundamental part of all human labors, cultural or otherwise: "Bloch's hermeneutic, on the contrary, finds its richness in the very variety of its objects themselves, while its initial conceptual content remains relatively simple, relatively unchanging: thus little by little wherever we look everything in the world becomes a version of some primal figure, a manifestation of that primordial movement toward the future and toward ultimate identity with a transfigured world which is Utopia."[85]

The challenge to recover this Utopian content is thus at its greatest, and most necessary, Jameson suggests, in places where our political values might lead us to be least likely to suspect it:

> In a more limited way, the problem of a Marxist hermeneutic arises whenever we are called upon to determine the place of what we may call right-wing literature, whether it be the traditional conservative literature of the past, of a Flaubert or a Dostoyevsky, or in our own time a Fascist literature of great quality, as is the case with Wyndham Lewis or Drieu, or with Céline. If it is as Marxism has always claimed, namely that there can be no such thing as a right-wing philosophy, that a Fascist system is a contradiction in terms, not thought but the optical illusion of thought only . . . then the official opinions and positions of such reactionary authors may be considered surface phenomena, rationalizations and disguises for some more basic source of energy of which, on the analogy of the Freudian model of the unconscious, they are unaware. A Marxist hermeneutic would then have the task of restoring to that energy the political direction which rightly belongs to it, of making it once more available to us.[86]

A small-scale model of this hermeneutic is on display in the discussion of Marcel Proust's *A la recherche du temps perdu* that concludes the chapter. Jameson shows how what appears in Proust's work as the thoroughly ideological vision of the *fin-de-siècle* French upper classes turns over into a more properly utopian projection:

> For it is precisely the leisure of this class, given over completely to interpersonal relationships, to conversation, art,

and social planning (if one may so characterize the energy that goes into the building of a salon), fashion, love, which reflects in the most distorted way the possibilities of a world in which alienated labor will have ceased to exist, in which man's struggle with the external world and with his own mystified and external pictures of society will have given way to man's confrontation with himself.[87]

Such a hermeneutic is further developed in Jameson's later work, notable, for example, in the still scandalous discussion of Wyndham Lewis's expressionism in *Fables of Aggression;* and, even later, in his beautiful lyrical musings on Franz Kafka's "Josephine the Singer, or the Mouse People" that concludes the chapter on Platonov's *Chevengur* in *The Seeds of Time.*

However, a more complete theoretical elaboration of the dialectic he touched upon in *Marxism and Form* would have to wait until the brief but absolutely central concluding chapter of *The Political Unconscious,* "The Dialectic of Utopia and Ideology." Throughout the book's earlier chapters, Jameson develops the three-part allegorical hermeneutic I outlined earlier, one deployed in this particular case to re-read the history of the novel, but clearly meant to be applicable to all cultural texts. In the book's long penultimate chapter on the fiction of Joseph Conrad, Jameson argues that modernist form more generally should be understood as "an ideological expression of capitalism, and in particular, of the latter's reification of daily life," *and* "as a Utopian compensation for everything reification brings with it."[88] Jameson then argues in the final chapter for the need to supplement this three-fold critical or

> Marxist negative hermeneutic, a Marxist practice of ideological analysis proper . . . with a Marxist positive hermeneutic, or a decipherment of the Utopian impulses of these same still ideological cultural texts . . . in which an *instrumental* analysis is coordinated with a *collective-associational* or *communal* reading of culture, or in which a *functional* method for describing cultural texts is articulated with an *anticipatory* one.[89]

This is the kind of double analysis I advanced in my discussion of *It's a Wonderful Life* earlier in this chapter: a reading of the film in terms of the condition of politics highlights its ideological dimensions, while an approach conditioned by the truth procedure of love illuminates its collective-associational and anticipatory aspects. This call is preceded a few pages earlier in *The Political Unconscious* by another of the fundamental axioms organizing Jameson's project: "*all* class consciousness— or in other words, all ideology in the strongest sense, including the most exclusive forms of ruling-class consciousness just as much as that of oppositional or oppressed classes—is in its very nature Utopian."[90] Utopia here means something different from what has been elaborated in the preceding Conrad chapter: not as compensation, what Bloch calls "abstract utopia," which is the only Utopianism available to those looking at the world from the perspective of the ruling classes, but rather a Utopianism of the consciousness of the global proletariat, a concrete and material figuration of a "beyond" of the present.[91]

Little in the way of examples of this positive hermeneutic appears in the chapter or even the book itself. However, such a labor is more fully on display in an essay that is one of the most influential companion pieces to *The Political Unconscious*, "Reification and Utopia in Mass Culture," originally published in the inaugural issue of the important radical theoretical journal *Social Text* (1979). In a recent institutional history of the journal, Anna McCarthy rightly points out that the readings in Jameson's essay "were not intended as works of criticism as much as heuristic examples of what a renewed practice of leftist cultural critique within the humanities might look like, a practice that pushed beyond paranoid models of manipulation, populist anti-intellectualisms, and the 'unsatisfactory' elements of Frankfurt School aesthetic hierarchies."[92] In order to achieve these goals, Jameson advances in the essay the axiomatic claim that *all* "works of mass culture cannot be ideological without one and the same time being implicitly or explicitly Utopian as well: they cannot manipulate unless they offer some genuine shred of content as a fantasy bribe to the public about to be so manipulated."[93] Jameson then recasts the notion of manipulation along the lines of the early work of the psychoanalytic theorist Norman Holland, such that the mass cultural text is now understood as one "which strategically arouses fantasy content within careful symbolic containment structures which defuse it."[94] Jameson goes on to exemplify the workings of these operations in three of the first Hollywood blockbuster films of the 1970s: Francis Ford Coppola's first two *Godfather* films (1972 and 1974) and Steven Spielberg's *Jaws* (1975).

One thing that has struck some readers as odd about this essay is the fact that the three films are treated in a mixed chronological sequence, a discussion of *Jaws* preceding that of the two *Godfather* movies. And yet, such a narrative *sujet* has a very significant function here, as it enables Jameson to conclude his analysis on this ringing affirmative note:

> [T]he ideological myth of the Mafia ends up generating the authentically Utopian vision of revolutionary liberation; while the degraded Utopian content of the family paradigm ultimately unmasks itself as the survival of more archaic forms of repressions and sexism and violence. Meanwhile, both of these narrative strands, freed to pursue their own inner logic to its limits, are thereby driven to the outer reaches and historical boundaries of capitalism itself, the one as it touches the pre-capitalist societies of the past, the other at the beginnings of the future and the dawn of socialism.[95]

This presentation thus enables Jameson to *interrupt* the recontainment operation he had outlined earlier—not only the recontainments that take place in these films (Michael Corleone's tragic descent into "evil"), but also in the larger institutional history of Hollywood film, where the political potential of the auteur films of the 1970s is cut short with the emergence of the blockbusters of the 1980s.[96] Jameson's story here thus takes the form of a what-if, or alternate history, where the lineaments of our own here and now appear in even starker relief.

In "Reification and Utopia," the efforts to figure a more Utopian horizon in Hollywood film immediately precedes the axiom concerning the "underlying impulse" of all contemporary works of art I cited earlier. The statement of this axiom then enables Jameson in the final line of the essay to issue this more general challenge to Marxist cultural critics:

> To reawaken, in the midst of a privatized and psychologizing society, obsessed with commodities and bombarded by the ideological slogans of big business, some sense of the ineradicable drive towards collectivity that can be detected, no matter how faintly and feebly, in the most degraded works of mass culture just as surely as in the classics of modernism—is surely an indispensable precondition for any meaningful Marxist intervention in contemporary culture.[97]

The very fact that this call occurs outside the borders of *The Political Unconscious* points toward the relative exteriority of this labor to the three-part hermeneutic that Jameson develops in this book. More recently, in the short Introduction to the collection of essays entitled *The Modernist Papers,* Jameson returns to this problem anew, as he works to locate a way beyond the contemporary impasse of formalism and historicism. I argue elsewhere, and will return to this question in the next chapter, that such an impasse—especially in its presentation in conservative and anti-Marxist disciplinary formations such as the New Formalism or surface reading, or in calls for the return to proper disciplinarity—unfolds on the level of the Imaginary, and in so doing masks the real challenge that is that of theory itself.[98] Jameson similarly argues that the other side of such an opposition is not to be found in a synthesis of these two terms ("form of the content") but rather in their *neutralization* ("content of the form"), an "attempt to escape that world's ideologies" that "must also be faithfully registered and counted as a Utopian one."[99] In so doing, Jameson splits the original formulation of the "ideology of the form" in order to produce a hermeneutic far more receptive to these Utopian dimensions of all cultural texts. A Greimasian presentation of these two schemas, that of the three-part hermeneutic of *The Political Unconscious* and that of the four-fold one alluded to in *The Modernist Papers,* would appear as in figure 23.[100]

In the final paragraph of the Introduction to *The Modernist Papers,* Jameson further elaborates on the project of the book and that of his larger intellectual endeavors at this moment:

> Utopia is another name for the persistence of that Absolute, in a social system which is either pure content—the infinite contingency of an endless collection of commodities—or pure form—in the abstractions of finance and the sheer relationality of the exchange system. But it is also, if you like, a name for the failure of their identification with each other, which is why the essays in this book tend to move back and forth between a focus on the form of the content—in the limits of a specific historical situation and its contradictions—and focus on the content of the form, or in other words the possibilities for figuration or representation.[101]

These observations point at once in two different directions. First, the "social system" Jameson references here is that which he has famously formulated as "postmodernism, or the cultural logic of late capitalism"; and in the book of that title, Jameson argues that the real challenge for a Marxist cultural criticism today is not so much a further elaboration

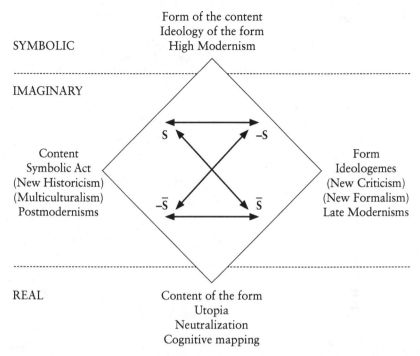

Figure 23. The hermeneutics of *The Political Unconscious* and *The Modernist Papers*.

on a "symptomology" of our current condition, important as such work remains, as the registering of the fitful, incomplete, and flawed efforts to produce a new form of the aesthetic he names *cognitive mapping*. I have already discussed the Utopian figurative dimensions of a cognitive mapping of a world to come in chapter 3; and Carolyn Lesjak now also shows how this project is further developed and extended in Jameson's formulation in *Valences* of a "spatial dialectic."[102] Second, to return to *The Modernist Papers*, with the reformulation of "content of the form" as *neutralization*, Jameson brings us back directly to the labors of the Greimasian schema that is at the center of our discussion. As we shall see again in the final chapter, the full figurative potential of this operation of neutralization will be explored in the most detail in *Archaeologies of the Future*.

Let me conclude this survey rather quickly then by reaffirming that Utopia, content of the form, cognitive mapping, and neutralization—the valences of Jameson's dialectic—these are the names for the challenge and invitation that his work issues to us as cultural critics. It is only by taking such a risk, looking at the world from the perspective of this void, or the condition of love, that, as Jameson writes in the final sentence of *The Political Unconscious,* "a Marxist cultural study can hope to play its part in political praxis, which remains, of course, what Marxism is all about."[103] How all of this relates more locally to our work as educators, intellectuals, and workers in the contemporary university will be the subject of the next chapter.

CHAPTER 5

Unfinished Business

On the Dialectic of the University in Late Capitalism

A significant trope that appears throughout Jameson's *Valences of the Dialectic* (2009) is that of the "unfinished." *Valences* is itself something of an unfinished book, a claim that may come as a surprise to many of the book's readers. At 625 pages, it is Jameson's longest book yet, nearly 200 pages longer than his two prior books, *Archaeologies of the Future* (2005) and *The Modernist Papers* (2007). Like these predecessors, *Valences* combines previously published essays and some significant original work. Of the book's six long sections, the first two, "The Three Names of the Dialectic" and "Hegel Without *Aufhebung*," and the final, "The Valences of History," offer what amount to original book-length studies in their own right. In between, Jameson reprints engagements "from a dialectical perspective" with the work of Derrida—a revised and expanded version of an essay originally published in *New Left Review* that now includes, among other things, an original discussion of Derrida's work on mourning—Deleuze, Sartre, Lenin, Rousseau, and others, as well as original and previously uncollected work on ideology theory, cultural revolution, commodification, Marxism, Utopia, and globalization.[1]

Even with this expansive scope, however, *Valences of the Dialectic* remains incomplete. In its manuscript form, the book included an extended discussion of Hegel's *Phenomenology of Spirit,* later published

separately as *The Hegel Variations* (2010). Moreover, in the final footnote of the first chapter, Jameson points toward related future books
on Heidegger's writings and Marx's *Capital*, the latter published as
Representing Capital: *A Reading of Volume One* (2011); and his most
recent essay on the work of Jacques Lacan, "Lacan and the Dialectic"—
subtitled "A Fragment"—was assumed by some of us to have been intended for, and even completed in, *Valences of the Dialectic*.[2] All of
these projects, past and to come, point toward the undiminished energy
of Jameson's ongoing intellectual project now in its sixth decade.

There are three different valences of the figure of the unfinished that
emerge in the course of the book. First, Jameson uses the figure in a
way that echoes Jürgen Habermas's now classic intervention in the
postmodernism debates, "Modernity—An Incomplete Project," an essay
printed alongside Jameson's "Postmodernism and Consumer Society"
in *The Anti-Aesthetic: Essays in Postmodern Culture* (1983), and which
Jameson engages with directly in the second chapter of *Postmodernism*.[3] In this first sense, Jameson thus means the unfinished to refer to
projects whose realizations still remain tasks for the future. Jameson describes the dialectic itself as "an unfinished project, as Habermas might
put it; a way of grasping situations and events that does not yet exist
as a collective habit because the concrete form of social life to which
it corresponds has not yet come into being."[4] In the rousing concluding lines of an essay whose title is "*History and Class Consciousness*
as an Unfinished Project," Jameson argues of Lukács's most influential
work, "I think that it would be better, however, to consider that, like
the *Manifesto*, it has yet to be written, it lies ahead of us in historical
time. Our task, as political intellectuals, is to lay the groundwork for
that situation in which it can again appear, with all the explosive freshness of the *Novum*, as though for the first time in which it can, once
again, become both real and true."[5] Similarly, of Althusser's influential
and widely debated essay "Ideology and Ideological State Apparatuses,"
Jameson notes, "Like much of Althusser's work, however, the essay is
programmatic and speculative: it is not a full-dress philosophical position, but rather an agenda, still incompletely fulfilled."[6] Finally, in his
discussion of the project of Marxism more generally, Jameson writes,
"What is Marxism? Or if you prefer, what is Marxism not? It is not,
in particular, a nineteenth-century philosophy, as some people (from
Foucault to Kolakowski) have suggested, although it certainly emerged
from nineteenth century philosophy (but you could just as easily argue that the dialectic is itself an unfinished project, which anticipates

modes of thought and reality that have not yet come into existence even today)."[7]

At the same time, Jameson suggests the *necessarily* unfinished nature of projects whose labors are interminable. For example, in "The Three Names of the Dialectic," Jameson notes that, as in Althusser's formulation of ideology, there is no world without the reified thinking of analytic reason, empiricism, or common sense (Hegel's "Understanding" or *Verstand*), and hence, the work of dialectical thinking (*Vernunft*) must remain unfinished:

> Yet it must also be clear from our description that insofar as it is critical, the dialectic is also what must be called reactive thought. That is, it depends for its operation on the normativity of a pre-existing thought mode, to which it is called upon to react: or to use a once popular theoretical expression, it is parasitic on *Verstand* itself, on the externalized thinking of a material world of objects, for its own operations of correction and subversion, of negation and critique.[8]

At the conclusion of a discussion of the second volume of Sartre's *Critique of Dialectical Reason*, Jameson suggests that it is the reality, or more precisely the real, of our existence in time, our very mortal finitude, that produces such incomplete endeavors: "Yet there are many scarcities in our world, among them the scarcity of life and the scarcity of time. This accounts for the repeated insistence, in late Sartre, that if everything is a project, if everything is totalization, then we must also acknowledge the inevitable failure of all totalizations, their finitude and their unfinished character, owing to the central fact of death."[9]

A beautiful illustration of these first two senses of the unfinished is on display in Jameson's brief engagement with the late work of the modernist painter, "preeminent among such dialectical artists," Piet Mondrian. Mondrian, Jameson argues, takes it upon himself to complete the critical assault begun earlier in the modernist revolution on what had become by the middle nineteenth century a reified and institutionalized painterly *Verstand* (the existence of a "highly formalized academicism" to react against being one of the three coordinates, along with the disorienting development of new industrial, communicational, and transportation technologies, and the "imaginative proximity of social revolution," in Perry Anderson's "conjunctural" explanation of the emergence of all modernisms).[10] Jameson writes, "What Mondrian realized was that cubism had stopped halfway in its move towards abstraction and that it had left intact and central a figure, a sculptural object, which continued to function as a representation and a mimesis, no matter how multiple its faces and dimensions. He resolved to dissolve even this figure itself."[11] However, Mondrian ultimately realizes that such a labor itself must remain interminable:

> One has not succeeded in neutralizing an opposition aesthetically unless one continues to keep that opposition and that tension alive: the very paradox of the aesthetic resolution of contradiction in the first place. So in his final canvas, *Victory Boogie Woogie,* the painter paints and repaints the extraordinary finished work, eliminating his own solutions one after another precisely because they have become solutions and have brought the process to a halt, and leaving the canvas unfinished at his death, a tragic relic of the insatiability of the dialectic, which here ends up destroying itself.[12]

Jameson then concludes, "It is interesting in this context to add that for Mondrian the vertical—the world, external human life—was essentially tragic and that the vocation of the abstract non-dimensional non-space of the painting was very precisely to destroy the tragic in the name of something else."[13]

This "something else" is, of course, an analogon for the larger Utopian project of the modernist revolution[14]—what Alain Badiou names its "passion for the real," the destruction of the world that currently exists and the production of the radically New: "When art is assigned a political vocation, what does 'political' signify? Ever since the twenties, the word dilates to the point of vaguely designating every radical break, every escape from consensus. 'Politics' is the common name for a collectively recognizable break. . . . The word 'politics' names the desire of beginning, the desire that some fragment of the real will finally be exhibited without either fear or law, through the sole effect of human intervention—artistic or erotic invention, for example, or the inventions of the sciences."[15]

The failure of the revolutionary "political" project of modernism, both in its original pre–World War manifestations and in its renewals in the counter-cultures and anti-colonial struggles of the 1960s, opens up in *Valences of the Dialectic* onto a final and much darker invocation of the unfinished. In this third sense, the "unfinished" designates those formations that stand as the last specters or undissolved remainders haunting the imaginary of a final and well-nigh dystopian victory (think here of the final pages of *Nineteen Eighty-Four*) of global neoliberalism and the concomitant "end of history": "late capitalism itself as ontology, the pure presence of the world market system freed from all the errors of human history and of previous social formations, including the ghost of Marx himself."[16] One of the fundamental challenges of dialectical thought Jameson suggests is to hold at once in our minds all three of these valences of the unfinished, and thereby keep this last project from coming to its dreadful completion.

This complex dialectical sense of the unfinished offers some productive ways to think about a theme that has been, albeit in a characteristically indirect fashion, of central concern to Jameson: the university and our work in it as intellectuals, teachers, and activists. Clint Burnham already finds a form of this indirection at work in *The Political Unconscious*—"the molecular *bouleversement* accomplished on pages 31 (pluralism) and 54 (alliance politics) means that the molar argument and narrative is already located in a maelstrom of specific and social contingencies: the academy and the state"[17]—and I suggested in part I a similar set of institutional engagements taking place in Jameson's work from *Marxism and Form* onward. Another more recent entry into these issues can be gleaned from Jameson's 1990 book, *Late Marxism: Adorno, or the Persistence of the Dialectic,* a work, not coincidently, that appears during an earlier moment of intensification of what the media would label the "culture wars": a series of Reagan- and Bush-era attacks on a public funding for a wide range of cultural institutions, including the NEA, NEH, public broadcasting, and, of course, the university.[18] I discussed in chapter 3 the ways *Late Marxism* unfolds as an "epistemo-critical" prologue to the project of Jameson's *Postmodernism.* However, in this context, the aspect of the book that is most relevant takes the form of a new reading of Max Horkheimer and Adorno's *Dialektik der Aufklärung (Dialectic of Enlightenment)* (1947) that forms *Late Marxism*'s centerpiece.

In the series of short chapters that compose the section of the book entitled, for reasons that will become clear in a moment, "Parable of the Oarsmen," Jameson demonstrates once again his commitment to a reading strategy at once sensitive to the "form of the content"—social representations that "can be said to encompass everything called ideology in the most comprehensive acceptation of the word"—and the "content of the form"—"the only productive coordination of the opposition between form and content that does not seek to reduce one term to the other, or to posit illicit syntheses and equally illicit volatilizations of an opposition whose tensions need to be preserved."[19] In *Late Marxism,* this unfolds through a careful mapping of the dialectical unity of what many readers take to be the discrete and fragmentary investigations that compose *Dialectic of Enlightenment*—the sketch of the dialectic of enlightenment itself, the allegorical reading of *The Odyssey,* a study prefiguring Lacan's more well-known essay on Kant with Sade, the infamous discussion of art and mass culture, and the analysis of anti-Semitism.

Jameson argues that the various components of the book are unified first and foremost by the particular context of their composition, a situation to which this study stands as a response, a symbolic act, and an intervention. As is well known, Horkheimer and Adorno wrote the book while in exile in the United States; moreover, "the anthropological shock of the contact of these Central European mandarins with the massdemocratic Otherness of the New World was uniquely conditioned by an unexpected historical conjuncture: the simultaneous rise, in Europe, of Hitlerian fascism."[20] It was the tremendous "originality of Adorno and Horkheimer first to have linked these two phenomena culturally."[21]

Secondly, on a more formal level, Jameson maintains that the book's arguments be re-cast in narrative terms, such that "the various positions become characters, and their abstract ballet turns out to be transferable to areas very different from art."[22] Art, the central figure in this dance, is for Adorno, Jameson stresses, a form of play, a creative exercise of the imaginative powers that define the human itself: "Fantasy, the capacity for fiction or for the mental entertainment of images of what is not (and even what is not yet, or what is past), is thus not some incidental, supplementary adjunct power of human consciousness but virtually its constitutive feature."[23] More specific to the present crisis, however, art is "the form, taken in the Aesthetic realm, of what Adorno elsewhere calls the 'determinate negation,' the only authentic form of critical thinking in our times—in other words, a consciousness of the contradiction which resists the latter's solution, its dissolution either into satiric positivism and cynical empiricism on the one hand, and into utopian positivity on the other."[24] In short, "art" can stand as a figure for the form of playful labor, "any dimension in which they might roam freely in imagination" and the sustained "thinking," which we and our students perform in the humanities classroom.[25]

Jameson's reading further brushes against the grain of the contemporary "common sense" reading of *Dialectic of Enlightenment,* that advanced by a populist cultural studies, which held up the work's most well-known chapter, "The Culture Industry," as exemplary of the high cultural mandarinism against which cultural studies then rightly react. Already in "Reification and Utopia in Mass Culture," Jameson shows the case to be a far more complicated one, an argument he develops in greater depth here. In *Late Marxism,* Jameson maintains of the culture industry analysis:

> This chapter can be clarified, I feel, and some of the more aimless polemics about it dispersed, by the realization that it does not involve a theory of culture at all, in any sense this word has come to have for us at least since Raymond Williams. . . . [T]he "Culture Industry" chapter has to do with individual works or signatures—from Toscanini to Victor Mature and Betty Grable; it also has very much to do with individual subjectivity and its tendential reduction and subsumption; but it does not include a concept of culture as a specific zone or structure of the social. This is why it is a mistake to suppose that Adorno's "elitist" critiques of the "Culture Industry" in any way define his attitude or position towards "mass culture", grasped now not as a group of commercial products but as a realm of social life. . . . [T]he Culture Industry, as Adorno and Horkheimer see it, is not art or culture but rather business as such, and indeed a place in which the tendential convergence between monopoly and instrumentalization can be observed more clearly than in other kinds of commodity exchange.[26]

This point is so important for Jameson that he reiterates a few chapters later, "Thus, the 'Culture Industry' is not a theory of culture but the theory of an *industry,* of a branch of the interlocking monopolies of late capitalism that makes money out of what used to be called culture."[27] Or, as Horkheimer and Adorno explicitly put it, "Films and radio no longer need to present themselves as art. The truth that they are nothing but business is used as an ideology to legitimize the trash they intentionally produce."[28]

Jameson stresses that for Adorno art is not fulfillment, "not bliss, but rather the latter's *promise*"—a formulation that expresses a thoroughly modernist commitment to keeping alive the Utopian possibility of a radically other way of being in our world. "This is, then," Jameson goes on to note, "one crucial thematic differentiation between 'genuine art' and that offered by the Culture Industry: both raise the issue and the possibility of happiness in their very being, as it were, and neither provides it; but where the one keeps faith with it by negation and suffering, through the enactment of its impossibility, the other assures us it is taking place."[29] Thus, as Horkheimer and Adorno argue, "The culture industry endlessly cheats its consumer out of what it endlessly promises."[30] In this way, the products of the Culture Industry become the very negation of art, or a form of what Jameson calls "anti-art."

This reading of *Dialectic of Enlightenment* as a unified narrative also offers an effective way of thinking about the nature and motivations of current assaults on the space of the university and our labors within it. A good deal of the significant and mounting critical analysis concerned with this phenomenon similarly focuses on the ways the university is being recast "not as art or culture but rather business as such"—what has in various venues been referred to as the "corporatization of higher education."[31] Even here, Horkheimer and Adorno's analysis, as Jameson presents it, offers an advance on many of these discussions, in that it enables us to recognize these efforts as only the latest phase in a longer capitalist cultural logic that they describe as *instrumentalization,* the reorganization of all activities and everyday life itself according to a monolithic ends orientation (that of profit, or as contemporary administrative thinking puts it, grants and patents, technology transfer, and other forms of "entrepreneurship"). In a statement that effectively captures the mindset of too many university administrators and their dim view of any form of critical humanities education, Horkheimer and Adorno note, "For enlightenment, anything which does not conform to the standard of calculability and utility [i.e. assessability and a counting] must be viewed with suspicion."[32] Current neoliberal assaults on the university are thus to be understood as an intensification, not unlike that taking place in 1930s fascist Germany, of a baleful process of modernization—the drive, in other words, to complete in our truly globalized world the last of capitalism's unfinished business. This is not an ethical judgment—nor, of course, does or should it suggest any equivalence between the suffering endured by contemporary university intellectuals and the victims of the Nazi state[33]—but rather a historical one. In both cases, these transformations are not exceptions to but rather the normal operation of capitalist expansion; or, to put it in another language—one that also first emerges from the context of fascism in the debates between Carl Schmitt and Walter Benjamin and which recently has experienced a revival of its fortunes—the "state of exception" (*der Ausnahmezustand*) is the norm.[34] (It is useful also to keep in mind that for Jameson, as for Marx before him, "modernity is simply capitalism itself," and modernization "the standardization projected by capitalist globalization.")[35]

However, Horkheimer and Adorno's discussion enables us to go further in our understanding of these assaults, especially when we acknowledge, as Jameson stresses we need to, the indispensability for their larger project of the book's chapter, "*Elemente des Antisemitismus. Grenzen der Aufklärung*" ("Elements of Anti-Semitism: Limits of Enlightenment"). Jameson points out that as conceived in Horkheimer and Adorno's book, art does not have one but rather three distinct others. In addition to the "anti-art" produced by the Cultural Industry, another option is what Jameson calls "non-art," the uncomprehending response of those whose class and educational status exclude them from the opportunity of developing the habits of, and equally significantly the resource of free time for engaging in, the imaginative play and sustained thought characteristic of art in the expanded sense we are using the term, a theme brilliantly treated in Isak Dinesen's great short story, "Babette's Feast" (1953). These excluded people are represented in *Dialectic of Enlightenment* allegorically by Odysseus's oarsmen. Finally, "the missing fourth term in this system," Jameson argues, "is secured less by a new form of culture (or its absence) than by a generalized negation of the other three terms."[36] It is this last position that is figured by the anti-Semite, or "the philistines in general," whose abiding and driving "passion" is "the very hatred of happiness itself."[37] In the conclusion to his discussion, Jameson illustrates the interrelationships among these four positions with the following Greimasian semiotic square (figure 24).

The final term of philistinism, when understood as also applying to the case of the contemporary university, enables us to account for an often veiled subjective dimension at work in the attacks on it: an *excess* of rage characteristic of many of the assaults on intellectual labor in all its forms. Anti-Semitism is according to Horkheimer and Adorno a subset of a larger cultural reaction formation, aimed at Jewish people, communists, gypsies, intellectuals, queer subjects, immigrants, and anyone marked as a powerless and marginal within the social body—a manifestation of a destructive envy directed toward the happiness *imagined* to be possessed by these others:

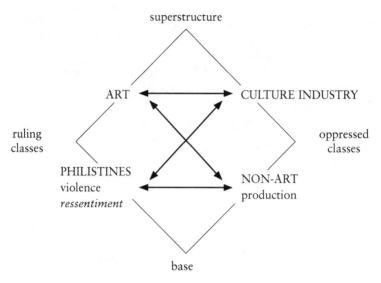

Figure 24. Fredric Jameson, *Late Marxism*, 154.

No matter what the makeup of the Jews may be in reality, their image, that of the defeated, has the characteristics
which must make totalitarian rule their mortal enemy: happiness without power, reward without work, a homeland
without frontiers, religion without myth. These features are
outlawed by the ruling powers because they are secretly cov-
eted by the ruled. The former can survive only as long as the
latter turn what they yearn for into an object of hate.[38]

A few pages earlier Horkheimer and Adorno make explicit the connection I am suggesting here:

The idea of happiness without power is unendurable because
it alone would be happiness. The fantasy of the conspiracy of
lascivious Jewish bankers who finance Bolshevism is a sign of
innate powerlessness, the good life an emblem of happiness.
These are joined by the image of the intellectual, who appears
to enjoy in thought what the others deny themselves and is
spared the sweat of toil and bodily strength. The banker and
the intellectual, money and mind, the exponents of circulation, are the disowned wishful image of those mutilated by
power, an image which power uses to perpetuate itself.[39]

Expressing a similar sentiment in relationship to the late 1980s attacks on funding for the arts and the university, Eve Kosofsky Sedgwick argues, "Millions of people today struggle to carve out—barely, at great cost to themselves—the time, permission, and resources, 'after work' or instead of decently-paying work, for creativity and thought that will not be in the service of corporate profit, nor structured by its rhythms. Many, many more are scared by the prohibitive difficulty of doing so. . . . I see that some must find enraging the spectacle of people for whom such possibilities are, to a degree, built into the structure of our regular paid labor."[40]

And yet, Jameson's analysis does not excuse this last group of people from culpability for the explosion of such destructive *ressentiment:* for the contemporary assault on intellectual labors is also, in no small part, a consequence of the failure of the collective project referred to as the 1960s to transform the world, and the retreat of so many of the survivors of these struggles into the spaces of relative freedom and autonomy represented by the university (the "tenured radicals" of a fevered conservative imagination). *Ressentiment* is, in short, an envy of Utopia; an envy of even tenuous and imperfect "pocket utopias" such as the university, from which, as the Horkheimer and Adorno's moving allegorical reading of the Sirens chapter of the *Odyssey* suggests, most are excluded, and which comes at a terrible cost for the intellectuals and academics who inhabit it:

> [Odysseus] knows only two possibilities of escape. One he prescribes to his comrades. He plugs their ears with wax and orders them to row with all their might. Anyone who wishes to survive must not listen to the temptation of the irrecoverable, and is unable to listen only if he is unable to hear. Society has always made sure that this was the case. Workers must look ahead with alert concentration and ignore anything which lies to one side. The urge to distraction must be grimly sublimated in redoubled exertions. Thus the workers are made practical. The other possibility Odysseus chooses for himself, the landowner who has others to work for him. He listens, but does so while bound helplessly to the mast, and the stronger the allurement grows the more tightly he has himself bound, just as later the bourgeois denied themselves happiness the closer it drew to them with the increase in their own powers. What he hears has no consequences for

him; he can signal to his men to untie him only by movement of his head, but it is too late. His comrades, who themselves cannot hear, know only of the danger of the song, not of its beauty, and leave him tied to the mast to save both him and themselves. They reproduce the life of the oppressor as part of their own, while he cannot step outside his social role. The bonds by which he has irrevocably fettered himself to praxis at the same time keep the Sirens at a distance from praxis: their lure is neutralized as a mere object of contemplation, as art. The fettered man listens to a concert, as immobilized as audiences later, and his enthusiastic call for liberation goes unheard as applause. In this way the enjoyment of art and manual work diverge as the primal world is left behind.[41]

According to Jameson, this allegory concerns "the sheer guilt of Art itself in a class society, art as luxury and class privilege."[42] It was the failure of the 1960s to bring this society and its privileges to an end—and the intellectual resistance in the years since to make, in Kathi Weeks's words, "the present configuration of the work society and its moralized configuration of work" a central concern[43]—that accounts for both the neoliberal intensification of the instrumentalization of all aspects of social life, including the corporatization of the university, *and* the growing *ressentiment* directed at it during the last thirty years of neo-conservative hegemony.

While Jameson's Adorno thus offers us a powerful means of thinking the complex situation we inhabit in the current moment, this negative dialectic itself remains at best a partial one. The limits of this negative dialectic can be brought into focus by way of Jameson's discussion of contemporary architectural practice found in the final chapter of *The Seeds of Time*. Jameson argues that within the diversity of postmodern architectural practices there are two residual modernist formations, exemplified for him by the work of Rem Koolhaas and Peter Eisenman. If the former continues, contrary to postmodern doxa, to think through the problem of the existent totality (as does Adorno, of course, in his earlier postmodernist moment), then the latter takes up the other half of the dialectic of modernism and celebrates innovation, the project of "making it new." The fundamental problem, and the way beyond the paralysis of the postmodern, Jameson suggests, is to place these two antimonies back into dialectical coordination, and thereby encourage the explosive re-emergence of the revolutionary energies of an earlier modernism, be it that expressed in the 1920s or the 1960s—the latter finding its testament and one of its most memorable monuments, as we saw in the first section of this book, in Jameson's *Marxism and Form*, and to which we can now recognize all his subsequent work as bearing an unqualified fidelity.

This opposition of Koolhaas and Eisenman pre-figures that formed by the two pre-eminent dialectical thinkers to which Jameson devotes single-author studies during the post–Cold War period of the 1990s: Adorno at its beginning, and Bertolt Brecht near its climax. Jameson's *Brecht and Method* (1998) can thus be understood as, among other things, an implicit criticism of the limits of the critical Adornoian symptomological project theorized in *Late Marxism* and put into effect in *Postmodernism*. However, as Jameson already acknowledges, to take the totalizing analysis advanced in *Postmodernism* in isolation from the innovative praxis he names cognitive mapping is ultimately to become what Brecht would describe as "'folgenlos'—what had no particular material consequences, and fostered no particular change," and to be *Tuis* ("Intellek-tuellen"), a position, Jameson notes, that Brecht "largely identified with the Frankfurt School."[44] Indeed, for Brecht, "it is precisely the preoccupation of leftist thinkers with various complex ('Western-Marxist') theories of ideology that mark them as *Tuis* in the first place."[45]

In order to break out of this deadlock, Jameson offers as a necessary dialectical rejoinder—and as I noted earlier, in a late footnote to *Brecht and Method*, Jameson refuses the false choice of either Adorno *or* Brecht—what he calls Brecht's "method," practices realized in both Brecht's diverse intellectual work and in his creation of the space of the theater itself. Jameson argues that Brecht's "'proposals' and his lessons—the fables and the proverbs he delighted in offering—were more on the order of a method than a collection of facts, thoughts, convictions, first principles, and the like. Yet it was an equally sly 'method,' which equally successfully eludes all the objections modern philosophy (as in Gadamer's *Truth and Method*) has persuasively made against the reifications of the methodological as such."[46] Jameson claims later in the book "that there existed a Brechtian 'stance' [*Haltung*] which was not only doctrine, narrative, or style, but all three simultaneously; and ought better to be called, with all due precautions, 'method.'"[47]

Some of the characteristic features of this stance or method include joy in an activity for its own sake and the dissolution of all reified things back into their human praxis. Indeed, at the very center of Brecht's method was the playful and necessarily interminable dialectical labor of *Verfremdungseffekt,* the V-effect, or what is often translated as *estrangement:*

> the whole political message and content of the V-effect itself—
> namely, to reveal what has been taken to be eternal or natural—
> the reified act, with its unifying name and concept—as merely
> historical, as a kind of institution which has come into be-
> ing, owing to the historical and collective actions of people
> and their societies, and which therefore now stands revealed
> as changeable. What history has solidified into an illusion of
> stability and substantiality can now be dissolved again, and
> reconstructed, replaced, improved, "umfunktioniert".[48]

A model of these reconstructed or refunctioned (*umfunktioniert*) institutional spaces can then be found in the experiment of Brecht's learning plays (*Lehrstücke*):

> What was specific to the *Lehrstücke*—and, indeed, unique
> in those experiments in stage dynamics—was the exclusion
> of the public and, at the same time, a rotation of the actors
> throughout the various roles. In other words, it is what in the
> theater is called a master class, but one which does not nec-
> essarily have a master director present either: even though
> we must imagine *Schiffbauerdamm* as one continuous mas-
> ter class, to which a paying public is invited only on selected
> occasions: Brecht's significance to the state was such, indeed,
> that he was given the money and the resources, including the
> personnel, not so much merely to create yet another theater,
> as to indulge the supreme wish of any true theater person:
> infinite rehearsals, in which, in true Brechtian fashion, all the
> alternatives can be tried out in turn and endlessly debated.[49]

In this way, Brecht effects a veritable reversal of the instrumentalization that Adorno helps us see as being a central tendency of modern life. Brecht does so through the indefinite open-ended extension of the means, the temporality of rehearsal, and the deferral of the ends, the final performance.

Finally, and as we might now anticipate, the fundamental form of this method is narrative: "If we can tell its story or narrative, in other words, that is a kind of proof, and it is better than the opinion: the narrative articulates the conceptual position, and thereby proves that it can have historical evidence—it is an alternative form of argument, implicitly as valid as the abstract philosophical."[50] It is on this basis that in *Valences* Jameson will effect one more unexpected dialectical resolution:

> The external world, however ugly or depressing, can never be inert or meaningless, if only because it has been historically produced and already has its meaning in historical production. Indeed, if seen in this way, Lukács may be said dialectically to rejoin his antagonist Brecht, for whom the very function of the so-called estrangement effect was to show how things considered natural (and thus inevitable or eternal) were in fact the results of human action (and could therefore be changed by other human beings). The presupposition of both aesthetics is the narratability of human action and human production.[51]

I would suggest that with all of this Jameson also means for Brecht's method to serve as an affirmative model for our own intellectual and pedagogical practices. Indeed, he makes clear the pedagogical dimensions of Brecht's method from the opening pages of his book: "Brecht offers us a world in which that practice is entertaining, and includes its own pedagogy as a member of the class it subsumes—the teaching of practice also being a practice in its own right, and thereby 'participating' in the very satisfactions it holds out to its student practitioners."[52] Shortly thereafter, Jameson suggests this fundamental lesson to be extracted from Brecht's entire project:

> This originality, however, takes on a somewhat different form—or rather, as I am tempted to say, finds itself productively *estranged*—when we consider "method" to be a kind of *gestus* and, above and beyond the "dramatistic" and interpersonal framework always implicit in rhetoric as such, restore to such acts the immanent or virtual narrative situation implied by them.
> So it is that what we were tempted to call "method" when we approached it as an abstract idea now, in some third dimension, unfolds itself, dramatically, into the very situation of pedagogy itself as it is variously staged, mocked, analyzed,

prophesied and utopianly projected, throughout a work single-mindedly obsessed with this concrete ideal, which—extending, to be sure, to that "educating of the educators" of which the third *Thesis on Feuerbach* speaks—can eventually be grasped as the very correlative and other face or *verso* of the theme of change itself. Running abreast of change, catching up with it, espousing its tendencies in such a way as to begin to inflect its vectors in your own direction—such is Brechtian pedagogy.[53]

I have written about the ways Jacques Lacan's late notion of analysis, especially as it is developed in his Seminar XVII, offers a similarly Utopian model of an alternative pedagogical practice; in both cases, the real challenge becomes how to enact this within an institutional structure inimical to it.[54]

Moreover, Jameson's (re)turn to Brecht highlights the "latest" dialectical development in the ongoing project of the thing Jameson calls "theoretical discourse," what I have argued throughout this book is one of the preeminent intellectual and cultural achievements of the decades following the 1960s. Indeed, in the Epilogue to *Brecht and Method,* Jameson effectively shows how, through the mediatory figure of Roland Barthes, Brecht influenced the very formation of what was later named theory: Barthes's "profound Brechtianism," Jameson argues, "is responsible for the most original interventions that constituted Barthes's historic significance in the 1950s and were influential in forming what one sometimes thinks of as the poststructural doxa of the 1960s and 1970s."[55] In a similar retrospective fashion, we can say that theory's impact was felt in three different waves. In the first wave, that of the neo-formalisms of structuralism and deconstruction, theory changed the nature of *how* we read. In the next wave, corresponding roughly to the landmark reconsiderations of value and evaluation by Barbara Herrnstein Smith and others, and the rising prominence of feminism, cultural studies, historicism, queer theory, and post-colonial theory, theory changed in a fundamental way *what* we read.[56] Finally, in its most recent moment, theory challenges the very *institutional space* of higher education itself.[57] Jacques Derrida already suggests in the 1970s such a trajectory for theory when he notes that the theoretical discourse of deconstruction in particular

attacks not only the internal edifice, both semantic and formal, of philosophemes, but also what one would be wrong to assign to it as its external housing, its extrinsic conditions of practice: the historical forms of its pedagogy, the social, economic or political structures of this pedagogical institution. It is because deconstruction interferes with solid structures, "material" institutions, and not only with discourses or signifying representations, that it is always distinct from analysis or a "critique." And in order to be pertinent, deconstruction works as strictly as possible in that place where the supposedly "internal" order of the philosophical is articulated by (internal *and* external) necessity with the institutional conditions and forms of teaching. To the point where the concept of institution itself would be subjected to the same deconstructive treatment.[58]

Each of these waves, I would further maintain, was also marked by an increasing scale of a conservative counter-assault and a growing national debate about the potential deleterious effects of the institutional changes theory helped usher in. The first round of debate was largely a concern of intellectuals and literary scholars themselves, unfolding in the pages of the new academic journals that, as I suggested earlier, occupied the place of the little magazines in the earlier moment of high modernism proper. One of the most explicit examples of this first wave of critical reaction was the "against theory" polemics of Steven Knapp and Walter Benn Michaels, issued in the pages of *Critical Inquiry* in the early 1980s, and of which Jameson writes in *Postmodernism,* "we feel very strongly that we are being told to *stop* doing something, that new taboos whose motivation we cannot grasp are being erected with passionate energy and conviction."[59] The second assault took the form of a national media debate about funding of the arts and scholarly research in the "culture wars" of the late 1980s and early 1990s.[60] Finally, the latest counter-assault, the one we continue to live through today, involves the staging, through what Kim Emery terms a strategy of "crisis management," of a direct attack on the governance and funding structures of the university itself. These are evident, for example, in David Horowitz's doublethink efforts to reign in free speech in the classroom, state legislative attacks on tenure, the de-professionalization of teaching, the increasingly casualization of academic labor, and a new corporate-style centralization of university administration.[61]

In a short essay published in *Critical Inquiry* in 2004, Jameson too suggests a number of different moments in the history of theory. The first moment, that of structuralism, occurs when the materiality of concepts "becomes inescapable; in which in other words, it slowly begins to dawn on us that concepts are not ideas but rather words and constellations of words at that."[62] In the second stage, poststructuralism, "this discovery mutates as it were into a philosophical problem, namely, that of representation, and its dilemmas, its dialectic, its failures, and its impossibility."[63] Finally, in the present, all this gives way to a turn to the political: "Under the tutelary deities of Machiavelli and Hobbes, and then of Spinoza and Carl Schmitt a whole new kind of discourse, a genuinely political theory, emerges, recast in the agonistic structure of Schmitt's 'friend or foe' and finding its ultimate figure in war."[64] However, Jameson concludes by observing that he remains "personally somewhat distant from this new moment, as I have always understood Marxism to mean the supersession of politics by economics"; and this leads him to "forecast yet a fourth moment for theory," one that "has to do with the theorizing of collective subjectivities."[65] The question remains then how to carry the small-scale model of totalizing innovation—in a word, cultural revolution—found in these waves of theory beyond the university and into the larger social and cultural sphere—a project, *Brecht and Method* optimistically announces, that might very much be on the table once more in the post–Cold War 1990s.

However, shortly after the publication of *Brecht and Method,* Jameson begins to take note of a disturbing challenge to this Utopian project that has emerged *within* the academic setting itself. This challenge comes to the fore in the Preface to his next book after *Brecht and Method,* and the first to be published following the watershed events of September 11, 2001, *A Singular Modernity* (2002).[66] Here, Jameson ruefully notes that "we have begun in the last few years to witness phenomena of a very different order, phenomena that suggest the return to and the reestablishment of all kinds of old things, rather than their wholesale liquidation" as seemed to be promised in the high moment of theory.[67] This includes the philosophical subfield of ethics and "the resuscitation of aesthetics." Jameson then makes the source of these "regressions" explicit: "The defeat of Marxism (if it really was defeated) checked the flow of much contemporary theory at its source. . . . Meanwhile the professionalization (and, increasingly, the privatization) of the university can explain the systematic recontainment of theoretical energy as such, as aberrant in its effects as it is anarchist in its aims."[68]

Jameson suggests that if theory represents an untimely form of modernism—a connection he again makes explicit in a number of places in *Valences of the Dialectic* as well—then these new formations are a reaction to, a negative judgment against, the radical energies of this most recent modernist formation: a reaction, as it unfolded in the post–World War II moment in response to the project of modernism proper, Jameson names *late modernism*.

> Late modernism is a product of the Cold War, but in all kinds of complicated ways. Thus, the Cold War spelled the end of a whole era of social transformation and indeed of Utopian desires and anticipations. . . . Politics must therefore now be carefully monitored, and new social impulses repressed or disciplined. These new forms of control are symbolically re-enacted in later modernism, which transforms the older modernist experimentation into an arsenal of tried and true techniques, no longer striving after aesthetic totality or the systemic and Utopian metamorphosis of forms.[69]

This then also suggests two very different visions of the relationship between art and culture (as well as a very different sense of artistic autonomy than that found in Kant's original formulation):

> Culture thus stands as the blurring of the boundaries and the space of passages and movements back and forth, the locus of transmutation and translation from one level or dimension to the other. If one sees this ambiguous space as mediation, as the greatest artists have always done, then the social pole of culture stands not only as content and raw material, it also offers the fundamental context in which art, even in its modernist form as the Absolute—especially in its modernist form as the Absolute—has a genuine function to redeem and transfigure a fallen society. If, on the other hand . . . one feels a malaise in the face of this blurring of the boundaries, an anxiety about the indeterminacy in which it necessarily leaves the work of art itself, it then becomes crucial to break the link, to sever this dialectical movement, to challenge and philosophically to discredit the concept of culture, in order to protect the space of art against further incursions or contamination.[70]

Moreover, this late modernism has been given new life in the contemporary university, something nowhere more evident than in the call for the return to a literary or film "canon," variously cloaked in the pleas for a renewed commitment to disciplinarity, aesthetics, ethics, or what Marjorie Levinson describes as a "normative formalism," a "campaign to bring back a sharp demarcation between history and art, discourse and literature, with form . . . the prerogative of art."[71] Thus, for example, we have Marjorie Perloff, in her 2006 MLA Presidential Address, extolling us to "to trust the literary instinct that brought us to this field in the first place and to recognize that, instead of lusting after those other disciplines that seem so exotic primarily because we don't really practice them, what we need is more theoretical, historical, and critical training in our own discipline."[72] Similarly, there are the self-identified "surface readers," whose efforts, Crystal Bartolovich argues, "not only mark a pointed withdrawal from politics and theory but also—while humanities departments are contracting—internalize the economic imperative to scale back," and which thereby, as Carolyn Lesjak further shows, stand alongside certain strands of the New Darwinism and champions of a return to beauty in signalling "the larger critical shift away from symptomatic readings or ideological critique," such that "a hermeneutics of suspicion is replaced by a suspicion of hermeneutics, a disavowing of interpretation itself, which is part and parcel of the so-called death of theory."[73] Finally, we have the case of disciplinary film scholars who subscribe to what Nico Baumbach usefully identifies as a "Grand anti-Theory" position that "reenacts the very move it criticizes by lumping a wide range of material into a single rubric that it then dismisses."[74]

Jameson suggests that we find the support for such retrenchments coming from "an alliance between the older philologists (if there are any left), who have a genuine historical interest in and commitment to the past, and the newer aesthetes who are the true ideologists of some (late) modern"—in other words, an alliance between the last remaining late modernist ideologues, including New Critical formalists, and an increasingly influential group of humanities scholars who believe we have come out on the "other side" of the theory revolution, and thus the time is ripe to return to our older more proper and dignified labors.[75] "The overarching message," Lesjak further notes, "seems to be: scale back, pare down, small aims met are better than grand ones unrealized, reclaim our disciplinary territory and hold on to it."[76] Such humanities scholarship thereby embraces what Steven Shaviro describes as the more general austerity logic of contemporary global neoliberalism: "at every turn, the demand for an exclusive *either/or* replaces the coziness and ease of *both/and*. In short, even as it produces greater material wealth than ever before in human history, capitalism also continually manufactures scarcity and want."[77]

In *The Prison-House of Language,* Jameson argues that the each of the "great modern formalisms"—structuralism, pragmatism, phenomenology, logical positivism, existentialism—has "helped to articulate the sense of this repugnance before content as such, by the nature of the particular type of content which it negates."[78] The content negated in these new formalisms is the very fact of the political nature of all culture labor, including that which takes place in the university itself. Thus, as in the original Cold War context of late modernism, such a return represents a retreat from the institutional political implications that theory represents. As early as *The Prison-House of Language,* Jameson already notes,

> This mode of thought, going back as it does to Locke, is, I believe, ultimately political in inspiration; and it would not be difficult, following the lines pursued by Lukács in *History and Class Consciousness* for rationalizing and universalizing thought, to show how such thinking is characterized by a turning away of the eyes, a preference for segments and isolated objects, as a means to avoid observation of those larger wholes and totalities which if they had to be seen would force the mind in the long run into uncomfortable social and political conclusions.[79]

In *Valences,* Jameson now argues that theory more generally, in its otherwise diverse manifestations, is first and foremost an operation of de-reification, of a drawing of "perverse" connections and a destabilization of established institutional practices (be they readings, canons, or classrooms and administrative boardrooms); and,

> Reification is what prevents the bourgeoisie from grasping society as a whole or totality, and thereby from experiencing the blinding reality of class struggle. . . . This analysis of bourgeois thought then makes clear the operation in Lukács of a conceptual opposition between reification and totality (or rather the "aspiration to totality"). The bourgeoisie must not confront society as a totality; the reification of its thinking makes it possible to remain within the semi-autonomous limits of this or that discipline, this or that limited thematization.[80]

Similarly, we could say that the adherents of new formalisms and surface readings refuse to confront the university and our work in it as a totality, one that has entered into a unprecedented crisis, lest arise uncomfortable social and political conclusions concerning their own positions; and in order to ward off these conclusions, they retreat to the limits of discipline and its limited thematizations. In this way, the new ideologists of an old late modernism fantasize about keeping at bay two extreme threats to ensconced institutional practices (what Jacques Rancière names the "distribution of the sensible"):[81] the threats represented by, on the one hand, what I described earlier as the corporatization/instrumentalization of the university, in which any form of reflective critical engagement has little place in the corporate research, pre-professional training, and entertainment complex that is the University, Incorporated; and at the same time, the challenge of humanist radicals—those working in the emergent fields of cultural studies, historicism, multiculturalism, interdisciplinarity, political criticism, and especially theory, which champions a thoroughgoing transformation of our scholarship, teaching, and institutions. Such a retreat cannot but fail to achieve its Utopian aim—to be sure, another example of Mannheim's "conservative utopian mentality"—of a restoration of the old order of a disciplined literary studies. As is now amply evident in institutions across the nation and the globe, the neoliberal restructuring of the university will not pass us by just because we choose to retreat within older institutional and disciplinary shells. "Once the idea of the humanities (or the university or theory) as an enclave becomes impossible to sustain," Lesjak maintains, "saving the university has no meaning if divorced from a larger, systemic politics."[82]

Valences of the Dialectic also provides us with tools to think together the seemingly antithetical developments of the neoliberal assault on the humanities and a neoconservative defense of the disciplines. In the "Three Names of the Dialectic," Jameson argues that one of the most powerful dialectical reading strategies lies in the construction of the "unity of opposites," and he shows the ways this unfolds in arguments by Lenin ("economism and terrorism," or "a gradualist social democracy [and a workerism based on trade unions] as well as 'extraparliamentary' activities of extreme-left activists"), Althusser ("Social Democracy and Stalinism [or, in ideological terms, between humanism and dogmatism]"), and Lukács ("naturalism and *symbolism*").[83] Jameson further notes, "What is more seriously dialectical in these analyses remains the 'paradoxical' proposition that the two positions under indictment are somehow 'the same.' But this is not only a union of opposites but also a union of negative terms."[84] A bit further on, he continues, "The dialectical feature of these polemics lies, not in the fight on two fronts which is characteristic of so many conceptual arguments, but rather in the way the bad opposites are identified by way of a single underlying flaw or ideological error which they share."[85]

The two recent developments in the academy that I noted earlier represent a similar unity of bad opposites, and a clue to their underlying connection is made available in Jameson's discussion of Althusser's critique of the couple of Social Democracy and Stalinism, or humanism (the current call for disciplinary retrenchment) and dogmatism (neoliberal corporate common sense):

> [B]oth these positions, and the politics they project, are politically and intellectually pernicious owing to a single great flaw they share, namely the omission of class struggle. And although he seems to have had some misgivings about the term, we may say that it is class struggle that restores a dialectical reading of history insofar as it necessarily proceeds by breaks and discontinuities, and not uninterrupted (or "homogeneous") temporality of progress or inevitability.[86]

Similarly, whether they take the form of an attack on the practices of a non-corporate university workplace now understood as out-of-date and disposable or of an appeal for a return to the traditional organization of that work, both these trends in higher education share a common loathing of what we might call the class struggle within the classroom, the so-called politicization of higher education and research fostered by a turn to theory, whose aim always already has been to change our institutional homes, practices, and identities in fundamental ways. Indeed, in a scathing critique contemporaneous with *Valences of the Dialectic* of the anti-theory polemic of Ian Hunter, Jameson writes, "so that where the appeal to modesty and pragmatism might well offer state or state university employment elsewhere, it must in the US remain sheer rhetoric and the injunction to intellectuals to behave themselves."[87]

The engagement with Hunter's argument is revealing in another way. Jameson maintains that in Hunter's assault on the theoretical turn, the latest manifestation of what Hunter names "university metaphysics,"

> it is the depth model in general and all manner of hermeneutic practices that are Hunter's targets here—the reduction,

in other words, of facts and historical realities to concepts that have no empirical object, like society, culture, revolution, class, language, history, capitalism, and so on. This particular line of attack is enough to link Hunter to the traditional Anglo-American empiricism that theory set out to demolish in the first place, and indeed the words *positive, empirical,* and *research* are here everywhere valorized and emphasized.[88]

A little later in the essay, Jameson further notes that for Hunter, "late capitalism is another of those claustral or periodizing concepts, like Foucault's episteme, or Kuhn's paradigm, that does not correspond to any empirical object (of research), and that is, to use the language of a different kind of attack on theory, totalizing."[89] In short, Jameson suggests that the contemporary assault on theory is also an expression of a more general suspicion of the cognitive operation of *abstraction,* which, as David Foster Wallace argues in his wonderful history of the changing fortunes of the mathematical concept of infinity, has been a target at least since Aristotle's "refutation of Zeno's Dichotomy."[90] Jameson makes this clear in his discussion in *Valences of the Dialectic* of Ricoeur's "polemic against Greimas" and his "critique of semiotics," which, he argues, "tends to turn anti-theoretical, implicitly to deplore theoretical jargon and the new kinds of 'inhuman' abstractions theory has brought to bear on the cultural world, and to express nostalgia for the older tradition of *belles lettres* and its cultivated or high literary discourse."[91]

Thus, in a classic dialectical reversal, it is Hunter's predictable dismissal and not theory itself that "has no history, consisting in a simple repetition, in 'improvisation,' on a single historical operation."[92] And it is these repetitions, again highlighting the inescapability of the reifications of *Verstand,* that mean theory's labors too remain necessarily unfinished:

At the same time [Hunter's] own ideological position expands well beyond the concerns of the professional historian of ideas to embrace the neopragmatism and Anglo-American empiricism and common sense that were the original targets of theory in all its forms and that have miraculously risen from the dead in the current "end of history" and triumph of free-market capitalism and globalization. Far from disabling theory, however, such an unexpected resurrection renews its original vocation to take up the weapons of criticism and to wage the old battles all over again (as one no doubt always must).[93]

This rousing invocation of the secular vocation of "theory in all its forms" points toward a new, more affirmative dimension in Jameson's ongoing project, one amply on display in both *The Modernist Papers* and *Valences of the Dialectic*.[94] On the one hand, Jameson engages in a form of a Benjaminian historical narration, encouraging us to strive to "fleetingly glimpse an alternate world alongside our own historical one: a world in which modernity in the current coinage did not occur, without our being able to discern clearly the outlines of what, equally supplanting precapitalist forms and relations, took its place"; or as he beautifully puts it a few lines later in the same essay, "an unfinished project that was also a missed opportunity."[95] Similarly, in the conclusion to *Valences of the Dialectic,* he issues this call to action:

> It would be best, perhaps, to think of an alternate world— better to say the alternate world, our alternate world—as one contiguous with ours but without any connection or access to it. Then, from time to time, like a diseased eyeball in which disturbing flashes of light are perceived or like those baroque sunbursts in which rays from another world suddenly break into this one, we are reminded that Utopia exists and that other systems, other spaces, are still possible.[96]

Such a project will struggle to restore the currently untimely but still vibrant radical energies of a rich array of modernist Utopian projects and formations, be they those of an early twentieth century high modernism, the 1960s, or even the post–Cold War 1990s, something exemplified in the sheer global and historical diversity of the modernisms Jameson discusses in *The Modernist Papers*; or, as in *Valences of the Dialectic,* of Walmart or Paolo Virno's figuration of the global multitude:

> There is so far no term as useful for the construction of the future as "genealogy" is for such a construction of the past; it is certainly not to be called "futurology," while "utopology" will never mean much, I fear. The operation itself, however, consists in a prodigious effort to change the valences on phenomena which so far exist only in our own present; and

experimentally to declare positive things which are clearly negative in our own world, to affirm that dystopia is in reality Utopia if examined more closely, to isolate specific features in our empirical present so as to read them as components of a different system. This is in fact what we have seen Virno doing when he borrows an enumeration of what in Heidegger are clearly enough meant to be negative and highly critical features of modern society or modern actuality, staging each of these alleged symptoms of degradation as an occasion for celebration and as a promise of what he does not—but what we may—call an alternate Utopian future.[97]

To this list, we might finally add the alternate world or "unfinished project that was also a missed opportunity" of the modern comprehensive university. Jameson points out, "Such a revival of futurity and of the positing of alternate futures is not itself a political program nor even a political practice: but it is hard to see how any durable or effective political action could come into being without it."[98]

Moreover, in *The Modernist Papers,* Jameson issues a call, in response to the double challenge we now face, for the formation of a new "Popular Front program of culture and the unification of Left intellectuals and writers generally."[99] Bosteels similarly concludes *Badiou and Politics* with the observation that

a renewed understanding of the common project to think an emancipatory politics would entail a radical overhaul of some of our most deeply engrained intellectual habits—such as the habit of polemicizing among factions within the left, always positioning oneself in terms of a neither/nor response to other thinkers, rather than in the inclusive terms of a both/ and stance, or the habit of preferring the self-destructive radicalism of an ever more vigilant deconstruction over and above the collective project of making a common front.[100]

Such a stance is exemplified in the deep listening (*l'écoute*) that I suggested in this book's opening and is characteristic of Jameson's project as a whole.

This labor takes the specific form in *Valences of the Dialectic* of a full-throated affirmation of the common project of the various practices of theory, those explicitly dialectical and otherwise. Early in the book's first chapter, Jameson revives an argument he originally developed in *The Prison-House of Language,* and celebrates structuralism's formulation of the "binary opposition" as "that breakthrough, with which, in my opinion, and unbeknownst to the structuralists themselves, dialectical thought was able to reinvent itself in our time."[101] A few pages later, Jameson locates a "family likeness" between deconstruction and the dialectic, "that is to say that kinship which allows the differences to be articulated and perceptible in the first place."[102] He then characterizes this dialectic of identity and difference in the following way, suggesting their differences lie primarily in the pace of the respective analysis:

> [B]oth work to bring into the light the structural incoherences of the "idea" or conceptual "positions" or interpretations which are their object of critique. But where the dialectic pauses, waiting for the new "dialectical" solution to freeze over in its turn and become an idea and ideology to which the dialectic can again be "applied" (as it were from the outside of the newly reformed system), deconstruction races forward, undoing the very incoherence it has just been denouncing and showing that seeming analytic result to be itself a new incoherence and a new "contradiction" to be unraveled in its turn.[103]

Finally, in the roaring climax of the chapter, Jameson identifies theory with the dialectic itself and the latter's unfinished projects:

> This is why the dialectic belongs to theory rather than philosophy: the latter is always haunted by the dream of some foolproof, self-sufficient, autonomous system, a set of interlocking concepts which are their own cause. This mirage is of course the afterimage of philosophy as an institution in the world, as a profession complicit with everything else in the status quo, in the fallen ontic realm of "what is." Theory, on the other hand has no vested interests inasmuch as it never lays claim to an absolute system, a non-ideological formulation of itself and its "truths"; indeed, always itself complicit in the being of current language, it has only the never-ending, never-finished task and vocation of undermin-

ing philosophy as such, of unraveling affirmative statements and propositions of all kinds.[104]

The "family" Jameson constructs here is, as Judith Butler would have it, definitely a "queer" one, bringing together projects often taken as antithetical to one another.[105] It has a kinship as well with the scintillating Utopian figure he formulates in *Late Marxism:*

> a Utopia of misfits and oddballs, in which the constraints for uniformization and conformity have been removed, and human beings grow wild like plants in a state of nature: not the beings of Thomas More, in whom sociality has been implanted by way of the miracle of the utopian text, but rather those of the opening of Altman's *Popeye,* who, no longer fettered by the constraints of a now oppressive sociality, blossom into the neurotics, compulsives, obsessives, paranoids, and schizophrenics whom our society considers sick but who, in a world of true freedom, may make up the flora and the fauna of "human nature" itself.[106]

This affirmation becomes the occasion for Jameson to enact a version of the dialectic he most closely associates with the work of Žižek, whom he identifies, along with Adorno, as one "of the most brilliant dialecticians in the history of philosophy." This dialectic is that of the paradox or "stupid first impression": "the paradox effect is designed to undo that second moment of ingenuity which is that of interpretation (it looks like this to you, but in reality what is going on is this . . .): the paradox is of the second order; what looked like a paradox was in reality simply a return to the first impression itself."[107] Thus, Jameson opens *Valences of the Dialectic* by claiming the kinship of theory and the dialectic, only in the second section, "Hegel Without *Aufhebung,*" to read Derrida and Deleuze as two of Hegel's most scathing "critics." However, this is immediately followed (negation of the negation) in the first two chapters of Section III with brilliant re-readings of Derrida and Deleuze as . . . dialectical thinkers!

This move then enables Jameson to resoundingly reaffirm the kinship of the various forms of theory, and, most significantly, in terms of their shared opponents within the university. For example, in chapter 5 Jameson notes that the project of Deleuze rejects in its very form the calls for return to a reified disciplinary thinking evident in new late modernist critiques of theory:

> But, in my opinion, the work of Deleuze gives no aid and comfort to such regressive efforts; indeed, the whole function of this work has been not to seal off the academic disciplines from the social, the political, and the economic, but rather to open them up precisely to that larger force field. Rather than attempting to contain those realities, in other words, and to send them back to the sterilized compartments of the appropriately specialized disciplines, Deleuzian analysis displays a realm of prodigious polymorphous coding in which desire restlessly invests across the boundaries; indeed, in which the libidinal cannot be confined to the narrower realm that bourgeois thought calls subjectivity or psychology (or even psychoanalysis), but shows how the social is also a tissue of phantasms, and the narrowly libidinal itself a web of social and political representations.[108]

Lesjak extends this operation, in showing the unexpected "dialectical" nature of Sedgwick's "nondualistic" strategies of "extreme or perverse reading" that encourage "'seeing what we know,' rather than knowing what we see, as surface readers would have it."[109]

The stress on these kinships is significant, Jameson suggests, for in them we are presented with a figuration of a collectivity whose Utopian energies are much in need today. In the final paragraph of his essay, "Globalization as Political Strategy," reprinted as the last chapter of the penultimate section of *Valences of the Dialectic,* Jameson argues,

> "Combination," the old word for labor organization, offers an excellent symbolic designation for what is at issue on this ultimate, social level; and the history of the labor movement everywhere gives innumerable examples of the forging of new forms of solidarity in active political work. Nor are such collectivities always at the mercy of new technologies: on the contrary, the electronic exchange of information seems to have been central wherever new forms of political resistance to globalization (the demonstrations against the WTO, for example) have begun to appear. For the moment,

we can use the word '"Utopian" to designate whatever programs and representations express, in however distorted or
unconscious a fashion, the demands of a collective life to
come, and identify social collectivity as the crucial center of
any truly progressive and innovative political response to
globalization.[110]

It is to this project too that the figure of what Emery calls the *queer
university* has a great deal to offer; and perhaps this exchange of energies and the new mobilizations it produces might lead to a renewal of
a diversity of very different unfinished projects that were also missed
opportunities.[111]

CHAPTER 6

Other Modernisms

On the Desire Called Utopia

True believers can, in other words, be exceedingly intelligent,
historicist and reflexive, without ceasing to be fanatics. The
commitment to the Absolute is an act of will, and not always
hospitable to pluralist fairness.
—Fredric Jameson, *Archaeologies of the Future*[1]

In the conclusion to *Postmodernism,* Jameson offers the following observation concerning the "Sartrean coinage" *totalization:* " 'From time
to time,' Sartre says somewhere, 'you make a partial summing up.' The
summing up, from a perspective or point of view, as partial as it must
be, marks the project of totalization as the response to nominalism."[2]
It is just such an act of totalization that takes place in Jameson's *Archaeologies of the Future: The Desire Called Utopia and Other Science
Fictions* (2005).[3] *Archaeologies* is, of course, neither his final book, nor
is it meant as the last word on the problems invoked throughout. It
is, rather, the culminating point, a "partial summing up," of a number of different historical and intellectual sequences unfolding within
Jameson's project. I will elaborate upon some of the most important of
these sequences in the pages that follow. Most significantly, in this final
chapter, I will draw upon the resources of Jameson's "modernist" classic, *The Political Unconscious,* to show how *Archaeologies* represents a
climactic moment in his extended engagement with the question of literary and cultural modernisms, one that clears the space for his (re)turn
in his most recent book, *The Antinomies of Realism* (2013), to the realism that had also been among his earliest concerns.[4]

Archaeologies of the Future is in reality two long books combined
into one; and in this regard it is much like the single "volume" composed

of the two books *A Singular Modernity* and *The Modernist Papers*. Like Thomas More's *Utopia*—a book that is central to the concerns of *Archaeologies*—the second part was composed before the first. It brings together for the first time many of Jameson's most significant essays on science fiction and Utopian literature, including studies of the work of Charles Fourier, Brian Aldiss, Ursula K. Le Guin, Boris and Arkady Strugatsky, Vonda MacIntyre, A. E. Van Vogt, George Bernard Shaw, Philip K. Dick, William Gibson, and Kim Stanley Robinson.[5] In making these essays available in this form—indeed, in making them widely available in any form, as a number were published in more obscure venues, and a 2000 essay, "History and Salvation in Philip K. Dick," had not appeared in print previously—this second "earlier" book demonstrates the centrality of science fiction and Utopia for Jameson's intellectual project. Among other things, these readings function as laboratory spaces wherein Jameson first develops many of the concepts—"generic discontinuity," "world reduction," and most significantly, if more indirectly, "cognitive mapping"—that will become central in his other writings.[6]

However, the very focus on science fiction and Utopian literature risks making *Archaeologies* one of the more under-appreciated of Jameson's texts. In the fourth chapter of *Archaeologies*' first book, entitled "The Desire Called Utopia," Jameson offers a Brechtian refunctioning (*Umfunktionierung*) of a series of conceptual oppositions: Coleridge's Fancy and Imagination (which he in fact first evokes at the beginning of his career in *Sartre: Origins of a Style*),[7] the distinction between the private fantasy and the work of art in Freud's "Creative Writers and Day-Dreaming," and Althusser's infamous couple of ideology and science. He does so in order to begin to think about the distinction in utopian fictions between "two very different types of wishes (or desires, to use the postcontemporary word)":[8] their individual narcissistic elements, and, what is of real interest, the more collective dimensions that enable the most successful of them to have such a magnetic hold on their audiences at certain times and places. In this sense, Jameson's interests in science fiction—and in these particular writers (after all, who reads Fourier, Van Vogt, or John Brunner any more?)—thus might be misperceived by some as a personal, even idiosyncratic, expression of taste, his "fancy" rather than the "imagination" at work in books like *The Political Unconscious* or *Postmodernism*.[9] (Of course, as Jameson notes too, this opposition is never that simple, because "as with all dualisms, the terms keep swapping places ceaselessly.")[10] If this were the case, the fate of *Archaeologies* could ultimately be the same as that of Jameson's other apparent work of fancy, *Fables of Aggression,* an extended engagement with the works of the modernist-turned-fascist Wyndham Lewis. *Fables of Aggression* remains the only one of Jameson's books to have been out of print for any extended period (Verso issued a new edition in the summer of 2008). It would be a sorry development if *Archaeologies* was similarly slighted by readers of Jameson's work and of critical theory more generally or relegated to a specialist audience of those involved in science fiction and Utopian studies, as both "The Desire Called Utopia" and the essays collected in the second part of *Archaeologies* address some of the most pressing cultural, social, and political concerns of the present moment.

In order to begin to make evident the importance of *Archaeologies* and to sort out the diverse interventions taking place in it, I take a page from the opening section of "The Desire Called Utopia," where Jameson presents a visual mapping of the various levels of the "Utopian allegory, of the investments of the Utopian impulse": these are, respectively, the levels of the text, the body, temporality, and the collective.[11] Jameson has already at this point differentiated this more general Utopian impulse from what he identifies as another trajectory emerging out of Thomas More's text, the "Utopian project" (spaces, communities, revolutions, and, of course, texts). The latter will be of central concern through the rest of the book. (However, in a subsequent essay, "Utopia as Replication," he again reminds his readers of the equal importance for Marxist cultural criticism of a hermeneutic sensitive to the Utopian impulse, "the allegorical stirrings of a different state of things, the imperceptible and even immemorial ripenings of the seeds of time, the subliminal and subcutaneous eruptions of whole new forms of life and social relations.")[12] This too is the first of the book's conceptual oppositions, a series that culminates, I will argue shortly, in the tension between Utopian enclaves and Utopian totality; or, in the political realm, between strategies of withdrawal and those of revolution.

In this mapping of the Utopian allegory, Jameson returns to the mechanism of the four-fold medieval hermeneutic that he had first invoked in his discussion of Walter Benjamin in *Marxism and Form,*[13] and which he then develops more fully a decade later in the first chapter of *The Political Unconscious.* In the latter, Jameson notes that such an allegorical interpretive approach has the advantage of opening up "the text to multiple meanings, to successive rewritings and overwritings which are generated as so many levels and as so many supplementary interpretations. . . . less as a technique for closing the text off and for repressing aleatory or aberrant readings and senses, than as a mechanism for preparing such a text for further ideological investment."[14] *Archaeologies* is available for a similar rewriting and overwriting, so that its project too can be understood to unfold simultaneously on four interrelated levels. First, on the literal level, that of the "historical or textual referent," the book attempts to come to grips with the specificity of the modernist genre of science fiction.[15] Second, on the allegorical level, the discussion of science fiction becomes a way of exploring some of the dilemmas faced in the construction of any Utopian representation. Third, on what traditionally was referred to as the moral level, that of a "psychological reading" of the individual subject, the book represents a significant intervention in and further extension of Jameson's larger intellectual project. And finally, on the anagogical level, that of the "political reading (collective 'meaning' of history),"[16] *Archaeologies* contributes to the reinvention of the collective project of Marxism, so that it might more effectively respond to the "historic originalities" of a post–Cold War "late capitalism—its cybernetic technology as well as its globalizing dynamics—and the emergence, as well, of new subjectivities such as the surcharge of multiple or 'parcellated' subject positions characteristic of postmodernity."[17]

I begin on the third level of investment in order first to situate *Archaeologies* within Jameson's ongoing project. Even on this level, however, a number of different narrative arcs emerge. On the one hand, *Archaeologies* represents Jameson's fourth milestone book, the earlier three being *Marxism and Form* (1971), *The Political Unconscious* (1981), and *Postmodernism* (1991). Each of these earlier books marks the conclusion of a distinct period in Jameson's intellectual development, which as I demonstrated in the first part of this book, can be productively characterized using his three-fold periodizing schema of realism, modernism, and postmodernism. What we see in *Archaeologies* then is the full elaboration of a fourth period in his project, a "cultural logic of globalization" or what we might call a "late postmodernism": a negation of the negation of postmodernism, whose intimations have been increasingly evident in the major work published between *Postmodernism* and *Archaeologies*. The historical period to which this work corresponds comes to its conclusion on September 11, 2001, and there is thus something decidedly "untimely" in our post-9/11 world about Jameson's intervention.[18] This becomes especially evident in the final chapters of "The Desire Called Utopia," an issue to which I will return in my discussion of the text's fourth allegorical level.

At the same time, this book, as the dust jacket to the hard cover edition notes, serves as the final volume of "Jameson's six-volume series on *The Poetics of Social Forms.*" With the 2007 publication of *The Modernist Papers,* the second half of the *Poetics* is complete. Volume four is composed of the books *A Singular Modernity: Essay on the Ontology of the Present* (2002) and *The Modernist Papers* (2007); and volume five, of *Postmodernism, or, The Cultural Logic of Late Capitalism* (1991), with *Late Marxism: Adorno, or the Persistence of the Dialectic* (1990), as I demonstrated in chapter 3, serving as its "epistemo-critical" prologue. The forthcoming volume one will deal with myth and narrative; volume two, whose title Jameson has given as *Overtones: The Harmonics of Allegory,* will take up the question of allegory;[19] and the recently published volume three, *The Antinomies of Realism*, offers an experimental effort "to come at realism dialectically" by locating the practice at the intersection between the older *récit* and newer narrative apparati designed to register affects.[20]

There is a way too that the already published volumes form a complete sequence in their own right, similar to what Jameson describes in *The Hegel Variations: On the* Phenomenology of Spirit (2010) as the "open-ended" dialectical totality that he finds exemplified by Hegel's *Phenomenology of Spirit.* In the first chapter of *Postmodernism,* Jameson suggests that the aesthetic practice he names "cognitive mapping"—"a pedagogical political culture which seeks to endow the individual subject with some new heightened sense of its place in the global system"— occupies the empty place of the Lacanian Symbolic in Althusser's opposition of ideology and science, the latter pair corresponding to "only two of Lacan's tripartite functions: the Imaginary and the Real, respectively."[21] A similar tripartite structure is formed by these volumes. If the last section of *A Singular Modernity* shows modernism becoming in the years after the Second World War a form of ideology, or an Imaginary (an issue I will return to in a moment), then *Postmodernism* develops both a symptomology of the present and a figuration of possible forms of the Symbolic of cognitive mapping appropriate to our new global reality.[22] *Archaeologies* in turn offers a "poetics" of the Real, "science" taking the form, as I will suggest in the final section of this chapter, of a particularly modernist "passion." If the open-ended totality formed here is understood in narrative terms, the sequence of Imaginary, Symbolic, and Real (the dialectic representing the fourth ring that Lacan describes in his late work as the sinthome), is similar to that at work in the Utopian German film *Lola rennt* (*Run Lola Run*) (1998). In this film, the first "realist" presentation of the lived immediacy of Lola's "run" occupies the place of the Imaginary (and thus, as with what Jameson notes of Balzac's earlier novelistic realism, the film narrative in this first iteration "does not really know what [it] will find beforehand"); the second, the Symbolic, a "naturalist" repetition wherein no escape from a closed order seems possible ("the novel in Zola's hands . . . has been degraded to a mere illustration of a thesis"); and the third, an encounter with the void of the Real, wherein a dramatic new possibility unexpectedly emerges.[23]

Finally, there is a more local connection, between *Archaeologies* and Jameson's two previous books, *Brecht and Method* and *A Singular Modernity,* as well as with its successor, *The Modernist Papers* (although the older essays that compose the latter also largely predate the composition of the first book of *Archaeologies*). Early on in *Archaeologies,* Jameson notes,

> The Utopian calling, indeed, seems to have some kinship with that of the inventor in modern times, and to bring to bear some necessary combination of the identification of a problem to be solved and the inventive ingenuity with which a series of solutions are proposed and tested. There is here some affinity with children's games; but also with the outsider's gift for seeing over-familiar realities in a fresh and unaccustomed way, along with the radical simplifications of the maker of models. But there is also the delight in construction to be taken into account.[24]

And a bit later he argues, "we need to grasp the Utopian operation in terms of home mechanics, inventions and hobbies, returning it to that dimension of puttering and active *bricolage*. . . . For it is precisely this dimension of a hobby-like activity, which anyone can do in their own spare time, at home, in your garage or workshop, that organizes the readership of the Utopian text, a better mousetrap which you can also emulate."[25] This resonates in an immediate way with what he describes in his earlier book as Brecht's method, and in particular Brecht's vision of "science and knowledge" as "not grim and dreary duties but first and foremost sources of pleasure: even the epistemological and theoretical dimensions of 'science' are to be thought in terms of *Popular Mechanics* and of the manual amusement of combining ingredients and learning to use new and unusual tools."[26] *Archaeologies* too offers a positive

Brechtian dialectic to complement the "negative dialectic" of Jameson's earlier approaches to the problem of representing Utopia. Moreover, the very title of *Archaeologies* first appears in the last line of *A Singular Modernity*—"Ontologies of the present demand archaeologies of the future, not forecasts of the past"[27]—and this suggests the ways this text immediately builds upon and dialectically transforms the discussion of its predecessor. What these books all share is an interest in the question of modernism in literary and cultural production.

This brings us back to the first or literal level on which we can map Jameson's intervention in *Archaeologies*. This book is literally, as its subtitle makes clear, about science fictions. The discussion of fantasy offered in chapter 5, for example, is meant as much to highlight the shared aspects between the two practices as to mark their formal differences—without devaluing either, a fact overlooked by some hasty early readers of the book. Indeed, fantasy is now to be understood as the practice that renders most evident the deepest drive of *all* science fiction, that "of forming and satisfying the Utopian wish."[28] Thus, Jameson takes the fundamental lesson of two of the great science fiction novels of the early 1970s, Le Guin's *Lathe of Heaven* (1971) and the Strugatskys' *Roadside Picnic* (1972) to be the following: "So it is that as Science Fiction approaches the condition of Utopia (as in the two novels currently under consideration here), a peculiar fairy-tale topology begins to rise towards the surface like a network of veins."[29] Even the discussion of older Utopian fictions such as More's *Utopia*, which Jameson examines in chapter 3, are on this level to be understood as discussions of science fiction. Indeed, Jameson notes early on that he follows the lead, in this as well as a number of other aspects, of Darko Suvin—the preeminent theorist of science fiction and, as the founding editor of *Science Fiction Studies*, the person responsible for the publication of some of Jameson's earliest writings on the genre—"in believing Utopia to be a socioeconomic sub-genre of that broader literary form."[30] One of this book's most original contributions is that it enables us to understand science fiction itself as a *modernist* practice.

Jameson points toward the parallels between science fiction and the canonical work of modernism at a number of other places as well. For example, in the opening of the chapter on fantasy, he notes, "In recent years, to be sure, the competition between SF and fantasy—which has evolved largely to the benefit of the latter, especially among younger readers of innumerable multi-volume series—has seemed to take on overtones of that bitter opposition between high and mass culture crucial to the self-definition of high modernism."[31] And later, in a footnote to his argument that "depersonalization" is "a fundamental or constituent feature of Utopia as such," he adds "it is also very central indeed in modernist aesthetics and in particular in modern poetry."[32]

There are dangers in such a proposition, as Jameson warns against the problems that arise when the specificity of any generic practice is ignored. For example, in his essay "Progress Versus Utopia, or, Can We Imagine the Future?" (reprinted in part 2 of *Archaeologies*), Jameson argues,

> It would in my opinion be a mistake to make the "apologia" for SF in terms of specifically "high" literary values—to try, in other words, to recuperate this or that major text as exceptional, in much the same way as some literary critics have tried to recuperate Hammett or Chandler for the lineage of Dostoyevsky, say, or Faulkner. SF is a sub-genre with a complex and interesting formal history of its own, and with its own dynamic, which is not that of high culture, but which stands in a complementary and dialectical relationship to high culture or modernism as such. We must therefore first make a detour through the dynamics of this specific form, with a view to grasping its emergence as a formal and historical event.[33]

To follow Jameson's lead here then, I would suggest that the formal specificity of science fiction as a modernist practice—a practice, needless to say, that is distinct from that of high art or "modernism as such"—is most effectively grasped in Suvin's influential definition, which Jameson draws upon directly: science fiction is "the literature of cognitive estrangement."[34] In his essay on Robinson's *Mars* trilogy, an essay that was reprinted as the final chapter of *Archaeologies,* Jameson notes,

> Indeed, Suvin's originality, as a theorist of both SF and utopias all at once, is (among other things) not merely to have linked the two generically; but also to have conjoined the SF and utopian critical tradition with the Brechtian one, centering on estrangement (the so-called V-effect); and to have insisted not merely on the function of SF and Utopia to "estrange," to produce a V-effect for the reader from a normal "everyday" common-sense reality, but also to do so "cognitively" (a no less Brechtian component of the definition). The

reassertion of the cognitive means, as we said at the outset, a refusal to allow the (obvious) aesthetic and artistic status of the SF or utopian work to neutralize its realistic and referential implications.[35]

Conversely, at other places in his earlier writings on science fiction, Jameson suggests the genre's practices, in its cognitive functions at least, are not unrelated to those of various forms of realism:

> One of the most significant potentialities of SF as a form is precisely this capacity to provide something like an experimental variation on our own empirical universe.... Only one would like to recall that 'high literature' once also affirmed such aims. . . . [T]he naturalist concept of the experimental novel amounted, on the eve of the emergence of modernism, to just such a reassertion of literature's cognitive function.[36]

Moreover, Jameson argues that the "formal and historical event" of SF's emergence occurs when and where it does, in the latter part of the nineteenth century, to fill the void left by the waning of the vitality of one of the most significant of the European realist genres, the historical novel: "We are therefore entitled to complete Lukács's account of the historical novel with the counter-panel of its opposite number, the emergence of the new genre of SF as a form which now registers some nascent sense of the future, and does so in the space on which a sense of the past had once been inscribed."[37]

However, it is precisely through its "realist" representation of the future that science fiction engages in the fundamental modernist operation of estrangement or defamiliarization (alternative translations of the Russian *ostranenie*), a concept that Jameson first discussed in *The Prison-House of Language.* In *Archaeologies,* Jameson notes, "For the apparent realism, or representationality, of SF has concealed another, far more complex temporal structure: not to give us 'images' of the future—whatever such images might mean for a reader who will necessarily predecease their 'materialization'—but rather to defamiliarize and restructure our experience of our own *present,* and to do so in specific ways distinct from all other forms of defamiliarization."[38] In short, Jameson shows how science fiction, not unlike Brecht's work, is a form of what we might call *realist* (cognitive) *modernism* (estrangement). The classics of high modernism—Joyce, Kafka, Mann, Soseki,

Baudelaire, Mallarmé, Rimbaud, Proust, Stein, Williams, and Stevens, the focus, along with outriders such as Oe Kenzaburo and Peter Weiss, of the essays collected together in *The Modernist Papers*—achieve these estranging effects through violations of formal expectations (and this was of the utmost importance to the originators of the concept of estrangement, Viktor Shklovsky and the Russian Formalists). Science fiction, on the other hand, estranges through its "realistic" content, a realism whose "referent," as Marc Angenot points out in a classic study, is an "absent" one.[39]

At the same time, Jameson's discussions help us grasp anew the historical specificity of science fictional modernisms. For the genre itself emerges, with the work of Wells, and especially the couple of *The Time Machine* (1895) and *The War of the Worlds* (1898),[40] in the period of modernism (or if you would push the origins back to Mary Shelley, then we might take Tony Pinkney's suggestion that romanticism was already a proto-modernism[41]—and Jameson too has some interesting things to say in the first essay of part 2 of *Archaeologies* about the moment of Romanticism and the parallels between Hegel and Fourier). In this way, science fiction, as an original representational technology, becomes as modernist as say, film, the two modernist developments not surprisingly converging early on in Georges Méliès's *Le Voyage dans la lune* (1902), an experimental short film inspired in part by Wells's *The First Men in the Moon* (1901).

Moreover, there is also a specific modernist period *within* the history of the practice, and here the connection between science fiction and film becomes even more suggestive. Jameson argues in *Signatures of the Visible* that film has two histories, that of silent era and that of sound, and that each of the two "evolutionary species" that results passes through similar developmental stages: from an early "realism" (of D. W. Griffith for silent and the Hollywood period for sound), a moment in which occurs "the conquest of a kind of cultural, ideological, and narrative literacy by a new class or group"; through a "modernist" period of formal experimentation (of "Eisenstein and Stroheim" on the one hand, and of the "great *auteurs*" on the other), and finally (although this occurs only in sound film), into a full-blown "postmodernism."[42]

I would suggest that something similar occurs in the history of science fiction.[43] Following its realist emergence in Wells, Forster, and Bogdanov, the first modernist moment of science fiction—the moment of Zamyatin, Tolstoi, Huxley, Čapek, and Stapledon, to name a few—is interrupted in the late 1920s, on the one hand, by the Soviet crackdown on all forms of literary experimentation, and, on the other, by the ascendancy in the U.S. of pulp magazine science fiction. The genre, now in its equivalent to film's "sound" era, subsequently passes through a second realist stage, the moment of the so-called Golden Age, its class or group readership being composed of young men and boys interested in science and technology and intent on producing a particular literary and cultural argot all their own. In the late 1950s, science fiction enters into its second modernist period, the "New Wave," a moment of radical experimentation in terms of both the genre's content and form that extends until the mid-1970s.[44] This is then followed in the early 1980s by the emergence of postmodern science fiction, this last stage signaled most dramatically by the appearance of cyberpunk and its subsequent dialectical rejoinder in what Tom Moylan names the "critical dystopias" of Robinson, Marge Piercy, and Octavia Butler.[45]

Jameson offers a different periodization of the genre in *Archaeologies,* although I think the two complement one another, as he further divides this second history into a number of stages: adventure and science for what I am calling the realist moment; sociology, subjectivity, and aesthetics for the modernist; and cyberpunk for the postmodern, "a general period break which is also consistent, not only with the neoconservative revolution and globalization, but also with the rise of commercial fantasy as a generic competitor and ultimate victor in the field of mass culture."[46] Not surprisingly, the majority of the writers that Jameson discusses in this book—Stanislaw Lem, Dick, Le Guin, Brunner, Aldiss, the Strugatsky brothers, MacIntyre, among others—come from this second modernist moment (although this is not to neglect the significant readings in *Archaeologies* of the Golden Age "realist" writers, Isaac Asimov in part 1 and Heinlein and Van Vogt in part 2, as well as of even earlier figures such as More, Fourier, and Shaw). Even the two chapters on contemporary fictions, Robinson's *Mars* Trilogy (1993–96) and Gibson's *Pattern Recognition* (2003)—and not, significantly, the latter's now canonical postmodern cyberpunk novel *Neuromancer* (1984)—concern texts that in fact offer intimations of a movement beyond high postmodern science fiction and into a new period in the practice's history.

The modernism we are talking about here is thus not that with which many of us were brought up, the modernism of the New Critics, with their privileging of unstable irony and a tortured self-reflexivity. Jameson confronts such a modernism head-on in *Archaeologies* in an engagement with Gary Saul Morson's category of the "meta-Utopia," an imaginary genre whose characteristic trait is self-reflexive Irony: "Irony is indeed the synthesis of opposites prescribed in the modernist period; and as a supreme modernist value (from Thomas Mann to Paul de Man) it is both distinct from and documented by all the specific individual ironies of the text."[47] Jameson further specifies the privileging of Irony as "the quintessential expression of late modernism and of the ideology of the modern as that was developed during the Cold War (whose traces and impasses it bears like a stigmata)."[48]

As we saw in the previous chapter, Jameson first theorizes late modernism in *A Singular Modernity* as "the survival and transformation of more properly modernist creative impulses after World War II."[49] Such a formation is marked by "the replacement of the varied and incomprehensible Absolutes of modernism by the far more modest and comprehensible aesthetic autonomies of the late modern."[50] Moreover, the "ideologists of modernism (as opposed to its genuine practitioners), from Greenberg to Adorno, and passing through the American New Criticism, are in agreement that the concept of culture is the true enemy of art as such; and that if one opens the door to 'culture', everything currently reviled under the term of cultural studies pours in and leaves pure art and pure literature irredeemably tainted."[51] Jameson further argues that the present moment has witnessed a revival of this late modernist stance, in the form of those who advocate a "return" to Literature or "the canon," variously cloaked in the calls for a renewed commitment to disciplinarity, aesthetics, or ethics.[52] Moreover, this ideological late modernism, whether in its older or new varieties, has no place for vulgar political writers (*plumpes Denken*) such as Brecht; or degraded "cultural" forms such as science fiction.

What we witness in *Archaeologies* then, as much as in Jameson's three books surrounding it, is an attempt to crack open this late modernist ideological entombment, and to recover a more radical modernism. Similarly, Jameson's interest in *The Seeds of Time* in Andrei Platonov's *Chevengur* lies in the fact that it too is a work that escaped these Cold War late modernist rewritings (unlike, say, Boris Pilnyak's *The Naked Year,* another modernist Soviet Utopian fiction whose veritable Deleuzian energies Jameson also might help us appreciate anew). *Chevengur,* first published in the late 1970s, comes to us as if out of a "time capsule," one of those "works whose existence was largely unexpected, works that express the Utopian energies of the great Soviet cultural revolution of the 1920s and the ferment and excitement, the well-nigh illimitable formal possibilities, of that period."[53] This is a modernism that is defined by its commitment to what Suvin in the science fiction

context calls—following the modernist theorist of Utopia, Ernst Bloch—
the *Novum:* "a totalizing phenomenon or relationship deviating from the
author's and implied reader's norm of reality."[54] Alain Badiou names this
the "situated void" making possible (without guaranteeing of course)
the event of a radical break with the status quo.[55] The only way to bring
about such a transformation—in short, to create a new world—is, Badiou suggests, through an absolute "fidelity" to one's project. A similar
sentiment is born out by the statement from Jameson's book that I used
as the epigraph to this essay. And again like Badiou's philosophical project, Jameson's most recent books attempt to mine the untimely lessons
that the radical cultural projects of modernism(s) have for our present, a
project that in both cases bears a striking resemblance to the one Slavoj
Žižek names "repeating."[56] Although Žižek's original point concerns
Lenin, his insight can be extended to any of the great modernist projects
of social and cultural transformation:

> As a result, *repeating* Lenin does not mean a *return* to
> Lenin—to repeat Lenin is to accept that "Lenin is dead," that
> his particular solution failed, even failed monstrously, but
> that there was a utopian spark in it worth saving. Repeating
> Lenin means that we have to distinguish between what Lenin
> actually did and the field of possibilities he opened up, the
> tension in Lenin between what he actually did and another
> dimension: what was "in Lenin more than Lenin himself."
> To repeat Lenin is to repeat not what Lenin *did* but what he
> *failed to do,* his missed opportunities.[57]

However, when we move to our next interpretive horizon, all this
gets reversed once again, as even the readings of modernist science fiction and fantasy texts become *allegories* of some of the fundamental
problems of the Utopian imagination. Jameson's analysis of Utopia in
this book moves across three central questions: first, that of wish fulfillment, which he argues is a fundamental aspect of Utopia's form, a fact
as I suggested earlier made most apparent in fantasy; second, that of
the representability of radical otherness, a question for which Jameson's
earlier investigations of Utopia became scandalous for many students of
the form, and which he revisits prominently here; and finally, that of the
content of Utopian texts.

The first discussion opens with the elaboration I discussed earlier of
the distinction between Utopian fancy and Utopian imagination, before

developing new readings of works such as B. F. Skinner's *Walden Two* and Le Guin's *The Lathe of Heaven.* Jameson then turns his attention to the sub-genre of fantasy whose attraction, as with religion as defined by Ludwig Feuerbach, lies in its status "as a projection . . . a distorted vision of human productive powers, which has been exteriorized and reified into a force in its own right."[58] Thus, for example, magic in fantasy, especially in such triumphs of the form as Le Guin's Earthsea novels, "may be read, not as some facile plot device (which it no doubt becomes in the great bulk of mediocre fantasy production), but rather as a figure for the enlargement of human powers and their passage to the limit, their actualization of everything latent and virtual in the stunted human organism of the present."[59]

The next section, exploring further the problem of representability, first approaches this question indirectly, examining the theme of alien "encounters" in such works as Lem's *The Invincible* and *Solaris* and Brunner's brilliant and neglected *Total Eclipse* (one of the additional bonuses of *Archaeologies* is that it may help revive interest in the prolific Brunner's work). This section also offers a new way to grapple with Jameson's claim in "Progress Versus Utopia" that the "deepest vocation" of science fiction is "over and over again to demonstrate and to dramatize our incapacity to imagine the future, to body forth, through apparently full representations which prove on closer inspection to be structurally and constitutively impoverished, the atrophy in our time of what Marcuse has called the *utopian imagination,* the imagination of otherness and radical difference."[60] The alien in all of these cases is also to be understood as an allegorical figure of this radically other future: "What, then, if the alien body were little more than a distorted expression of Utopian possibilities? If its otherness were unknowable because it signified a radical otherness latent in human history and human praxis, rather than the not-I of a physical nature?"[61]

However, there is an even more important dialectical turn that begins to take place in these chapters: the reading of Brunner's novel revises in a significant way the stringent adherence to the Adornoian "unknowability thesis" evident in Lem's fiction and in Jameson's earlier essay. For while Brunner's novel still demonstrates the ultimate unrepresentability of the radical other, be it an alien culture or Utopia, it also suggests the possibility of lateral approximations, of particular kinds of allegorical figurations, through affective, "empathetic" identifications. In Brunner's case, this involves the construction of a model of the alien body "large enough to contain the investigator himself, and to allow

him the freedom, but also the constraints, of the characteristic movements of this species."[62] Jameson will return to these operations and
their significant pedagogical role in his final discussions of the kinds of
global Utopias being envisioned today.

It is only with the third aspect of his discussion of Utopia that we
encounter the concerns of utopian studies proper. Moreover, we also
get in this section a demonstration of the power of Jameson's mode of
dialectical thought. Jameson begins by organizing the contents of various Utopias into dualisms—the city and the country (space, or perhaps
circulation), work and leisure (production), abundance and poverty
(consumption), complexity and simplicity (politics), to name the central
ones he touches upon here. We may extend the series further, without reducing it to any master code (to do so "would be to ontologize solutions
to specific historical situations in the form of some timeless metaphysical dualism such as that between materialism and idealism"), to include,
for example, the happiness and freedom couple of Zamyatin and Bloch,
or Deleuze and Guattari's smooth and striated spaces.[63] Jameson then
rewrites theses pairs as a series of conceptual antinomies, wherein each
pole is understood not as a positive position in its own right, but rather
as the negation of the other.

At this point, the importance for Jameson's project of Louis Marin's
Utopiques: jeux d'espaces (1973) once again returns to the fore, as he
suggests that Marin's real breakthrough was precisely *not* to conceive
Utopia as the synthesis of these competing poles. Such a synthesis would
become as ideological as the endorsement of either pole, only now in
the form of an "ideology of modernism": "Irony is thus also a way of
unifying opposites; and with it you can at one and the same time believe
in the importance of politics and embrace everything we might lose if
we indulged in political practice."[64] Rather, Jameson argues that Marin
enables us to think Utopia in a non-ideological fashion only if Utopia
is understood in terms of the figure of the *neutral,* the bottom position
on A. J. Greimas's semiotic square and the place I have identified with
the void of the unrepresentable Lacanian Real. This is the place of the
"synthesis" of the two negatives, the neither-nor as opposed to the both/
and of the schema's top or "complex" term. In the example touched on
at this juncture, the neutral is produced by way of the synthesis of the
"critique of the city" and "the critique of the country," resulting in an
unthematizable figuration of "collective free choice," a "space of freedom beyond nature," or a "neither materialism nor idealism."[65] A bit
later, and in another context, Jameson uses the power of the neutral

to think about "figures of the invention of collective entities beyond either empire or secession"[66]; in other words, a Utopian collective defined in the negative, as at once neither Empire nor secession. In this presentation, Empire and secession—on the one hand, the new global sovereignty theorized by Michael Hardt and Antonio Negri, and on the other, the delinking strategies offered by an older underdevelopment theory and critiqued by Hardt and Negri[67]—are figures for the system and the withdrawal from it, two alternatives, a systemic and an anti-systemic one, that equally thwart the movement toward Utopia. But this is to be distinguished, Jameson maintains, from the very different kind of negation represented by the anti-Utopia, the latter expressions of fear that he argues "derive from the formal properties of this genre, and in particular from that closure on which we have so often insisted: closure in space, closure in time, the closure of the Utopian community and its position beyond history, or at least beyond Marx's 'pre-history' as we know it."[68]

With this invocation of Marx, we arrive at last at our final interpretive horizon, that of the anagogical: the reflection in this text upon the nature and work of Marxism today. Jameson reiterates in this book a point that has in fact been consistent throughout his writings: Marxism is Utopianism, and Utopianism is Marxist, or they are both no more than ideologies, expressions of particular fancies. To begin to understand what he means by this we need first to set aside any lingering clichés about "what Marxism is" (economic determinism, working classism, centralization, state planning, forced collectivization, dictatorship, and totalitarianism), an Imaginary picture held even by some students of Utopia. These stereotypes might all better be understood as dimensions of a different social and cultural project championed by some Marxists (and many others besides), and even at times endorsed by Marx himself: that of a forced *modernization,* of which the former Soviet Union was exemplary (state socialism paving the way for capitalism). In *A Singular Modernity,* Jameson concludes, "Radical alternatives, systemic transformations, cannot be theorized or even imagined within the conceptual field governed by the word 'modern'. . . What we really need is a wholesale displacement of the thematics of modernity by the desire called Utopia."[69] It is just such a displacement that takes place in *Archaeologies.*

In the opening pages of *Archaeologies,* Jameson offers the following definition: "Utopian form is itself a representational meditation on radical difference, radical otherness, and on the systemic nature of the social totality, to the point where one cannot imagine any fundamental change in our social existence which has not first thrown off Utopian visions like so many sparks from a comet."[70] There are two points in this statement worth emphasizing further: those of "radical difference" and the "systemic nature of the social totality." In Jameson's view both are fundamental aspects—along with the questions of social class, the economic, and the transition from one totality to another (in other words, revolution)—of the problematic known as Marxism. Jameson has long stressed that Marxism should be understood as such a "problematic," "not a set of propositions about reality, but a set of categories in terms of which reality is analyzed and interrogated, and a set of 'contested' categories at that."[71] Only when one abandons a fidelity to this set of categories—falling into the form of ethical evil Badiou names "betrayal"[72]—does one truly break with the Marxist problematic. Moreover, with this vision of Marxism as a problematic, Jameson also hints at one way of negotiating the old impasse of Marxism and anarchism, the latter now understood as a set of political strategies and one side of a Utopian antinomy, and which can have both Marxist and non- or post-Marxist variants.[73]

In this way, what Jameson has been describing throughout this book as the "desire called Utopia" becomes available for rewriting as "the passion for totality" that Negri sees as fundamental to Marx's most radical text, the *Grundrisse* notebooks.[74] Jameson has long stressed the totalizing thinking processes that take place in utopian and science fictional world making. For example, he concludes his earlier essay on Vonda McIntyre with the "proposition that the distinctiveness of SF as a genre has less to do with time (history, past, future) than with space."[75] It is this spatial dimension of the concept of totality that Jameson also emphasizes early on in *Archaeologies:* "Totality is then precisely this combination of closure and system, in the name of autonomy and self-sufficiency and which is ultimately the source of that otherness or radical, even alien, difference already mentioned. . . . Yet it is precisely this category of totality that presides over the forms of Utopian realization: the Utopian city, the Utopian revolution, the Utopian commune or village, and of course the Utopian text itself."[76] Moreover, this "passion for totality" marks the difference between what Jameson describes as the Utopian impulse and the Utopian program, and which distinguishes the radically original invention that occurs in Book Two of More's text from the more tentative sketches featured in Book One: "The latter are, to be sure, imagined as enclaves within our existent world; whereas, despite the positioning and the supplementary explanations, Utopia is somehow felt to replace our world altogether."[77]

And finally, it is the passion for totality that accounts for the tremendous fear of Utopia expressed in the anti-Utopia: "For it is this seamless closure of the new system that renders it alien and existentially threatening, and which clothes the radically New in the lineaments of a sublime terror before which we necessarily pause and hesitate, or draw back."[78] It is the passion for totality too that Žižek describes as Kant's "radical evil," in the context of a discussion that has special resonance here: "So, although the motivations of Thomas More were undoubtedly 'good,' *the very formal structure of his act was 'radically evil'*: his was an act of radical defiance which disregarded the Good of community. And was it not the same with Christ himself, whose activity was experienced by the traditional Hebrew community as destructive of the very foundations of their life?"[79]

Jameson's reading of the differences between the "utopias" of More's Book One and the Utopia of the earlier Book Two suggests that we see already in More's work the two opposed political conclusions that might be drawn from the passion for totality or the desire called Utopia. These are also at work in an earlier exchange that will be of interest here, and which is reprinted in the final chapter of Marin's book: that which occurs in the middle of the nineteenth century between the French Utopian author and radical political activist Etienne Cabet and the editors of *Kommunistische Zeitschrift,* the official newspaper of the then recently founded Communist League to which Marx and Engels belonged and for whom they would shortly write their most well-known work, *Manifest der Kommunistischen Partei.* This exchange occurred following Cabet's announcement in the spring of 1847 of a plan to migrate with his followers to the U.S. to form a community based on the principles outlined in his utopia, *Voyage en Icarie* (1842). In an open letter to Cabet, the anonymous authors plead with him to remain in Europe as part of the fight to establish Utopia, a "community of wealth"; for, they conclude, "this community will be established here or it will be nowhere (*sera établie ici ou ne le sera nulle part*)."[80] These writers maintain that the realization of this new community must be "now-here," in the totality of "our old Europe" (*notre vieille Europe*), or it will remain nowhere, a utopia in the bad sense of an idle daydream or fancy. Any attempt to found it as an alternative beyond or even within the horizon of this totality will be short-lived, ultimately reabsorbed into the dominant and effective order, or, if viewed as a more direct challenge, violently suppressed (the former would be the fate of Cabet's Icarian community).[81] This too suggests that the scale of totality, and hence the horizon of revolution and Utopia, changes in time. Hence, in our moment such a totality can only be global; and the revolutionary process of bringing it into being—which Jameson, in one of the final footnotes of "The Desire Called Utopia," argues we need to distinguish from a self-defeating "terrorism"—must likewise be global in nature.[82]

This leads Jameson to a concluding section on contemporary efforts to generate new global Utopian visions. Of these, Jameson notes, "if it were not so outworn and potentially misleading a term, federalism would be an excellent name for the political dimensions of this Utopian figure, until we have a better one."[83] These new forms of global Utopia are figured in works like Robinson's *Mars* trilogy and its recent sequel 2312 (2012), or Ken MacLeod's "fall revolution" quartet;[84] or in the various urban and spatial imaginaries of the late-postmodern architect Rem Koolhaas, another intellectual whose obsessive working through of the antinomy of freedom and necessity in his architectural and urban schemas also plays an important role in Jameson's thinking about Utopia.[85] In fact, when Jameson describes these new global imaginaries, he may have in mind Koolhaas's figure of the "City of the Captive Globe," which appears at the climax of *Delirious New York* (1978). In Jameson's reworking, Koolhaas's city is expanded to a global scale: "autonomous and non-communicating Utopias—which can range from wandering tribes and settled villages all the way to great city-states or regional ecologies—as so many islands: a Utopian archipelago, islands in the net, a constellation of discontinuous centers, themselves internally decentered."[86]

However, federalism is a limited figure in our moment because it "would seem to lack that passionate investment which nationalism preeminently possesses." By "naming"—"constituting the object as such, no matter how vast or minute, isolating it within a perceptual field"—a process with a kinship to the aesthetic of cognitive mapping, these new Utopias promise to make this federal model available for such "libidinal investment," much as an earlier tradition of Utopian fiction had done for the nation-state.[87] Similarly, in the work of "naming" new forms of collectivity, forms that may flourish in a global rather than older national totalities, the science fiction and utopian writings of figures as diverse as Fourier, Platonov, Dick, and Robinson, discussed here and elsewhere, again become so vital for the present.[88] All of this is a fundamental part of the pedagogical labor of the Utopian form that E. P.

Thompson describes as "the education of desire," a means to "open a way to aspiration."[89]

We also here come full circle in the history of the genre of Utopia, as Jameson now suggests that More's vision of the abolition of money has become significant once again today: "It is the decision to abandon money, to place this demand at the forefront of a political program, that marks the rupture and opens up a space into which Utopia may enter, like Benjamin's Messiah, unannounced, unprepared by events, and laterally, as if into a present randomly chosen but utterly transfigured by the new element."[90] This then immediately opens up onto a concluding discussion of the political role of Utopian imagination in our global world. Following the lead of Jürgen Habermas's discussion of Benjamin's messianism, Jameson names this labor "disruption:"

> Disruption is, then, the name for a new discursive strategy, and Utopia is the form such disruption necessarily takes. And this is now the temporal situation in which the Utopian form proper—the radical closure of a system of difference in time, the experience of the total formal break and discontinuity—has its political role to play, and in fact becomes a new kind of content in its own right. For it is the very principle of the radical break as such, its possibility, which is reinforced by the Utopian form, which insists that its radical difference is possible and that a break is necessary. The Utopian form itself is the answer to the universal ideological conviction that no alternative is possible, that there is no alternative to the system. But it asserts this by forcing us to think the break itself, and not by offering a more traditional picture of what things would be like after the break.[91]

Such a radical other way of being in the world can be figured only, as I noted earlier, through "an absolute formalism, in which the new content emerges itself from the form and is a projection of it."[92] Or as he put it in his earlier essay on Robinson, in what now serves as one of the concluding statements in *Archaeologies* as a whole, "utopia as a form is not the representation of radical alternatives; it is rather simply the imperative to imagine them."[93] The trajectory Jameson traces out here thus resonates with what Negri sees at work in the *Grundrisse* notebooks, where the inevitable momentum of the analysis carries us from "the world market to communism," from the final spatial horizon of the capitalist mode of production to its global Utopian other.[94]

This then casts the project of *Archaeologies* in a new and unexpected light. The discussion of the representational difficulties of the Utopian form can now be understood as nothing less than a figure for two of the most significant hurdles faced by contemporary Marxism. The first is the challenge to keep faith with a project of revolution that, though in our fully global reality may be nearer than before, nevertheless sometimes feels more distant than ever—especially in the moment of the book's original publication, in the nadir between 9/11 and the Arab-Madison-Occupy spring and falls. The second task is that of inventing new forms of social and cultural collective life appropriate to such a global world. In this respect, Jameson's project in *Archaeologies* becomes one with a number of other "untimely interventions," all of which engage in their own form of Utopian thinking and work to formulate a move beyond the closures and pieties of the postmodern—I am thinking here for example of the theoretical projects of Hardt and Negri, Badiou, Žižek, and Judith Butler, among others; the recent Utopian visions and projects touched on above; and the political activities of the counter-globalization "movement of movements," the World Social Forum, Occupy, and so forth.[95] Jameson's project too struggles to put the question of Utopia back on the table precisely in a moment that seems allergic to such radical totalizing visions—Utopia now conceived not only as a literary genre, but as among the most significant political challenges for our own and all other times.

Afterword: Representing Jameson

I opened this book with a claim that Jameson advances in *Marxism and Form* concerning the "peculiar difficulty of dialectical writing," which, he maintains, lies "in its holistic, 'totalizing' character: as though you could not say any one thing until you had first said everything; as though with each new idea you were bound to recapitulate the entire system."[1] While I stressed earlier the problems this characterization of dialectical writing creates for readers of Jameson's work, it brings up another set of concerns in trying to bring my own study of that work to a close: how does one conclude a portrait, one with holistic or totalizing aspirations of its own, of an intellectual project that is itself very much an ongoing proposition? One of the immense pleasures of reading Jameson's work in the present is that his scholarly productivity continues on unabated, and major studies, including the first three volumes of *The Poetics of Social Forms,* are already well under way.

This concern came home to me the very week I completed the first full draft of this manuscript, as another significant and original work by Jameson then appeared, *Representing* Capital: *A Reading of Volume One* (2011). On the one hand, this slim volume, along with its immediate predecessor *The Hegel Variations,* fulfills the promise made in the conclusion of the opening section of the already monumental but also "unfinished" *Valences of the Dialectic:* "To be sure, *Valences* is something of a *Hamlet* without the prince, insofar as it lacks the central chapter on Marx and his dialectic which was to have been expected. Two complementary volumes, commentaries on Hegel's *Phenomenology* and Marx's *Capital* (volume 1), respectively, will therefore complete the project."[2]

In good dialectical fashion, such a "completion" necessarily changes in some significant ways how we should read not only *Valences of the Dialectic* but also Jameson's entire project as it has developed up to this moment. For example, with the appearance of this pair of volumes—unique in their own right in Jameson's oeuvre in that they are his first books dedicated to a close reading of a single text—we might now glimpse the larger plan of *Valences of the Dialectic,* wherein the opening section, "The Three Names of the Dialectic," is to be followed by three dialectical "specifications" (to use Karl Korsch's term that Jameson invokes in the later pages of *Representing* Capital), those at work, respectively, in Hegel's *Phenomenology* and *Encyclopedia Logic* (the topic of *Valences'* second chapter, "Hegel and Reification"), and Marx's first volume of *Capital.*[3]

Crucially, however, in no way should *Capital* be taken as the telos, or the moment of synthesis, in this three-part schema. In both *The Hegel Variations* and *Representing* Capital, Jameson confronts head on "one of the most notorious and inveterate stereotypes" of not only Hegel's work but also of dialectical thinking more generally, "namely the thesis-antithesis-synthesis formula."[4] Such a conceptual reification, on occasion encouraged by even Hegel himself, is, Jameson points out, "instructively undercut by Hegel's addition of a fourth term in the greater Logic, which now replaces 'synthesis' with another old friend, 'the negation of the negation.' The latter, officially inscribed in their dialectical philosophy by Engels and then Stalin, and attracting about as much opprobrium as 'base and superstructure,' is in reality a formal and future-oriented move, which, unlike the regressive idea of a 'synthesis' or return to the original qualities, leaves the nature of the latter open."[5] This is the same operation that is given such a brilliant figuration, as we saw in the interlude, in Jameson's later deployments of Greimas's semiotic square. Moreover, even the tripartite formula, if understood itself as a figure, "can suggest the all-important unity of opposites by way of its first two terms, and provided we abandon the obsessive search for syntheses."[6]

Similarly, "the form of the syllogism," which Jameson locates as the origin of the tripartite schema, "can also be useful if we focus attention not on its results or conclusions, but rather on that 'middle term' shared by both subject and predicate."[7] The latter is the approach Jameson takes in *Valences of the Dialectic* to the particular dialectic of Hegel's *Logic,* locating it as the mediating link between the *Phenomenology* and *Capital:* "Hegel's analysis of *Verstand*—so subtle and wide-ranging—thereby proves to be his most fundamental contribution to some properly Marxian theory of reification. We have indeed many studies—negative and positive alike—of Marx's Hegelianism; but this particular transmission does not seem to me to bring more grist to a mill still very much in business, however antiquated its technology. I would rather propose for current purposes a more unusual version, namely Hegel's Marxism."[8]

Finally, all these examples, Jameson concludes, "suggest yet a further lesson, namely the need to stress an open-ended Hegel rather than the conventionally closed system which is projected by so many idle worries about Absolute Spirit, about totality, or about Hegel's allegedly teleological philosophy of history."[9] These are all lessons that only become possible when all three elements of this dialectic are seen in relationship to one other—that is, as a figure of totality.

In chapter 2 I pointed to some of the potential ways that this new book might change our understanding of earlier aspects of Jameson's project. I suggested that what Jameson indicates to be one of the most "scandalous opinions" advanced in *Representing* Capital—*Capital* "is not a book about politics"[10]—also revises our understanding in some productive ways of the project of his major intervention published three decades earlier, *The Political Unconscious.* For *The Political Unconscious* is similarly not a political book: as with *Capital,* it offers neither a "political theory"—a practice Jameson now also concludes "has become extinct in capitalism"—nor "politics in the tactical or strategic sense," beyond "a few scattered and occasional remarks."[11] To view it otherwise, as does Edward Said in his influential early review essay "Opponents, Audiences, Constituencies, and Communities," is to engage in a generic mistake, confusing this unique specimen of an orange for a very inadequate apple.

However, as Jameson again emphasizes in his reading of *Capital,* the intent of such an approach is neither "to demoralize political readers" of Jameson's earlier book "nor in any way to argue against political practice as such," the latter so passionately and rightly called for by Said. Rather, it is to re-frame our investigations around the "practical political results" that such a reading "may produce, despite the fact that results are always (perhaps even by definition) unforeseeable."[12] It was this question that I took up when I discussed the institutional consequences of theory more generally, and the real political consequences of the so-called (re)turn from it, and the retreat to disciplinarity, if not a full-blown embracing of aesthetics and liberal ethics.

The other major claim advanced in *Representing* Capital may prove to be even more controversial: in his Introduction, Jameson argues that it is "not even a book about labor: it is a book about unemployment."[13] This is what Jameson takes to be the key lesson of *Capital*'s climactic twenty-fifth chapter, "The General Law of Capitalist Accumulation": "What is irrefutable is that the general law enunciated here has to do with non-work: not with the production of a working proletariat (let alone its reproduction), but with a 'reserve army' which includes people who will never work and who are indeed incapable of working."[14] It is this fundamental insight that then accounts for a new relevance of *Capital* in the present moment:

> Along with Marx's intimations of globalization, these analyses seem to renew the actuality today of *Capital* on a world scale. In another sense they designate a stage of "subsumption" in which the extra-economic or social no longer lies outside capital and economics but has been absorbed into it: so that being unemployed or without economic function is no longer to be expelled from capital but to remain within it. Where everything has been subsumed under capitalism, there is no longer anything outside it; and the unemployed— or here the destitute, the paupers—are as it were employed by capital to be unemployed; they fulfill an economic function by way of their very non-functioning (even if they are not paid to do so).[15]

This resonates in a profound way with what Richard Dienst means by the concept of indebtedness: "indebted bodies are precisely what capital takes for granted on every level. Here is the legacy of originary accumulation, renewed at every turn: indebtedness is the primary 'enclosure' of the lived body, the inaugural biopolitical event. . . . In sum, debts are the means by which misery becomes socialized."[16] Jameson returns to this insight again in his final chapter, where he speculates on its political significance and historical relevance in relationship to "globalization as such": "It suggests that those massive populations around the world who have, as it were, 'dropped out of history,' who have been deliberately excluded from the modernizing projects of First World capitalism and written off as hopeless or terminal cases . . . our reading suggests that these populations, surely the vessels of a new kind of global and historical misery, will look rather different when considered in terms of the category of unemployment."[17] In short, Jameson argues that we rethink "all such lost populations of the world in terms of exploitation rather than domination."[18]

This potentially reorients in a profound way not only our theory but also our practices. Jameson maintains that the latter coding, with its "emphasis on domination," invariably leads to the proposal of a political or democratic set of solutions, "a program and a language only too easily and often coopted by the capitalist state"; while "the outcome of an emphasis on exploitation is a socialist program," a thorough-going economic or totalizing, in short a revolutionary, change of affairs.[19] Jameson goes on to suggest, " 'Imperialism' is indeed a useful conceptual space in which to demonstrate the way in which an economic category can so easily modulate into a concept of power or domination (and it is clear that the word 'exploitation' is itself scarcely immune from such slippage either)."[20] As a case in point, I would suggest that it is to the category of domination that many of the reductive critiques of Michael Hardt and Antonio Negri's biopolitical concept of Empire implicitly appeal, and especially those that assert an unmodified persistence into the global present of older structures of imperialism and the continued centrality of the nation-state. In their narrow focus on the domination of third world nations by the first, or even more specifically by the United States (for Hardt and Negri too, the chief policing arm of Empire), they run the danger both of underplaying, or missing altogether, the significance of the forms of capitalist economic exploitation emerging in former third world and even state socialist locales (China, India, and so forth), and of reimposing models of national revolution, with the racial or ethnic alliances of bourgeoisie and the exploited, under the leadership of the former of course (today, only a first-world intellectual's fantasy to be sure). This is a model of political mobilization that Franz Fanon already pointedly cautioned against during the mid-twentieth-century wave of decolonization: "Because it is bereft of ideas, because it lives to itself and cuts itself off from the people, undermined by its hereditary incapacity to think in terms of all the problems of the nation as seen from the point of view of the whole of that nation, the national middle class will have nothing better to do than to take on the role of manager for Western enterprise, and it will in practice set up its country as the brothel of Europe."[21] Jameson concludes his book, "To think of all of this in terms of a kind of global unemployment rather than of this or that tragic pathos is, I believe, to be recommitted to the invention of a new kind of transformatory politics on a global scale"—Dienst's and Hardt and Negri's goals as well as those of Jameson's earlier experiments with Utopia, cognitive mapping, the content of the form, and neutralization I discussed earlier.[22]

Along with these myriad revisionist readings and estranging propositions, *Representing* Capital is also very much a book about the problems of narrative closure, and so it is an appropriate place at which I can conclude, for the time being at least, my engagement with Jameson's ongoing project. Such closure is crucial for Marx, Jameson argues, because *Capital* "stands or falls as the representation of a system."[23] The analysis in Marx's book takes the form of an "implacable demonstration of the systemic nature of capitalism itself—which is to say, which reinstates the advantages of a totalizing analysis of this system (using totality and system here interchangeably)."[24] Capitalism is in Marx's presentation "a peculiar machine whose evolution is (dialectically) at one with its breakdown, its expansion at one with its malfunction, its growth with its collapse."[25] At once a totality *and* in constant flux, and even subject to a more revolutionary overturning: here the twin imperatives of Jameson's dialectical project—always historicize and always totalize—come once more to the fore.

Such a dialectical bifocality, or what Žižek characterizes as a parallax view, is similarly at play in Jameson's reflections on the form of *Capital.* Marx's book, he suggests, should be understood as composed of three distinct sections. The first and most well-known, "Part One: Commodities and Money," stands "as a small but complete treatise . . . a related yet semi-autonomous discussion in its own right, one which lays the ground and frees the terrain for the principal task to come."[26] Similarly, *Capital*'s concluding section, "Part Eight: So-Called Primitive Accumulation," serves as a coda to the primary discussion, one that poses "problems of periodization and historical causality which had been bracketed during the preceding inquiry (just as the analysis of exchange value in Part One bracketed the question of use value)."[27] Only with Part Two does the analysis proper begin, starting off with the positing of "a real problem which it then eventually solves. The problem is this: how can the exchange of equals or equivalents produce a profit, or in other words, simplifying it even further, how money can beget more money?"[28] This far-reaching question inaugurates Jameson's own breathless representation of Marx's work, one replete with all the narrative energies, twists and turns, and surprises of any great mystery thriller. At one point, Jameson wonders, "Have we not now completed the investigation, and Marx his analysis of capital?" only a few lines later to observe "But now unexpectedly we confront a sudden explosion of new problems."[29] A few paragraphs further on, Jameson again notes, "Our long investigation is thus not nearly at its end; the story must continue."[30]

And yet, like any satisfying story, this is one whose forward momentum is not indefinite. Thus, a mere ten pages later, Jameson observes,

> But none of the hesitations and tentativities prepare us for what is about to happen next: for now at the beginning of Part Seven, presumably the climactic, and on my reading the concluding section of *Capital,* and after some six hundred pages of this eight-hundred-page work, suddenly and altogether unexpectedly Marx lets us in on the secret and outlines the plan for *Capital* as a whole, including the projected content of the next two volumes (709–10), along with a brief summary of everything that has been thus far achieved.[31]

It is at this point that the sheer originality of the form of Marx's masterpiece becomes apparent: "In reality, however, and to be dialectical about it, the unexpected forecast now allows us to grasp *Capital,* Volume One as both finished and unfinished all at once. What this means in fact is that we can expect both boundaries and lines of flight simultaneously, climaxes along with unfinished business." In its very form then, *Capital* the book models the thing it tries to describe, "the mechanism of capital" similarly now grasped "as both a structure and an open-ended historical development at one and the same time."[32] What *Capital* unleashes, however, is precisely the Utopian potentiality in such a form, potentiality that emerges only through Marx's rigorous practice of an "absolute formalism."[33]

What is most significant here is that such an impossible conclusion can only come into focus by Jameson's unreserved commitment "to be dialectical." Thus, the deepest lesson of this short book, as it is of all of his work, and of which we might now finally be in some better place to conclude, is the continued necessity of and unwavering fidelity to the strenuous labors of dialectical thinking and writing—really the only authentic form of thinking and writing available to us. But what does it mean, after all this, to be dialectical? Jameson's invocation of this stance at the climax of *Representing* Capital, though not the book's last page or insight—expect both boundaries and lines of flight simultaneously, climaxes along with unfinished business—is a scintillating one, and I would like to help bring my book to its close by citing it in full:

> The dialectic is in that sense a kind of self-consciousness of what is already second-degree thinking (philosophizing, abstracting): no dialectic without realizing that we are practicing the dialectic; no spontaneous and unself-conscious dialectical thinking as such (even though it is the return to that which the "analytic Marxists" invited us). Dialectical thinking can never become common sense thinking (or ideology), as Aristotelian or Kantian thinking did. It would, however, be incorrect to say that we must grasp our thought as an *example* of the dialectic: but this incorrect formulation puts us on the right track, inasmuch as there can be an example, a particular, only in the presence of a universal or a generality of some kind. All dialectical thinking is, however, singular: the dialectic is not a universal or a generality of that kind, of which there might be examples. Each dialectical moment is unique and ungeneralizable, and this is why we are able to describe what is dialectical only in terms of its various shapes (unity of opposites, contradictions, etc.) and not in terms of abstract concepts. Meanwhile, as Korsch understood, this specificity or singularity, this non-abstractable and ungeneralizable, unique but concrete thought is therefore to be characterized in another way, namely that it is historical. It is only history which is unique but meaningful in this dialectical way; capitalism is not a concept but a historical phenomenon (with its twin faces of structure and event); *Capital* is itself a unique historical event, and this constitutes its dialectic.[34]

Similarly, each of Jameson's own works should be understood as a unique historical event, an experience rather than a representation—"In all that concerns truths, there must be an *encounter*"—and it is something of the evental nature of these myriad interventions, their daring leaps into the void of their particular and concrete situations, that I have tried to convey in the preceding pages.[35]

At the same time, if none of his books or essays can be taken as examples of dialectical writing and thinking, they all remain exemplary in another and far more profound sense. Evan Watkins concludes his meditation on Jameson's project by noting that Jameson's work is an "anomaly" among that of the "'masters' of theory" for the simple reason that "you can't follow this act. The historicizing of retrospective generalization doesn't open new territories in which to work, nor does it promise a still further specificity to engage."[36] This doesn't mean that there have not been heroic attempts, as with Hegel and Marx before him, to systematize aspects of his work, to create a named Jamesonian theory, or to recast its unique and ungeneralizable interventions into a form "of what Lacan called the 'discourse of the university,' which is to say the irrepressible urge to identify all thoughts with a named source (as when we speak of the Hegelian dialectic or, indeed, of Marxism)."[37] This is particularly the case as we saw with his groundbreaking work on postmodernism, and the results can be at times extremely productive. However, such a faithfulness to the letter of his texts always betrays their deepest energies; and hence, the only real fidelity would be paradoxically, as Žižek also reminds us, a betrayal of them. Watkins further notes, "Maybe you can't do this for yourself; it's not exactly clear what it might mean to 'follow Jameson's direction.' But it is always possible to learn from his work how to do what you do far better and in more historically responsible ways."[38] It is this joyful possibility that in a large part accounts for the inexhaustible richness of Jameson's legacy—a legacy from which we would benefit greatly by listening to it as deeply as possible as it continues to grow in nuance and complexity. May we prove equal to the task!

Notes

PREFACE

1. Fredric Jameson, *Marxism and Form: Twentieth-Century Dialectical Theories of Literature* (Princeton: Princeton University Press, 1971), 306.

2. Adam Roberts, *Fredric Jameson* (New York: Routledge, 2000), 152.

3. Colin MacCabe, preface to *The Geopolitical Aesthetic: Cinema and Space in the World System,* by Fredric Jameson (Bloomington: Indiana University Press, 1992), ix.

4. Ian Buchanan, *Fredric Jameson: Live Theory* (New York: Continuum, 2006), 1.

5. For a discussion of Jameson's pedagogical strategies, see Fredric Jameson, "Marxism and Teaching," *New Political Science* 1, no. 2/3 (1979–80): 31–6; and Christopher Wise, "The Case for Jameson, or, Towards a Marxian Pedagogy of World Literature," *College Literature* 21 (1994): 173–89.

6. For further information on the Holberg, see "Holberg Prisen," http://www.holbergprisen.no/en/holberg-international-memorial-prize.html (accessed April 17, 2013); and for the MLA Award for Lifetime Scholarly Achievement, see *MLA Newsletter* 43, no. 4 (Winter 2011): 1.

7. In addition to the works by Roberts, MacCabe, and Buchanan cited above, also see Clint Burnham, *The Jamesonian Unconscious: The Aesthetics of Marxist Theory* (Durham: Duke University Press, 1995); Christopher Wise, *The Marxian Hermeneutics of Fredric Jameson* (New York: Peter Lang, 1995); Sean Homer, *Fredric Jameson: Marxism, Hermeneutics, Postmodernism* (New York: Routledge, 1998); Perry Anderson, *The Origins of Postmodernity* (New York: Verso, 1998); Michael Hardt and Kathi Weeks, introduction to *The Jameson Reader,* by Fredric Jameson (Oxford: Blackwell, 2000), 2–29; Steven Helmling, *The Success and Failure of Fredric Jameson: Writing, the Sublime, and the*

Dialectic of Critique (Albany: SUNY Press, 2001); and the essays collected in Douglas Kellner and Sean Homer, eds., *Fredric Jameson: A Critical Reader* (New York: Palgrave, 2004), and Caren Irr and Ian Buchanan, eds., *On Jameson: From Postmodernism to Globalization* (Albany: State University of New York Press, 2006).

8. Louis O. Mink, *Mind, History, and Dialectic: The Philosophy of R. G. Collingwood* (Middletown, CT: Wesleyan University Press, 1987), 2. In a 2011 inteview, Jameson talks about the key influence of Collingwood on his formation: "I was convinced at a very early point that what was very interesting about philosophy, really interesting in a certain contemporary philosophy, was the idea of question and response, problem and situation. The first thinker I identified with this, that I learned this from, was not Hans-Georg Gadamer but long before Gadamer, R. G. Collingwood, a very unusual English philosopher, who saw all philosophy not as a set of concepts but as a set of responses to situations, and his idea was that you could never really understand a philosophical concept in the abstract, you had to reconstruct the problem from which it sprang or the situation from which it emerged and in which it tried to intervene." Maria Elsa Cevasco, "Imagining a Space That Is Outside: An Interview with Fredric Jameson," *Minnesota Review* 78 (2012): 90.

9. Fredric Jameson, *Valences of the Dialectic* (New York: Verso, 2009), 15.

10. Mink, *Mind, History, and Dialectic*, 3.

11. I give an overview, confirmed by Jameson, of the complete schema for the *The Poetics of Social Forms* in the final chapter's discussion of *Archaeologies of the Future*.

12. The distinction between *fabula* and *sujet* is drawn from Russian Formalism. For Jameson's most extensive discussion of Russian Formalism, especially in terms of the movement's treatment of narrative, see *The Prison-House of Language: A Critical Account of Structuralism and Russian Formalism* (Princeton: Princeton University Press, 1972), 43–98.

13. Fredric Jameson, *The Political Unconscious: Narrative as a Socially Symbolic Act* (Ithaca: Cornell University Press, 1981), 13.

14. Fredric Jameson, "Foreword to A. J. Greimas' *On Meaning: Selected Writings in Semiotic Theory*," in *The Ideologies of Theory* (New York: Verso, 2008), 523 and 534.

15. Jameson, *The Prison-House of Language*, 62.

16. Jameson, *The Political Unconscious*, 13; Jameson, *Valences of the Dialectic*, 484.

17. Jameson, *Valences of the Dialectic*, 486.

18. Fredric Jameson, Introduction to *The Ideologies of Theory, Essays 1971–1986*, vol. 1, *Situations of Theory* (Minneapolis: University of Minnesota Press, 1988), xxviii.

19. Fredric Jameson, "Imaginary and Symbolic in Lacan," in *The Ideologies of Theory, Essays 1971–1986*, vol. 1, 115.

20. Fredric Jameson, *The Modernist Papers* (New York: Verso, 2007), xi.

21. Bruno Bosteels, *Badiou and Politics* (Durham: Duke University Press, 2011), 251.

22. See Toril Moi, *Simone de Beauvoir: The Making of an Intellectual Woman* (Oxford: Blackwell, 1994); Slavoj Žižek, *Looking Awry: An Introduction to Jacques Lacan Through Popular Culture* (Cambridge, MA: MIT Press, 1991); Geoffrey Bennington and Jacques Derrida, *Jacques Derrida* (Chicago: University of Chicago Press, 1999); Jodi Dean, *Žižek's Politics* (New York: Routledge, 2006); and Bosteels, *Badiou and Politics*.

23. On the contemporary renewal of dialectical materialism, see Bosteels, *Badiou and Politics*, 13–15, and Slavoj Žižek, *Less than Nothing: Hegel and the Shadow of Dialectical Materialism* (New York: Verso, 2012).

24. Helmling, *The Success and Failure of Fredric Jameson*, 2.

25. Fredric Jameson, *Postmodernism, or, The Cultural Logic of Late Capitalism* (Durham: Duke University Press, 1991), 209.

26. Jameson, "Foreword to A. J. Greimas" in *The Ideologies of Theory,* 517.

27. Walter Benjamin, *The Arcades Project,* trans. Howard Eiland and Kevin McLaughlin (Cambridge, MA: Harvard University Press, 1999), 473.

28. Bennington and Derrida, *Jacques Derrida,* 7–8.

29. See Fredric Jameson, *Brecht and Method* (New York: Verso, 1998); and below, chapter 4.

30. My thinking in this regard remains indebted to the brilliant critique of the ideologeme of obsolescence developed in Evan Watkins, *Throwaways: Work Culture and Consumer Education* (Stanford: Stanford University Press, 1993).

31. Jameson, *The Prison-House of Language,* 132.

32. Jameson, *Postmodernism,* 182.

33. See Jameson, *Postmodernism,* 181–217.

34. "Indeed, in its emphasis on the paradoxical structure of the present or of consciousness, always already in place and in situation, always somehow preceding themselves in time and being, Derrida's thought here rejoins Althusser's notion of the '*toujours-déjà-donné*': 'In the place of the ideological myth of a philosophy of origins and its organic concepts, Marxism establishes as its guiding principle the recognition of the givenness of the complex structure of every concrete 'object,' a structure which governs both the development of the object itself and the development of that theoretical praxis which produces knowledge of the object. We thus no longer have to do with some original essence, but with something always given in advance [*un toujours-déjà-donné*], no matter how far back into the past knowledge may go.'" Jameson, *The Prison-House of Language,* 184.

35. Jameson, *The Political Unconscious,* 102.

36. Jameson, *Postmodernism,* 307.

37. Jameson, *The Political Unconscious,* 299.

38. Fredric Jameson, "Symptoms of Theory or Symptoms for Theory?" *Critical Inquiry* 30 (Winter, 2004): 406.

39. Fredric Jameson, *Archaeologies of the Future: The Desire Called Utopia and Other Science Fictions* (New York: Verso, 2005), 9.

40. Fredric Jameson, *Representing* Capital: *A Reading of Volume One* (New York: Verso, 2011), 61–62.

INTRODUCTION

1. Jameson, *Postmodernism*, xvii.

2. Slavoj Žižek, *In Defense of Lost Causes* (New York: Verso, 2008), 140. I thank John P. Leavey, Jr., for first suggesting the trope of betrayal as a central to my engagement with Jameson's work.

3. For Jameson's reflections on Žižek's version of the dialectic, which he presents as the "comic" other to Adorno's "tragic" dialectic, see *Valences of the Dialectic*, 51 and 57–62. Jameson also now has interesting things to say about "fidelity" and "unfaithfulness" in relationship to the specific question of film adaptation in "Adaptation as a Philosophical Problem," afterword to *True to the Spirit: Film Adaptation and the Question of Fidelity*, ed. Colin MacCabe, Kathleen Murray, and Rick Warner (Oxford: Oxford University Press, 2011), 215–33.

4. Burnham, *The Jamesonian Unconscious*, 88.

5. See Marjorie Levinson, "What Is New Formalism?" *PMLA* 122, no. 2 (2007): 558–69. I return to this issue in chapter 5.

6. Jameson, *The Political Unconscious*, 115. Also see "Imaginary and Symbolic in Lacan," in *The Ideologies of Theory;* and the George Eliot chapter of *The Antinomies of Realism* (New York: Verso, 2013), 114–37. For some speculations on the possibility of an alternative collective ethics, see "Morality Versus Ethical Substance; or, Aristotelian Marxism in Alasdair MacIntyre," in *The Ideologies of Theory, Essays 1971–1986*, vol. 1, 181–85.

7. Jameson, *Valences of the Dialectic*, 408.

8. Jameson, *Postmodernism*, 297. See Burnham's effective response to some of these characterizations in *The Jamesonian Unconscious*, 217–32.

9. Jameson, *Brecht and Method*, 163.

10. Jameson, *Valences of the Dialectic*, 279.

11. Jameson explicitly engages with Brecht's concept of *Unfunktionierung* in *The Geopolitical Aesthetic: Cinema and Space in the World System* (Bloomington: Indiana University Press, 1992), 209–11; and *Brecht and Method*, 38. I discuss this further in part II.

12. Fredric Jameson, "Introductory Note," in *The Ideologies of Theory, Essays 1971–1986*, vol. 2, *Syntax of History* (Minneapolis: University of Minnesota Press, 1988), viii–ix. Jameson first mentions Greimas's use of the term on the final page of *The Prison-House of Language*, 216. Jameson further develops the concept of transcoding in *Postmodernism*, 120–21, 238, 270, 394–95. For a useful retooling of Jameson's notion of transcoding, or what he refers to as overcoding, see Jeffrey T. Nealon, *Post-postmodernism, or, The Cultural Logic of Just-in-Time Capitalism* (Stanford: Stanford University Press, 2012), 22–24.

13. Burnham, *The Jamesonian Unconscious*, 23.

14. Ibid., 138.

15. Burnham does present one Greimasian semiotic square of his own (*The Jamesonian Unconscious*, 213), a schema that, for reasons that will become clear later, I would suggest also might be productively inverted.

16. For another significant deployment of the Kuhnian terms for thinking about the labors of contemporary theory, see Yannis Stavrakakis, *The Laca-*

nian Left: Psychoanalysis, Theory, Politics (Edinburgh: University of Edinburgh, 2007), especially 6–11.

17. Burnham, *The Jamesonian Unconscious*, 22.

18. Ibid., 23.

19. Ibid., 21.

20. Ibid., 23. A not unrelated four-fold schema—that of the idiot, moron, imbecile, and . . . becile!—appears in the opening pages of Žižek's *Less than Nothing*, 1–3.

21. See Phillip E. Wegner, "Lacan avec Greimas: Formalization, Theory, and the 'Other Side' of the Study of Culture," *Minnesota Review* 77 (2011): 62–86.

22. Fredric Jameson, "Imaginary and Symbolic in Lacan," in *The Ideologies of Theory, Essays 1971–1986*, vol. 1, 114; emphasis added.

23. Jameson, "Science Versus Ideology," *Humanities in Society* 6 (1983): 288. Beginning with *The Prison-House of Language*—whose project he claims is "to lay bare what Collingwood would have called the 'absolute presuppositions' of Formalism and Structuralism taken as intellectual totalities" (x)—Jameson deploys Collingwood's concepts at a number of key junctures throughout his career. See also *The Prison-house of Language*, 137; "The Ideology of the Text," in *Ideologies of Theory, Essays 1971–1986*, vol. 1, 18; "Marxism and Historicism," *Ideologies of Theory, Essays 1971–1986*, vol. 2, 156–7; *Late Marxism: Adorno, or the Persistence of the Dialectic* (New York: Verso, 1990), 192; and *The Seeds of Time*, 37–39. For a recent statement on Collingwood's influence on Jameson's work, see above, note 8 to Preface.

24. Mink, *Mind, History, and Dialectic*, 143. This rigorous aximotizization of theory may also suggest an interesting kinship, which unfortunately I will not be able to explore further here, with François Laruelle's practice of *non-philosophy*. For two useful overviews of Laruelle's project, see Ray Brassier, "Axiomatic Heresy: The Non-philosophy of François Laruelle," *Radical Philosophy* 121 (2003): 24–35; and John Mullarkey, *Post-Continental Philosophy: An Outline* (New York: Continuum, 2006).

25. For the classic study, see Elizabeth McCutcheon, "Denying the Contrary: More's Use of Litotes in the *Utopia*," *Moreana* no. 31–32 (1971): 107–22. Jameson's most recent use of the litote could also be understood as offering the beginnings of a theorization of the figure's dialectical force: "The paradoxical, we may even say dialectical, originality of Marx's analysis is that in *Capital*, 'system' is characterized as a unity of opposites, and it is the open system of capitalism which proves to be closed. In other words, what is open about capitalism is its dynamic of expansion (of accumulation, of appropriation, of imperialism). But this dynamic is also a doom and a necessity: the system cannot not expand; if it remains stable, it stagnates and dies; it must continue to absorb everything in its path, to interiorize everything that was hitherto exterior to it. Thus, by a chiasmus that has become dialectical, everything bad about the qualification of the closed has been transferred to the open, without the opposite necessarily also being true." Jameson, *Representing Capital*, 146.

26. Jameson, "Marxism and Historicism," *Ideologies of Theory, Essays 1971–1986*, vol. 2, 150.

27. Jameson, "Metacommentary," in *The Ideologies of Theory, Essays 1971–1986,* vol. 1, 5. Also see the discussion of this operation in Buchanan, *Fredric Jameson: Live Theory,* 12–18.

28. Jameson, *The Prison-House of Language,* 207.

29. Fredric Jameson, *The Hegel Variations: On the* Phenomenology of Spirit (New York: Verso, 2010), 27–28. Also see Žižek's discussion of Jameson's reading of Hegelian positing in *Less than Nothing,* 269–73.

30. Jameson, *The Political Unconscious,* 80.

31. Ibid.

32. I discuss this film in some detail in "A Fine Tradition: The Remaking of the United States in *Cape Fear,*" in *Life Between Two Deaths, 1989–2001: U.S. Culture in the Long Nineties* (Durham: Duke University Press, 2009), 85–116.

33. Ian Stewart, *The Great Mathematical Problems: Marvels and Mysteries of Mathematics* (London: Profile Books, 2013), 10.

34. Ibid., 10–11.

35. Ibid., 11.

36. Roland Barthes, *Mythologies,* trans. Annette Lavers (New York: Hill and Wang, 1972), 35.

37. Ibid., 114–15.

38. Jameson, *Valences of the Dialectic,* 417.

39. Jameson, "Imaginary and Symbolic in Lacan," in *The Ideologies of Theory, Essays 1971–1986,* vol. 1, 115.

40. Karin Boye, *Kallocain,* trans. Gustaf Lannestock (Madison: University of Wisconsin Press, 1966), 162–63.

41. Alexandre Kojève, *Introduction to the Reading of Hegel: Lectures on the* Phenomenology of Spirit, trans. James H. Nichols, Jr. (Ithaca: Cornell University Press, 1969), 183. See also Wegner, "Lacan avec Greimas."

42. Buchanan, *Fredric Jameson: Live Theory,* 27.

43. Jameson, *Postmodernism,* xvi.

44. Jameson, "The Ideology of the Text," in *The Ideologies of Theory, Essays 1971–1986,* vol. 1, 56. In 2008, Verso published a combined and expanded version of *The Ideologies of Theory,* with the addition of thirteen essays, largely published in the intervening two decades. For reasons that will be apparent shortly, I want to consider this later volume a distinct collection in its own right.

45. Jameson, "Periodizing the 60s," in *The Ideologies of Theory, Essays 1971–1986,* vol. 2, 193.

46. Helmling, *The Success and Failure of Fredric Jameson,* 147.

47. Friedrich Nietzsche, *Untimely Meditations,* trans. R. J. Hollingdale (Cambridge: Cambridge University Press, 1997), 60. Jameson engages with the meditation from which this quotation is taken, "On the Uses and Disadvantages of History for Life," in his essays "Benjamin's Readings" and "Marxism and Historicism," both reprinted in *The Ideologies of Theory,* 222–42 and 451–82. For a useful role of the concept of the untimely in the work of Gilles Deleuze, see Paul Patton, *Deleuzian Concepts: Philosophy, Colonization, Politics* (Stanford: Stanford University Press, 2010), 88–93.

48. I return to this issue in chapter 5 below. Perry Anderson, in his significant essay on modernism (see chapter 5 below), also argues for another persistence of modernism in the 1960s, when "something like a brief after-glow of the earlier conjuncture that had produced the classical innovatory art of the century flared into life again" in the "cinema of Jean-Luc Godard." "Marshall Berman: Modernity and Revolution," in *A Zone of Engagement* (New York: Verso, 1992), 39. Finally, also see Alain Badiou's more recent major periodizing assessment of modernism, *The Century*, trans. Alberto Toscano (Cambridge: Polity Press, 2005), as well as his useful notes on this project in Alain Badiou, "Beyond Formalization," reprinted in Bruno Bosteels, *Badiou and Politics*, 318–24.

49. Jameson, *Postmodernism*, xvi.

50. For an overview of the "new modernist studies," see Douglas Mao and Rebecca L. Walkowitz, "The New Modernist Studies," *PMLA* 123, no. 3 (May 2008): 737–48.

51. Jameson, *The Political Unconscious*, 9.

52. Burnham, *The Jamesonian Unconscious*, 2.

53. Jameson, *Postmodernism*, 403.

54. Evan Watkins, "Generally Historicizing," in *On Jameson*, 23. For more on the figure of the network, see Wesley Beal and Stacy Lavin, "Theorizing Connectivity: Modernism and the Network Narrative," *Digital Humanities Quarterly* 5, no. 2 (2011), http://www.digitalhumanities.org/dhq/vol/5/2/000097/000097 .html; and Steven Shaviro, *Connected, or What It Means to Live in the Network Society* (Minneapolis: University of Minnesota Press, 2003). I explore the role of the Benjaminian constellation in Jameson's presentation of postmodernism in chapter 3.

55. Jameson, *The Political Unconscious*, 82. Also see "Marxism and Historicism," in *Ideologies of Theory, Essays 1971–1986*, vol. 2, 148–70. For some of the consequences of the New Historicist axiom that all culture is text, see Catherine Gallagher and Stephen Greenblatt, *Practicing New Historicism* (Chicago: University of Chicago Press, 2000), especially 8–15.

56. Jameson, *The Political Unconscious*, 102.

57. Ibid., 28.

58. Fredric Jameson, *Signatures of the Visible* (New York: Routledge, 1990), 203.

59. Jameson, *Postmodernism*, 4 and 159. See Raymond Williams, "Base and Superstructure in Marxist Cultural Theory," in *Problems in Materialism and Culture* (New York: Verso, 1980), 38; the further elaboration of these ideas in *Marxism and Literature* (Oxford: Oxford University Press, 1977), 55–141; and Jameson, *Valences of the Dialectic*, 43–48. Interestingly, the year of the original publication of Williams's essay, 1973, also marks for Jameson the moment of the "crystallization" of the postmodern period (*Postmodernism*, xx).

60. Jameson, *The Political Unconscious*, 99. On the concept of cultural revolution, also now see *Valences of the Dialectic*, 267–78; and for further discussion of its role in Jameson's project, see Robert Seguin, "Cultural Revolution, the Discourse of Intellectuals, and Other Folk Tales," in *On Jameson*, 95–115. Finally also see Robert Seguin, "Cosmic Upset: Cultural Revolution and the

Contradictions of Zora Neale Hurston," *Modernism/Modernity* 16, no. 2 (April 2009): 229–54.

61. Fredric Jameson, *A Singular Modernity: Essay on the Ontology of the Present* (New York: Verso, 2002), 28.

62. Ibid., 94.

63. Ibid., 62.

64. Ibid., 24.

65. Ibid., 64.

66. Jameson, *The Political Unconscious*, 98–99.

67. Jameson, *The Modernist Papers*, xiv–xv.

68. Helmling, *The Success and Failure of Fredric Jameson*, 19. For another brief discussion of the dialectical sentence, see Hardt and Weeks, introduction to *The Jameson Reader*, 7–8. For a synopsis of other comments on Jameson's sentences, see Burnham, *The Jamesonian Unconscious*, 47.

69. Jameson, *Marxism and Form*, 53.

70. For a useful reading of the Jamesonian paragraph, see Caren Irr, "The American Grounds of Globalization: Jameson's Return to Hegel," in *On Jameson*, 229–30.

71. Jameson, *Marxism and Form*, xiii.

72. Jameson, "Interview with Xudong Zhang," in *Jameson on Jameson: Conversations on Cultural Marxism*, ed. Ian Buchanan (Durham: Duke University Press, 2007), 194. Also see Jameson's pointed "On Jargon," reprinted in *The Jameson Reader*, 117–18.

73. Jameson, *Valences of the Dialectic*, 22–23.

74. Georg Wilhelm Friedrich Hegel, *Hegel's Preface to the* Phenomenology of the Spirit, trans. Yirmiyahu Yovel (Princeton: Princeton University Press, 2005), 160. Also see the translator Yovel's useful discussion of this issue here and on 89–92. Jameson discusses this tripartite schema in *The Hegel Variations*, 18–22.

75. Jameson, *Valences of the Dialectic*, 45. For an effective defense of the modern intellectual vocation, see Bruce Robbins, *Secular Vocations: Intellectuals, Professionalism, Culture* (New York: Verso, 1993).

76. Fredric Jameson, Foreword to Jean-François Lyotard, *The Postmodern Condition: A Report on Knowledge*, trans. Geoff Bennington and Brian Massumi (Minneapolis: University of Minnesota Press, 1984), xx and xix.

77. For a discussion of this issue, see Fredric Jameson, "Transformations of the Image in Postmodernity," in *The Cultural Turn: Selected Writings on the Postmodern, 1983–1998* (New York: Verso, 1998), 93–135.

78. Jameson, *Signatures of the Visible*, 6.

79. Ibid., 157.

80. Ibid., 156.

81. Ibid. For a discussion of the issue of scale in spatial geographical analysis that has important lessons for cultural criticism as well, see Neil Smith, "Homeless/Global: Scaling Places," in *Mapping the Futures: Local Cultures, Global Change*, ed. Jon Bird et al. (New York: Routledge, 1993), 87–119. Also see Neil Smith, *Uneven Development: Nature, Capital, and the Production of Space*, 3rd ed. (Athens: The University of Georgia Press, 2008), especially chapter 5.

82. Burnham briefly entertains such an approach before moving elsewhere in his analysis. *The Jamesonian Unconscious,* 165.

83. Jameson, *The Political Unconscious,* 106.

84. Ibid., 106–7.

85. Ibid., 9.

86. Hardt and Weeks, introduction to *The Jameson Reader,* 20. Also see my review of this collection in *Utopian Studies* 12, no. 2 (2001): 316–19.

87. See Giovanni Arrighi, *The Long Twentieth Century: Money, Power, and the Origins of Our Times* (New York: Verso, 1994); and Michael Hardt and Antonio Negri, *Empire* (Cambridge, MA: Harvard University Press, 2000). Jameson discusses Arrighi's work in "Culture and Finance Capital," reprinted in *The Cultural Turn,* 136–61. For the differences between Arrighi and Hardt and Negri's characterization of the present moment, see *Empire,* 238–39.

88. Jameson, *Signatures of the Visible,* 155.

89. Helmling, *The Success and Failure of Fredric Jameson,* 147–48. Burnham argues "that many intellectuals of my generation read the work of Jameson, and theory in general (Jameson means something else) as mass culture; by my generation I suppose I mean those born in the late-fifties or in the sixties, Generation X as my fellow Canadian put it. . . . in this milieu, Jameson and Butler and Spivak and Barthes are on the same plane as Shabba Ranks and PJ Harvey and *Deep Space Nine* and John Woo." *The Jamesonian Unconscious,* 244. Rather than forming a contradiction, these statements by Helmling and Burnham can be understood dialectically as the "unity of opposites" I discuss in chapter 5. They also at once signal what Jameson describes in *Late Marxism* and elsewhere as a tremendous mutation in mass culture, such that "so-called popular culture now becomes technically advanced (very much in the spirit of Adorno's description of modernism)" (141); and the postmodern mutation in the Bourdieuian hierachy of taste so famously elaborated in *Distinctions* (1979), such that elite cultural consumption is no longer so much defined by what one consumes as the ability to "performatively" move across as wide a range of different cultural forms as possible. Also see Watkins, *Throwaways.*

CHAPTER 1

1. For a discussion of the particular importance of Sartre, Adorno, Brecht, and Barthes for Jameson's project, see Buchanan, *Fredric Jameson: Live Theory,* chapter 2.

2. Fredric Jameson, *Sartre: The Origins of a Style* (New York: Columbia University Press, 1984), xii. The pagination of the main body of this text is identical with the 1961 original, published by Yale University Press.

3. Buchanan, *Fredric Jameson: Live Theory,* 120.

4. Martin Jay, "Adorno in America," in *Permanent Exiles: Essays on the Intellectual Migration from Germany to America* (New York: Columbia University Press, 1986), 127.

5. Jameson, *Sartre,* 206.

6. Ibid., 8.

7. Ibid., 43.

8. Ibid., 201.

9. Ibid., 202.

10. Ibid., 211.

11. Ibid., 55.

12. Ibid., 181.

13. Jameson, *Marxism and Form*, 196.

14. Ibid., 195. Jameson will return to the question of literary naturalism in each of his next major period texts: see *The Political Unconscious*, chapter 4; and *Postmodernism*, chapter 7, part 1. There is an interesting migration here too from French (Zola) to British (George Gissing) and then U.S. (Theodore Dreiser and Frank Norris) practices of naturalism. Jameson comes full circle and once again adresses Zola's work in *The Antinomies of Realism*, 45–77.

15. Hegel, *Hegel's Preface to the* Phenomenology of the Spirit, 118 and 122.

16. Jameson, *Marxism and Form*, 195.

17. Ibid., xi.

18. Ibid., 198.

19. See *Marxism and Form*, 198–201, as well as "Reflections on the Brecht-Lukács Debate" in *The Ideologies of Theory, Essays 1971–1986*, vol. 2, 133–47.

20. Jameson, *Marxism and Form*, 204.

21. Ibid., xi.

22. Fredric Jameson, "Architecture and the Critique of Ideology," in *The Ideologies of Theory, Essays 1971–1986*, vol. 2, 40.

23. Jameson, *Marxism and Form*, 36.

24. Ibid., 35.

25. Ibid., 42.

26. Max Horkheimer and Theodor W. Adorno, *Dialectic of Enlightenment: Philosophical Fragments*, trans. Edmund Jephcott (Stanford, CA: Stanford University Press, 2002), 213. I will discuss Jameson's engagement with *Dialectic of Enlightenment* in more detail in chapter 5.

27. Jameson, *Marxism and Form*, 72. For his brief invocation of the fourfold schema, see *Marxism and Form*, 60–61.

28. Jameson, *Marxism and Form*, 77.

29. Ibid., 80.

30. Ibid., 84. For more on the impact of Marcuse's presence on the San Diego campus, see the wonderful documentary *Herbert's Hippopotamus* (1996; dir. Paul Alexander Juutilainen), now available online at http://gseis.ucla.edu/faculty/kellner/Illumina%20Folder/marc.htm. Jameson makes a brief appearance in the film. I also touch on this context in my introduction to Robert C. Elliott, *The Shape of Utopia* (Oxford: Peter Lang, 2013). Elliott was another of Jameson's colleagues at UC, San Diego.

31. Jameson, *Marxism and Form*, 105.

32. Ibid., 110.

33. Ibid.

34. Ibid., 112 and 113.

35. Ibid., 116.

36. For further discussion of Bloch's importance for Jameson, see Phillip E. Wegner, "Horizons, Figures, and Machines: The Dialectic of Utopia in the Work

of Fredric Jameson," *Utopian Studies* 9, no. 2 (1998): 58–73. I will return to these issues again in chapter 5.

37. Jameson, *Marxism and Form*, 120.

38. Ibid., 126 and 137.

39. Ibid., 129.

40. Ibid., 159.

41. Ibid., 161.

42. Ibid., 184.

43. Ibid., 187.

44. Ibid., 189.

45. Jay, *Marxism and Totality*, 108.

46. Jameson, *Sartre*, 183.

47. Jameson, *Marxism and Form*, 208.

48. Ibid., 292–93. There is an interesting resonance here with the argument Antonio Negri advances in his discussion of the difference between the projects of Marx's *Grundrisse* and *Capital* in *Marx Beyond Marx: Lessons on the* Grundrisse, trans. Harry Cleaver, Michael Ryan and Maurizio Viano (New York: Autonomedia, 1991).

49. Jameson, *Marxism and Form*, 294.

50. Ibid., 297.

51. Ibid., 207 and 304.

52. Ibid., 304.

53. Ibid., 305.

54. Ibid., 299.

55. Jameson, *Sartre*, 214.

56. Fredric Jameson, "Periodizing the 60s," in *The Ideologies of Theory, Essays 1971–1986*, vol. 2, 207.

57. Jameson, *Late Marxism*, 4–5.

58. Jameson, "Periodizing the 60s," in *The Ideologies of Theory, Essays 1971–1986*, vol. 2, 208.

59. Fredric Jameson, "Beyond the Cave: Demystifying the Ideologies of Modernism," in *The Ideologies of Theory, Essays 1971–1986*, vol. 2, 128. For further development of this idea in terms of a close reading of a passage from Flaubert's "*Un coeur simple*," see Fredric Jameson, "The Realist Floor-Plan," in *On Signs*, ed. Marshall Blonsky (Baltimore: The Johns Hopkins University Press, 1985), 373–83.

60. Jameson, *Marxism and Form*, ix.

61. See Barbara Foley, *Radical Representations: Politics and Form in U.S. Proletarian Fiction, 1929–1941* (Durham: Duke University Press, 1993); Michael Denning, *The Cultural Front: The Laboring of American Culture in the Twentieth Century* (New York: Verso, 1996); Caren Irr, *The Suburb of Dissent: Cultural Politics in the United States and Canada during the 1930s* (Durham: Duke University Press, 1998); and William J. Maxwell, *New Negro, Old Left: African-American Writing and Communism Between the Wars* (New York: Columbia University Press, 1999).

62. See Hazard Adams, ed., *Critical Theory Since Plato* (San Diego: Harcourt Brace Jovanovich Publishers, 1971), 819–27 and 905–13.

63. Jameson addresses the limitations of the New Criticism directly in *Marxism and Form,* 332–33.

64. Jameson, *Marxism and Form,* 374.

65. Jameson, *The Prison-House of Language,* 206.

66. Already in a brief discussion of Dante's *Paradiso* aimed at testing out the Formalist method, Jameson argues, "Yet the events of *Paradiso* are, when juxtaposed with those of the other canticles, curiously sef-referential. I do not only mean by that the absence in them of any genuine resistance or stubbornness in the matter itself—an absence which they share with other forms of science fiction, whether the sublime and theological as in Milton or Wyndham Lewis, or the everyday interplanetary kind, and whose result is a kind of double pretense on the part of the writer that he is straining to render with precision a 'world' which he has himself just finished inventing out of whole cloth." *The Prison-House of Language,* 85–86. For a discussion of the science fictional dimensions of Milton's and Lewis's work, see Fredric Jameson, *Fables of Aggression: Wyndham Lewis, the Modernist as Fascist* (Berkeley: University of California Press, 1979).

67. Jameson, *The Prison-House of Language,* 132.

68. Jameson, "Beyond the Cave," 129.

CHAPTER 2

1. Jameson, *Marxism and Form,* 306.

2. Ibid., 307 and 308.

3. Jameson, *The Prison-House of Language,* 51.

4. Jameson, *Marxism and Form,* 309.

5. Ibid., 319.

6. Ibid., 314.

7. Ibid., 331 and 338.

8. Ibid., 340.

9. Jameson, "Metacommentary," in *The Ideologies of Theory, Essays 1971–1986,* vol. 1, 5. Also see the discussion of this operation in Buchanan, *Fredric Jameson: Live Theory,* 12–18.

10. Jameson, *Marxism and Form,* 348.

11. Ibid., 378.

12. Ibid., 382–83.

13. Ibid., 385.

14. Ibid., 404.

15. Ibid., 307.

16. Ibid., 44–45.

17. Ibid., 48.

18. Ibid., 47.

19. Jameson, "Beyond the Cave," 129.

20. Jameson, *The Political Unconscious,* 280. This concept of the modernist text is already at work in the 1976 essay, "Modernism and Its Repressed; or, Robbe-Grillet as Anti-Colonialist," reprinted in *The Ideologies of Theory, Essays 1971–1986,* vol. 1, 167–80.

21. Jameson, *The Political Unconscious,* 35.

22. Ibid., 207. Also see Jameson's essay, "Reification and Utopia in Mass Culture," reprinted in *Signatures of the Visible,* 9–34. I discuss the latter essay in chapter 4.

23. Fredric Jameson, *Fables of Aggression,* 3.

24. Ibid., 20.

25. Ibid., 57; *Postmodernism,* 303. The essay he refers to here is "Modernism and Imperialism," in *Nationalism, Colonialism, and Literature* (Minneapolis: University of Minnesota Press, 1990), 41–66. Also see "*Ulysses* in History," in *James Joyce and Modern Literature,* ed. W. J. McCormack and Alistair Stead (London: Routledge, 1982), 126–41. Both are now reprinted in *The Modernist Papers,* 137–69, along with a third original essay, "Joyce or Proust?" 170–203. For his most recent musings on the relationship of *Ulysses* to the four realist genres, see "A Note on Literary Realism," in *Adventures in Realism,* ed. Matthew Beaumont (Oxford: Blackwell, 2007), 261–71, a revised version of which appears in *The Antinomies of Realism,* 145–54.

26. T. S. Eliot "*Ulysses,* Order, and Myth," in *Modernism: An Anthology,* ed. Lawrence Rainey (Oxford: Blackwell, 2005), 166.

27. Jameson, *The Political Unconscious,* 118.

28. Jameson, *Valences of the Dialectic,* 532.

29. Jameson, *The Political Unconscious,* 75.

30. Jameson, *Fables of Aggression,* 10.

31. Buchanan, *Fredric Jameson: Live Theory,* 125–26.

32. Jameson, *The Political Unconscious,* 75.

33. Ibid., 166. For Jameson's first provisional engagement with Lévi-Strauss's model of myth work, see *Marxism and Form,* 383–84. This is then formalized in *The Political Unconscious,* 77–80.

34. Jameson, *The Political Unconscious,* 76.

35. Ibid., 185.

36. Ibid., 204.

37. Ibid., 98–99.

38. Ibid., 99 and 225.

39. Ibid., 226–27.

40. Jameson, *Signatures of the Visible,* 204.

41. Ibid., 205.

42. Ibid. Also see the discussions of "separation" and "autonomy" in *Brecht and Method,* 43–51; and *A Singular Modernity,* part I.

43. Jameson, *Signatures of the Visible,* 207–8.

44. Ibid., 208.

45. Jameson, *The Political Unconscious,* 144.

46. For a useful discussion of Marx's "regressive-progressive" dialectic, see Henri Lefebvre, *The Production of Space,* trans. Donald Nicholson-Smith (Oxford: Blackwell, 1991), 65–68. For Jameson's first exploration of the concept of "generic discontinuity," see "Generic Discontinuities in SF: Brian Aldiss' *Starship,*" *Science Fiction Studies* 1, no. 2 (1973): 57–68, reprinted in *Archaeologies,* 254–66. Contemporaneous with this essay is Jameson's review of Bakhtin's colleague V. N. Volosinov's *Marxism and the Philosophy of Language* (a text of

which Bakhtin claimed himself to be the author): the review appears in *Style* 8, no. 3 (Fall, 1974): 535–43.

47. Jameson, *Signatures of the Visible*, 208.

48. Jameson, *The Political Unconscious*, 36–37.

49. Fredric Jameson, "Imaginary and Symbolic in Lacan," in *The Ideologies of Theory, Essays 1971–1986*, vol. 1, 104.

50. In *Postmodernism*, Jameson observes, "the foundational description and the 'working ideology' of the new politics, as it is found in Chantal Mouffe and Ernesto Laclau's fundamental *Hegemony and Socialist Strategy*, is overtly postmodern and must be understood in the larger context we have proposed for this term" (319). See also *Valences of the Dialectic*, 374 and 389.

51. See Terry Eagleton, *Against the Grain: Selected Essays, 1975–1985* (London: Verso, 1986), 65. This essay was originally published in the special Fall 1982 issue of *Diacritics* devoted to *The Political Unconscious*.

52. Jameson, *Postmodernism*, 16.

53. Ibid., 306.

54. Andreas Huyssen, *After the Great Divide: Modernism, Mass Culture, Postmodernism* (Bloomington: Indiana University Press, 1986), 206–16; and Fredric Jameson, "'End of Art' or 'End of History'?" in *The Cultural Turn*, 84–85.

55. See *Diacritics* 12, no. 3 (Fall, 1982); and William C. Dowling, *Jameson, Althussser, Marx: An Introduction to* The Political Unconscious (Ithaca: Cornell University Press, 1984). This interview, along with an intriguing introduction entitled "On Not Giving Interviews" (1–9), is republished in the collection *Jameson on Jameson*, 11–43.

56. Jameson, *Postmodernism*, 307. For a productive application of this idea to a reading of the specific situations of U.S. modernism, see Susan Hegeman, *Patterns for America: Modernism and the Concept of Culture* (Princeton, NJ: Princeton University Press, 1999).

57. Jameson, *Postmodernism*, 311.

58. Cited in T. S. Eliot, "*Ulysses*, Order, and Myth," 166.

59. Jameson, *Signatures of the Visible*, 75–76. Jameson advances an earlier version of this argument in *The Prison-House of Language*, 133.

60. Jameson, "Beyond the Cave," 130. Also see Jameson's refinement of this notion in *A Singular Modernity*, 158.

61. Fredric Jameson, "Baudelaire as Modernist and Postmodernist: The Dissolution of the Referent and the Artificial 'Sublime'," in *Lyric Poetry Beyond the New Criticism*, ed. Chaviva Hosek and Patricia Parker (Ithaca: Cornell University Press, 1985), 252; the essay is reprinted in *The Modernist Papers*, 223–37.

62. Jameson, *Signatures of the Visible*, 77.

63. Jameson, *The Political Unconscious*, 17.

64. Also see Jameson's reflections on "late modernism" in *A Singular Modernity*, especially 198–200. I will return to this argument in chapter 5.

65. Edward Said, "Opponents, Audiences, Constituencies and Community," reprinted in *The Anti-Aesthetic: Essays on Postmodern Culture*, ed. Hal Foster (Port Townsend, WA: Bay Press, 1983), 135. This essay was originally published in *Critical Inquiry* 9 (September, 1982).

66. Said, "Opponents," 147.

67. Jameson, *The Political Unconscious*, 54.

68. Said, "Opponents," 147.

69. Ibid., 149.

70. Ibid., 155.

71. Jameson, *The Political Unconscious*, 280.

72. Said, "Opponents," 157.

73. Jameson, *Representing* Capital, 37–38.

74. For a sampling of Jameson's engagements with the voluntarism and determinism question, see *Postmodernism*, 326–29; "Religion and Ideology: A Political Reading of *Paradise Lost*," in *Literature, Politics and Theory: Papers from the Essex Conference, 1976–84*, ed. Francis Barker et al. (London: Metheun, 1976), 35–56, especially 41–45; "The Experiments of Time: Providence and Realism," in *The Novel*, vol. 2: *Forms and Themes*, ed. Franco Moretti (Princeton, NJ: Princeton University Press, 2006), 99–101; and *Representing* Capital, 87 and 144–47. Also see Slavoj Žižek's important engagement with these issues in "Georg Lukács as the Philosopher of Leninism," Postface to *A Defence of History and Class Consciousness: Tailism and the Dialectic*, by Georg Lukács, trans. Esther Leslie (New York: Verso, 2000), 151–82. Interestingly, Said turns more to the latter position—that context shapes and limits in significant ways the possibility of expression—in his monumental study, *Culture and Imperialism* (New York: Knopf, 1993).

75. Jameson, *The Political Unconscious*, 236.

76. Ibid., 236–37.

77. Jameson, "Architecture and the Critique of Ideology," 68.

CHAPTER 3

1. Fredric Jameson, "Postmodernism and Consumer Society," in *The Anti-Aesthetic*, 111–25; now reprinted in *The Cultural Turn*, 1–20. The publication of the Italian edition of *The Anti-Aesthetic* (*L'antiestetica: Saggi sulla cultura postmoderna* [Milano: Postmedia Books, 2012]) has served as the inspiration for Luca del Baldo's ongoing gallery of portraits of contemporary living philosophers, "The Visionary Academy of Ocular Mentality," http://www.lucadelbaldo .com/art/work/THE+VISIONARY+ACADEMY+OF+OCULAR+MENTALITY/ (accessed April 17, 2013).

2. Fredric Jameson, "Postmodernism, or, The Cultural Logic of Late Capitalism," *New Left Review* 146 (July–August, 1984): 52–92; reprinted in a slightly modified form in *Postmodernism*, 1–54.

3. Anderson, *The Origins of Postmodernity*, 54.

4. Jameson, "Postmodernism and Consumer Society," 113.

5. See Fredric Jameson, "On Raymond Chandler," *The Southern Review* 6, no. 3 (Summer, 1970): 636–39.

6. Jameson, "Postmodernism and Consumer Society," 123. For a productive overview of Jameson's use of Perelman, see Burnham, *The Jamesonian Unconscious*, 239–41. At this same moment in San Francisco, the New Narrative movement was spawned in response to what they took to be the apoliticism

and the marginalization of experience, the body, and narrative in the Language Poetry. One of the movement's founders, Bruce Boone, published in 1980 a fascinating experimental autobiography, *Century of Clouds,* that deals in part with his involvement in the late 1970s with the Marxist Literary Group (MLG), founded by Jameson and a group of his students at the University of California, San Diego. Long unavailable, *Century of Clouds* has been republished with a useful overview of the New Narrative movement by Rob Halpern. See Bruce Boone, *Century of Clouds* (Callicoon, NY: Nightboat Books, 2009). For more on the New Narrative, see the interview with Kevin Killian in *Readme* no. 4 (Spring/Summer 2001), http://home.jps.net/~nada/issuefour.htm. For more on the early years of the MLG, see Sean Homer, "A Short History of the MLG," *The Marxist Literary Group,* http://mlg.eserver.org/about/a-short-history-of-the-mlg/ (accessed April 17, 2013).

7. Jameson, *Postmodernism,* 21.

8. Ibid., 27.

9. Ibid., 25.

10. Ibid., 365.

11. Burnham also marks the continuity between *Signatures of the Visible* and *Postmodernism* in *The Jamesonian Unconscious,* 217.

12. Jameson, *Late Marxism,* 52.

13. Ibid., 54.

14. Ibid., 55–56. For a brief introduction to Badiou's notion of naming, see Peter Hallward, *Badiou: A Subject to Truth* (Minneapolis: University of Minnesota Press, 2003), 124–25.

15. Jameson, *Late Marxism,* 62.

16. Jameson, *Postmodernism,* 418.

17. Ibid., vii.

18. See Walter Benjamin, *The Arcades Project,* trans. Howard Eiland and Kevin McLaughlin (Cambridge, MA: Harvard University Press, 1999), 29.

19. See for example his essays "History and the Death Wish: *Zardoz* as Open Form," *Jump Cut* 3 (1974): 5–8; and "Towards a Libidinal Economy of Three Modern Painters," *Social Text* 1 (1979): 189–99. The latter is now reprinted in *The Modernist Papers,* 255–68.

20. Fredric Jameson, "Postmodernism and Marxism," *New Left Review* 176 (1989): 32.

21. Jameson, *Postmodernism,* 48. For Jameson's engagement with Habermas's statements on the postmodern, see *Postmodernism,* 58–61. For further discussion of the importance of the culture concept in the postmodern moment, see Susan Hegeman, *The Cultural Return* (Berkeley: The University of California Press, 2012).

22. Jameson, *Postmodernism,* 99, 94, and 186. Gallagher and Greenblatt note, "The notion of culture as text has a further major attraction: it vastly expands the range of objects available to be read and interpreted." *Practicing New Historicism,* 9. The idea of the "retroactive manifesto" comes from Rem Koolhaas, *Delirious New York* (New York: Oxford University Press, 1978), 6.

23. Jameson, *Postmodernism,* 321.

24. Ibid., 151.

25. See the discussion of these symptoms in Anderson, *The Origins of Post-modernity*, 55–66; and Buchanan, *Fredric Jameson: Live Theory*, 89–102.

26. Jameson, *Postmodernism*, 45–46.

27. Ibid., 3.

28. Ibid., 46.

29. Ibid., xvii.

30. Ibid., xx.

31. Ibid., 407.

32. Caren Irr, "The American Grounds of Globalization," 215. According to Irr, it is the Hegel of the *Logic* rather than *The Phenomenology* that is foundational for Jameson's thought at this conjuncture, a fact that now seems to be confirmed by Jameson's extended engagement with Hegel's *Logic* published alongside his more recent essays on globalization in *Valences of the Dialectic*.

33. Jameson, *The Political Unconscious*, 36. I am referring here to Jameson's extensive discussion of mechanical, expressive, and structural causality in *The Political Unconscious*, 23–58. Burnham further claims, "Althusser's concept of overdetermination functions as a master-code for *The Political Unconscious*: it both explains the variety of methodologies Jameson brings together and functions as the 'last instance' of how the absent cause of history will affect cultural products." *The Jamesonian Unconscious*, 105.

34. See, for example, the passing comments in Meaghan Morris's *Too Soon Too Late: History in Popular Culture* (Bloomington: Indiana University Press, 1998), 130–31.

35. Fredric Jameson, "Cognitive Mapping," in *Marxism and the Interpretation of Culture*, ed. Cary Nelson and Lawrence Grossberg (Urbana: University of Illinois Press, 1988), 347. He uses this formulation again in "Periodizing the 60s," where he notes, "Althusser's proposal seems the wisest in this situation: . . . the historian should reformulate her vocation—not any longer to produce some vivid representation of History 'as it really happened,' but rather to produce the *concept* of history" (180).

36. Jameson, "Cognitive Mapping," 356.

37. Jameson, *Postmodernism*, 409.

38. I explore the relationship between Jameson's and Althusser's Lacanian inspired tripartite schemas, as well as that found in Henri Lefebvre's monumental *The Production of Space*, in my "Horizons, Figures, and Machines," and *Imaginary Communities: Utopia, the Nation, and the Spatial Histories of Modernity* (Berkeley: University of California Press, 2002).

39. Jameson, *Postmodernism*, 54.

40. Ibid., 128.

41. Ibid., 120.

42. Ibid., 128.

43. Chad Barnett, "Reviving Cyberpunk: (Re)Constructing the Subject and Mapping Cyberspace in the Wachowski Brothers' Film *The Matrix*," *Extrapolation* 41, no. 4 (2000): 359–74. Also, see Jameson's discussion of *The Matrix*, "The Iconographies of Cyberspace," *Polygraph* 13 (2001): 121–27; and my dis-

cussion of the periodizing logic unfolding in *The Matrix* trilogy in *Life Between Two Deaths*, 38–42.

44. Jameson, *Postmodernism*, 409.

45. For Jameson's response to these criticisms, see *Postmodernism*, 331–34.

46. Jameson, Foreword to *The Postmodern Condition*, xix.

47. Likewise, Carolyn Lesjak claims that cognitive mapping "functions as Jameson's version of a new realism" (28). "History, Narrative, and Realism: Jameson's Search for a Method," in *On Jameson*, 28.

48. Jameson, *Postmodernism*, 51.

49. Ibid.

50. Slavoj Žižek, *Tarrying with the Negative: Kant, Hegel, and the Critique of Ideology* (Durham, N.C.: Duke University Press, 1993), 201. I discuss this passage further in *Imaginary Communities*, 54.

51. See Mikhail Bakhtin, *The Dialogic Imagination*, trans. Caryl Emerson and Michael Holquist (Austin: University of Texas Press, 1981), 366–415. And also see Franco Moretti, "The Novel, the Nation-State," in *Atlas of the European Novel, 1800–1900* (New York: Verso, 1998), 11–73.

52. Jameson, *Postmodernism*, 330.

53. The debate began almost as soon as the essay was published, with Aijaz Ahmad, "Jameson's Rhetoric of Otherness and the 'National Allegory'," *Social Text* 17 (1987): 3–25, reprinted in Ahmad, *In Theory: Classes, Nations, Literatures* (New York: Verso, 1992); and Jameson, "Brief Response," *Social Text* 17 (1987): 26–27. Also see Michael Sprinker, "The National Question: Said, Ahmad, Jameson," *Public Culture* 6 (1993): 3–29.

54. Fredric Jameson, "Third World Literature in the Era of Multinational Capitalism," *Social Text* 15 (1986), 69.

55. Jameson, *Fables of Aggression*, 90.

56. Ibid., 94.

57. Ibid., 103.

58. Anderson, "Marshall Berman: Modernity and Revolution," 39.

59. Jameson, "Third World Literature," 85–86.

60. See my "As Many as Possible, Thinking as Much as Possible: Figures of the Multitude in Joe Haldeman's *Forever* Triology," in *Life Between Two Deaths*, chapter 7. For other useful discussions of this essay, see Burnham, *The Jamesonian Unconscious*, 154–59; Christopher Wise, "The Case for Jameson, or, Towards a Marxian Pedagogy of World Literature," *College Literature* 21 (1994): 173–89; Tang Xiaobing, *Chinese Modern: The Heroic and the Quotidian* (Durham: Duke University Press, 2000); Ian Buchanan, "National Allegory Today: A Return to Jameson," and Imre Szeman, "Who's Afraid of National Allegory? Jameson, Literary Criticism, Globalization," in *On Jameson*, 173–212; Neil Lazarus, "Fredric Jameson on 'Third-World Literature': A Qualified Defense," in *Fredric Jameson: A Critical Reader*, 41–62; and Robbins, *Secular Vocations*, 126–27.

61. Jameson, "Third World Literature," 88.

62. Burnham too notes a shift in Jameson's writings at this point: "a thematic theoretical figuration of totality and space that confronts more fully and radically the unrepresentability of those systems even as it pushes the mass cultural

objects—primarily film, but also cyberpunk and Raymond Chandler—in the direction of meta-intepretive allegories." *The Jamesonian Unconscious,* 245.

63. Jameson, *Postmodernism,* 38.

64. Burnham, *The Jamesonian Unconscious,* 238. I discuss the conspiracy form in my essay "The Beat Cops of History; or, the Paranoid Style in American Intellectual Politics," *Arizona Quarterly* 66, no. 2 (2010): 149–67; reprinted in *Shockwaves of Possibility: Essays on Science Fiction, Globalization, and Utopia* (Oxford: Peter Lang, 2014).

65. Jameson, *The Geopolitical Aesthetic,* 78–79.

66. Ibid., 155.

67. Fredric Jameson, "New Literary History After the End of the New," *New Literary History* 39, no. 3 (2008): 386.

68. Jameson, *The Geopolitical Aesthetic,* 3–4.

69. Ibid., 184.

70. Ibid., 199.

71. Ibid., 210. Jameson continues to develop many of the themes announced here in *Brecht and Method.* Also see the discussion of Jameson's reading of the film in Lesjak, "History, Narrative, and Realism," in *On Jameson,* 34–35 and 39–40; and for more on Tahimik's body of work, see Christopher Pavsek, *The Utopia of Film: Cinema and Its Futures in Godard, Kluge, and Tahimik* (New York: Columbia University Press, 2013).

72. Jameson, *Valences of the Dialectic,* 453.

73. Fredric Jameson, *The Seeds of Time* (New York: Columbia University Press, 1994), 191–92 and 202.

74. Fredric Jameson, "Globalization as a Philosophical Issue," in *Globalization and Culture,* ed. Masao Miyoshi and Fredric Jameson (Durham: Duke University Press, 1998), 62; reprinted in *Valences of the Dialectic,* 442. For a further discussion of this essay, see Irr, "The American Grounds of Globalization," in *On Jameson,* 231–35.

INTERLUDE

1. Fredric Jameson, Foreword to *On Meaning: Selected Writings in Semiotic Theory* by Algirdas Julien Greimas (Minneapolis: University of Minnesota Press, 1987), xiv. Reprinted in *The Ideologies of Theory,* 516–33; citation from 524. Greimas first fully develops this tool in his classic essay, co-authored with François Rastier, "The Interaction of Semiotic Constraints" (1968), reprinted in *On Meaning,* 48–62. In the essay, Greimas notes, "The preceding model is simply a reworked formulation of one formerly proposed by the author in *Sémantque structurale.* This new presentation makes it possible to compare the model to Robert Blanché's *logical hexagon* . . . as well as to the structures called the Klein group in mathematics and the Piaget group in psychology" (49–50).

2. Paul de Man, "The Resistance to Theory," *Yale French Studies* 63 (1982): 14–15; and Paul Ricoeur, *Time and Narrative,* vol. 2, trans. Kathleen McLaughlin and David Pellauer (Chicago: University of Chicago Press, 1985), 46. Also see Ricoeur, "Greimas's Narrative Grammar," *New Literary History* 20, no. 3 (1989): 581–608, especially the long notes on the semiotic square in footnotes

5 and 12; and Jameson's reassessment of Ricoeur's project in *Valences of the Dialectic,* 484–545.

3. Dylan Evans, *An Introductory Dictionary of Lacanian Psychoanalysis* (Philadelphia: Brunner-Routledge, 2001), 132.

4. Slavoj Žižek, *The Parallax View* (Cambridge, MA: The MIT Press, 2006), 399.

5. Ibid., 94.

6. Let me add that something similar could be said to occur in many of the other great structuralist systems. For example, in Tzetvan Todorov's structuralist genre study, *Introduction à la literature fantastique* (1970), the genre's fundamental rhetorical device of "hesitation"—"the duration of uncertainty" between the acceptance of a world of magic, and hence the shift into the kin genre of the marvelous, or the introduction of a "scientific" explanation for the narrative's strange occurrences, characteristic of the related genre Todorov names the "uncanny"—has the effect, as long as it is sustained (indefinitely, as is the case in a work not discussed by Todorov, James Hogg's masterpiece of the form, *The Private Memoirs and Confessions of a Justified Sinner* [1824]), of undermining the "grammar" of the genre's "themes" that Todorov elaborates in the second half of the book. Tzetvan Todorov, *The Fantastic: A Structural Approach to a Genre* (Ithaca, N.Y.: Cornell University Press, 1975), 25.

7. See for example Fredric Jameson, "Imaginary and Symbolic in Lacan," in *The Ideologies of Theory, Essays 1971–1986,* vol. 1, 75–115; and Fredric Jameson, "Lacan and the Dialectic: A Fragment," *Lacan: The Silent Partners,* ed. Slavoj Žižek (New York: Verso, 2006), 365–97.

8. Jameson, *The Geopolitical Aesthetic,* 211.

9. Fredric Jameson, "Foreword to A. J. Greimas," in *The Ideologies of Theory,* 516. Jameson also wrote for the THL series the forewords to Jean-Francois Lyotard's *The Postmodern Condition* (1984) and Jacques Attali's *Noise: The Political Economy of Music* (1985), both of which are reprinted in *The Ideologies of Theory,* 243–63.

10. Jameson, "Foreword to A. J. Greimas," in *The Ideologies of Theory,* 525.

11. Žižek, *In Defense of Lost Causes,* 140.

12. Jameson, *Archaeologies,* 11.

13. Jameson, *The Political Unconscious,* 166.

14. Jameson, "Foreword to A. J. Greimas," in *The Ideologies of Theory,* 525.

15. Ibid., 526.

16. Jameson, *The Prison-House of Language,* 166–67.

17. Ibid., 167.

18. Ibid., 168. For another deployment of the Greimasian semiotic square that develops in some richly productive ways the dialectical or "explosive" possibilities of the internal fourth term, see Ronald Schleifer, *A. J. Greimas and the Nature of Meaning: Linguistics, Semiotics and Discourse Theory* (Lincoln: University of Nebraska Press, 1987). Schleifer's superb study has the additional value of already calling into question the stereotypical characterization of Greimas's work, and exploring in brilliant detail its dynamic dimensions, as well as its kinship with the later work of Derrida, de Man, and Lacan.

19. Jameson, *The Political Unconscious,* 13.

20. Jameson, *The Prison-House of Language,* 62.

21. Fredric Jameson, "The Synoptic Chandler," in *Shades of Noir: A Reader*, ed. Joan Copjec (New York: Verso, 1993), 45.

22. See Fredric Jameson, "The Vanishing Mediator; or, Max Weber as Storyteller," in *The Ideologies of Theory, Essays 1971–1986*, vol. 2, 3–34; "After Armageddon: Character Systems in *Dr. Bloodmoney*," in *Archaeologies*, 349–362; and "Imaginary and Symbolic in Lacan," in *The Ideologies of Theory, Essays 1971–1986*, vol. 1, 75–115. For an insightful discussion of the first essay, see Robbins, *Secular Vocations*, 118–27.

23. Jameson, *The Political Unconscious*, 79.

24. Mary Shelley, *Frankenstein; or, The Modern Prometheus* (New York: Signet Classic, 1983), 36–37.

25. Ibid., 49.

26. William Wordsworth, "The Tables Turned" (1798); reprinted in *English Romantic Writers*, ed. David Perkins (New York: Harcourt Brace Jovanovich, 1967), 209.

27. Shelley, *Frankenstein*, 133. Interestingly, the novel suggests earlier a similar failure on the part of Victor's father: "If, instead of this remark, my father had taken the pains to explain to me that the principles of Agrippa had been entirely exploded and that a modern system of science had been introduced which possessed much greater power than the ancient . . . I should certainly have thrown Agrippa aside and have contented my imagination, warmed as it was, by returning with greater ardour to my former studies" (38–39).

28. Greimas, "The Interaction of Semiotic Constraints," 53–54.

29. Also now see the discussion of other levels of monstrosity in the novel offered in Žižek, *In Defense of Lost Causes*, 73–81. For a discussion of more positive figurations of modern monstrosity, see Wegner, *Life Between Two Deaths*, chapter 8.

30. Shelley, *Frankenstein*, 190.

31. Ibid., 39 and 101.

32. Franco Moretti, *Signs Taken for Wonders: Essays in the Sociology of Literary Forms*, rev. ed. (New York: Verso, 1988), 88. Also see the provocative reading of the way the work stages the "unrepresentability" of the proletariat in this specific historical conjuncture in Warren Montag, "'The Workshop of Filthy Creation': A Marxist Reading of *Frankenstein*," in *Case Studies in Contemporary Criticism: Mary Shelley*, Frankenstein, ed. Johanna M. Smith (Boston: Bedford, 1992), 300–311.

33. Jameson, *The Political Unconscious*, 168.

34. "Henry Clerval is both an alter-ego of Victor Frankenstein and the embodiment of all the qualities of Percy Shelley that Mary most loved." Anne K. Mellor, *Mary Shelley: Her Life, Her Fiction, Her Monsters* (New York: Routledge, 1989), 74.

35. Shelley, *Frankenstein*, 149.

36. Also see Jameson's discussion of the similar impossible resolution represented by the figure of the Comte de Troisville in Balzac's *La Vieille Fille* (1836), in *The Political Unconscious*, 168–69.

37. I discuss Gibson and Sterling's novel in "The Last Bomb: Historicizing History in Terry Bisson's *Fire on the Mountain* and Gibson and Sterling's *The Difference Engine*," *The Comparatist* 23 (1999): 141–51.

38. Shelley, *Frankenstein*, 175.

39. Darko Suvin, *Metamorphoses of Science Fiction: On the Poetics and History of a Literary Genre* (New Haven: Yale University Press, 1979), 133.

40. I discuss the conservative mentality in *Imaginary Communities*, chapter 6.

41. For an insightful analysis of Scott's figuration of the new imperialism in his earlier novel *Waverley* (1814), see Saree Makdisi, *Romantic Imperialism: Universal Empire and the Culture of Modernity* (Cambridge: Cambridge University Press, 1998), 70–99.

42. Wayne Booth, *The Rhetoric of Fiction* (Chicago: University of Chicago Press, 1961), 264–65. Jameson cites this passage in full in his discussion of Booth's book in *Marxism and Form*, 356. Booth was a teacher at Haverford while Jameson was an undergraduate in the early 1950s. As an undergraduate, Jameson also published a short story, "Journal," in *Haverford Revue* (May, 1953): 36–39.

43. See Franco Moretti, *Atlas of the European Novel, 1800–1900* (New York: Verso, 1998).

44. See Nancy Armstrong, *Desire and Domestic Fiction: A Political History of the Novel* (Oxford: Oxford University Press, 1987); as well as her discussion of Scott and Shelley in *How Novels Think: The Limits of Individualism from 1719–1900* (New York: Columbia University Press, 2005). Interestingly, some of Armstrong's earliest essays offer explorations of the value and limits of Greimasian semiotics for reading the novel, and include a Greimasian mapping of Austen's *Pride and Prejudice* that resonates with my discussion of *Emma*. See "Inside Greimas's Square: The Game of Semiotic Constraints in Jane Austen's Fiction," *The Sign in Music and Literature*, ed. Wendy Steiner (Austin: University of Texas Press, 1981), 52–66; and "Domesticating the Foreign Devil: Structuralism in English Letters a Decade Later," *Semiotica* 42 (1982): 243–75. The latter essay also has the additional benefit of offering a Greimasian mapping, akin to that deployed in Schleifer's work, of "the relationship among contending structures of discourse within literary criticism" (*A. J. Greimas and the Nature of Meaning*, 272), the resolution of whose final opposition—"poststructuralism" and "Marxism and psychoanalysis"—effectively characterizes the original methodology Armstrong deploys in her influential subsequent book.

45. Jameson does however already note in *The Prison-House of Language*, 165, fn. 74, the deployment of the operation of "neutralization" by Marin—who was at that time a colleague of Jameson's at the University of California, San Diego—in Marin's earlier study, *Sémiotique de la Passion* (1971).

46. Fredric Jameson, "Of Islands and Trenches: Neutralization and the Production of Utopian Discourse," in *The Ideologies of Theory, Essays 1971–1986*, vol. 2, 79.

47. Ibid., 91. For a valuable discussion of the life and work of this important post-war artist, see Nouritza Matossian, *Xenakis* (Nicosia, Cyprus: Moufflon Publications, 2005).

48. Jameson, "Of Islands and Trenches," 92.

49. Fredric Jameson, *Seeds of Time*, xiii.

50. Ibid., xvi. Also now see the discussion of *Chevengur* in Jonathan Flatley, *Affective Mapping: Melancholia and the Politics of Modernism* (Cambridge, MA: Harvard University Press, 2008), 158–90.

51. Jameson, *Seeds of Time*, xiii–xvi.

52. Fredric Jameson, "Marx's Purloined Letter," *New Left Review* 209 (1995): 86–120. A revised and expanded version appears in *Valences of the Dialectic*, 127–80.

53. Jameson, *Seeds of Time*, 190.

54. Ibid., 201.

55. Ibid., 202.

56. Jameson, *Archaeologies*, 177–179. Also see Fredric Jameson, *A Singular Modernity*, 161–210; and the essays in part II below. Perry Anderson similarly notes, "It was now, however, when all that had created the classical art of the early twentieth century was dead, that the ideology and cult of modernism was born." "Marshall Berman: Modernity and Revolution," 39.

57. Jameson, *Archaeologies*, 179–80.

58. Ibid., 224.

59. Žižek, *The Parallax View*, 121.

60. Jacques Lacan, *The Seminar of Jacques Lacan, Book II: The Ego in Freud's Theory and in the Technique of Psychoanalysis, 1954–1955,* trans. Sylvana Tomaselli (New York: Norton, 1991), 29.

61. Jameson, "Lacan and the Dialectic," 376.

62. Jacques Lacan, *Le séminaire Livre I, Le écrits techniques de Freud, 1953–1954,* ed. Jacques-Alain Miller (Paris: Éditions du Seuil, 1975), 80; Jacques Lacan, *The Seminar of Jacques Lacan, Book I: Freud's Papers on Technique, 1953–1954,* trans. John Forrester (New York: Norton, 1991), 66; Jameson, *The Ideologies of Theory, Essays 1971–1986,* vol. 1, 104.

63. Lorenzo Chiesa, *Subjectivity and Otherness: A Philosophical Reading of Lacan* (Cambridge, MA: The MIT Press, 2007), 105.

64. See Jacques Lacan, *Le séminaire Livre XXIII, Le sinthome, 1975–1976,* ed. Jacques-Alain Miller (Paris: Éditions du Seuil, 2005); and Evans, *An Introductory Dictionary,* 18–20 and 188–190.

65. The proposition that it would be possible to read "Lacan's schematization in relation to A. J. Greimas's semiotic square" is also briefly alluded to in James M. Mellard, *Using Lacan, Reading Fiction* (Urbana: University of Illinois Press, 1991), 60–61.

66. I show in "Lacan avec Greimas" how Lacan comes to rethink the labor of analysis in his late work.

67. Chiesa, *Subjectivity and Otherness,* 107.

68. Ibid., 108.

69. Jacques Lacan, *Écrits,* trans. Bruce Fink (New York: Norton, 2006), 671 and 693.

70. Chiesa, *Subjectivity and Otherness,* 119.

71. Ibid., 191–92. For a further elaboration on the radical political potential of Lacan's thought, see Yannis Stavrakakis, *Lacan and the Political* (London: Routledge, 1999), and *The Lacanian Left.*

72. Jameson, "Foreword to A. J. Greimas," in *The Ideologies of Theory*, 531.

73. Ibid.

74. Jameson, *Postmodernism*, 287.

75. Ibid., 291.

76. Ibid., 293. In the conclusion of his essay "Class and Allegory in Contemporary Mass Culture: *Dog Day Afternoon* as a Political Film," Jameson explores the narrative labor performed by the 1975 film's mobilization of the analogon of the star system, and I would suggest that we might also profitably apply the schema he develops there to the cognitive mapping taking place in *Something Wild*. See *Signatures of the Visible*, 52–54.

77. Jameson, *Postmodernism*, 291 and 293.

78. Ibid., 291.

79. Susan Jeffords, *Hard Bodies: Hollywood Masculinity in the Reagan Era* (New Brunswick, NJ: Rutgers University Press, 1994), 153.

80. Michael McKeon, *The Origins of the English Novel, 1600–1740* (Baltimore: The Johns Hopkins University Press, 1987), 4.

81. Ibid., 267.

82. Ibid. Also see Michael McKeon, "A Defense of Dialectical Method in Literary History," *Diacritics* 19, no. 1 (Spring, 1989): 83–96.

83. McKeon, *The Origins of the English Novel*, 394. Also see M. M. Bakhtin, *The Dialogic Imagination: Four Essays*, trans. Caryl Emerson and Michael Holquist (Austin: University of Texas Press, 1981), 366–415.

84. McKeon, *The Origins of the English Novel*, 266.

85. Raymond Williams, *Marxism and Literature*, 131–32. Also see Williams, *The Country and the City* (Oxford: Oxford University Press, 1973).

86. McKeon, *The Origins of the English Novel*, 418–19.

87. T. S. Eliot, "*Ulysses*, Order, and Myth," *Modernism: An Anthology*, ed. Lawrence Rainey (Oxford: Oxford University Press, 2005), 166.

88. Jameson, *The Prison-House of Language*, 77.

89. See Bosteels, *Badiou and Politics*, 246 and 237–38. For Badiou's most recent detailed discussion of the Commune, see *The Communist Hypothesis*, trans. David Macey and Steve Corcoran (New York: Verso, 2010), 168–228.

90. Alain Badiou, "Can Change Be Thought?" in Bosteels, *Badiou and Politics*, 301.

91. Žižek, *The Parallax View*, 4. Also see Kojin Karatani, *Transcritique: On Kant and Marx*, trans. Sabu Kohso (Cambridge, MA: The MIT Press, 2003). Jameson deploys another such double Greimasian schema in *The Hegel Variations*, 113–14.

92. See Jameson, "The Vanishing Mediator; or, Max Weber as Storyteller," in *The Ideologies of Theory, Essays 1971–1986*, vol. 2, 3–34; and Jacques Lacan, *The Seminar of Jacques Lacan, Book VII: The Ethics of Psychoanalysis 1959–1960*, trans. Dennis Porter (New York: Norton, 1992).

93. I discuss in some detail the significance of, among other factors, the "end" of the Cold War, the publication of these crucial theoretical interventions, and the increasing importance of the concept of globalization for an understanding of this historical context, in *Life Between Two Deaths*.

94. Žižek, *Tarrying with the Negative,* 222.

95. Ibid. Also see David Harvey, *The New Imperialism* (Oxford: Oxford University Press, 2005); and Naomi Klein, *The Shock Doctrine: The Rise of Disaster Capitalism* (New York: Henry Holt, 2007).

96. Jameson, *Valences of the Dialectic,* 445.

97. Jameson, "The Experiments of Time: Providence and Realism," in *The Novel,* vol. 2, 96; reprinted in *The Antinomies of Realism,* 196.

98. Ibid., 95, 195.

99. Jameson, *Signatures of the Visible,* 31.

100. Žižek, *Tarrying with the Negative,* 223–24.

101. Ibid., 96–97.

102. Ibid., 224.

103. Ibid., 225. Let me note that another Greimasian dialectical schema emerges more recently in Slavoj Žižek, "Against the Populist Temptation," *Critical Inquiry* 32 (Spring 2006): 551–74; now included in, "Why Populism Is (Sometimes) Good Enough in Practice, but Not in Theory," *In Defense of Lost Causes,* 264–333. And finally, see the discussion of "divine violence" in Slavoj Žižek, *Violence* (New York: Picador, 2008).

104. Cited in Esther Leslie, *Walter Benjamin* (London: Reaktion, 2007), 115.

105. Jameson raises the question of the opposition of voluntarism and determinism in relationship to the providential plot structure invoked above in "The Experiments of Time: Providence and Realism," in *The Novel,* vol. 2, 100–101; and *The Antinomies of Realism,* 200–201.

106. Jameson, *Archaeologies,* 212.

107. Jameson, *Valences of the Dialectic,* 409. This essay was originally published in *Polygraph* 6/7 (1993): 70–195.

CHAPTER 4

1. Raoul Vaneigem, *The Revolution of Everyday Life,* trans. Donald Nicholson-Smith (Oakland, CA: PM Press, 2012), 11. Also see the related important discussions of radical love in Michael Hardt and Antonio Negri, "De Singularitate 1: Of Love Possessed," in *Commonwealth* (Cambridge, MA: Harvard University Press, 2009), 179–99; and Rosemary Hennessey, "Identity, Need, and the Making of Radical Love," in *Profit and Pleasure: Sexual Identities in Late Capitalism* (New York: Routledge, 2000), 203–32.

2. Alain Badiou, *Conditions,* trans. Steven Corcoran (New York: Continuum, 2008), 23.

3. However, another significant continuity between Jameson and Badiou lies in the fact that both begin their intellectual trajectory through a sustained engagement with the problematic of Sartre. Badiou notes that in relationship to structuralism in particular, "I entered into this debate from the point of view of Sartre, whereas for most others in my generation this question of structure has been their immediate philosophical education so that they really entered the debate *against* Sartre and not *from* Sartre." Bosteels, *Badiou and Politics,* 295.

4. Bosteels, *Badiou and Politics,* 204.

5. Ibid., 205.

6. See Wegner, "Lacan avec Greimas."

7. See Badiou, "Anti-Philosophy: Plato and Lacan," in *Conditions*, 228–47. Badiou maintains that his project, understood again as a deeply dialectical one, attempts to stand "at the crossroads of all that these two names refer to that I consider essential. To stand in a crossing in torsion, without any unity of plane, between anti-philosophy and philosophy." *Conditions*, 246. For the concept of non-philosophy, see François Laruelle, *Principles of Non-Philosophy*, trans. Nicola Rubczak and Anthony Paul Smith (London: Bloomsbury, 2013), and above Introduction, footnote 24.

8. Badiou's *Theory of the Subject*—maintaining, as Bosteels demonstrates, a deep fidelity to the events of May 1968 and the Chinese Cultural Revolution and thus "out-of-place" in a situation of an emerging postmodernism and Thatcher–Reagan neo-conservatism—is contemporaneous with three other similarly untimely works: Rem Koolhaas's *Delerious New York* (1978), Antonio Negri's *Marx Beyond Marx* (1979), and Jameson's *The Political Unconscious* (1981). I invoke this connection and discuss the untimeliness of Koolhaas's book in particular in "'The Mysterious Qualities of This Alleged Void': Transvaluation and Utopian Urbanism in Rem Koolhaas's *S,M,L,XL*," in *Imagining and Making the World: Reflections on Architecture and Utopia*, ed. Nathaniel Coleman (Oxford: Peter Lang, 2011), 283–98.

9. Badiou invokes the four discourses in *Conditions*, 239. Approaching this question from a different direction, Bosteels touches on the differences between Badiou's conditions and Lacan's four discourses, as well as the earlier four discourses Althusser theorizes in his research notes from the mid-1960s. See Bosteels, *Badiou and Politics*, 62–64.

10. Hallward, *Badiou: A Subject to Truth*, 185.

11. Žižek, *The Parallax View*, 406.

12. Cited in Jameson, *Valences of the Dialectic*, 13.

13. Bosteels, *Badiou and Politics*, 34.

14. Ibid., xviii. Later, in one of the main corollaries to arise from the second of the three presuppositions or axioms of his rich and detailed reading of Badiou's project, Bosteels asserts, "all of Badiou's subsequent work can be read as a giantic polemical effort to untie the eclectic doctrinal knot that even today binds together the works of Marx, Freud, Nietzsche, and Heidegger as read by Althusser, Lacan, and Derrida." *Badiou and Politics*, 75–76. Here again the four conditions obliquely re-appear, as Badiou is understood to launch a politically inflected philosophical critique of Althusser's, and even more so conservative structuralism's tangential suture to the condition of science; the antiphilosophy of Lacan, to love; and Derrida, following Nietzsche and Heidegger, to art.

15. Alain Badiou, *The Incident at Antioch: A Tragedy in Three Acts*, trans. Kenneth Reinhard (New York: Columbia University Press, 2013).

16. Alain Badiou, *In Praise of Love*, trans. Peter Bush (London: Serpent's Tail, 2012), 16.

17. Ibid., 26–27. For an important early study of the evental nature of Rimbaud's poetry, see Kristin Ross, *The Emergence of Social Space: Rimbaud and the Commune* (Minneapolis: University of Minnesota Press, 1988).

18. Raymond Williams, *Keywords: A Vocabulary of Culture and Society*, rev. ed. (New York: Oxford University Press, 1983), 87.

19. Badiou, *In Praise of Love*, 21–22.

20. Ibid., 38.

21. Ibid., 34.

22. Bosteels, *Badiou and Politics*, 362.

23. Badiou, *In Praise of Love*, 73.

24. Ibid., 80. In her discussion of Žižek's reading of the Pauline suspension of the law, Jodi Dean similarly claims, "The love Paul advocates involves active work and struggle." *Žižek's Politics*, 163.

25. See Stanley Cavell, *Pursuits of Happiness: The Hollywood Comedy of Remarriage* (Cambridge, MA: Harvard University Press, 1981). I discuss the "evental genre" of the comedy of remarriage in *Life Between Two Deaths*, 31–32; "If Everything Means Something Else: Technology, Allegory, and Event in *Roadside Picnic* and *Stalker*," in *Shockwaves of Possibility*; "'The Great Sea Voyage Which Marriage Can Be': Repetition, Love, and Concrete Utopia in *50 First Dates*" (forthcoming).

26. Badiou, *In Praise of Love*, 89; emphasis added. Also see Badiou, *The Communist Hypothesis*.

27. Jameson briefly touches on Lenin's two-stage theory in Jameson, "A New Reading of *Capital*," *Mediations* 25, no. 1 (2011), http://www.mediationsjournal.org/articles/a-new-reading-of-capital (accessed April 17, 2013); and in an unpublished talk presented at the Society for Utopian Studies meeting in 2009, "Utopia and Marxism Today." I discuss the latter in my essay "Hegel or Spinoza (or Hegel); Spinoza and Marx," *Mediations* 25, no. 2 (2011), http://www.mediationsjournal.org/articles/hegel-or-spinoza-or-hegel (accessed April 17, 2013).

28. On the concept of *le service des biens* (the service of goods) and its relationship to psychoanalysis, see Lacan, *The Seminar of Jacques Lacan, Book VII*, 302–10. In a 2007 interview with Rosa Moussaoui, Badiou defines the concept as "the key to our society. The service of goods today is, to paraphrase Lacan, the service of liberal capitalism. Goods are produced and distributed in the regime of the market economy. If one is in the service of the service of goods, one supports it. However, I repeat that, in my opinion, liberal capitalism offers no collective orientation. The citizen is the one who appears in the market, the consumer defined by the circulation of merchandise. Consequently, our society as it currently exists is unable to represent its collective future. People who find themselves in such an existence are unable to construct real projects outside the universe of consumption and accumulation. This is, in a word, disorientation." (My translation.) Alain Badiou, "L'hypothèse de l'émancipation reste communiste," *L'Humanité* (6 novembre 2007), http://www.humanite.fr/node/66520 (accessed April 17, 2013).

29. Badiou, *Ethics*, 79.

30. Ibid.

31. See John A. Noakes, "Bankers and Common Men in Bedford Falls," *Film History* 10, no. 3 (1998): 311–19. The entire memo is reproduced in Will Chen, "FBI Considered 'It's a Wonderful Life' Communist Propoganda," *Wise Bread: Living Large on a Small Budget* (December 24, 2006), http://www.wisebread

.com/fbi-considered-its-a-wonderful-life-communist-propaganda#memo1 (accessed April 17, 2013).

32. Jameson, "Science Versus Ideology," 283.

33. Karl Marx, *A Contribution to a Critique of Political Economy* (New York: International Publishers, 1970), 22; Karl Marx and Friedrich Engels, *The German Ideology, Part One*, ed. C. J. Arthur (New York: International Publishers, 1970), 46. German original from Karl Marx and Friedrich Engels, *Die deutsche Ideologie*, http://www.mlwerke.de/me/meo3/meo3_009.htm (accessed April 17, 2013). For a useful discussion of some of the difficulties raised by the standard English translation of this passage, see Paul Riceour, *Lectures on Ideology and Utopia*, ed. George H. Taylor (New York: Columbia University Press, 1986), 74–75.

34. Marx and Engels, *The German Ideology*, 47.

35. Marx, *A Contribution to a Critique of Political Economy*, 20–21.

36. Ibid., 21.

37. Étienne Balibar, *The Philosophy of Marx*, trans. Chris Turner (New York: Verso, 1995), 42. Catherine Gallagher and Stephen Greenblatt fail to acknowledge the distinction between ideology and fetishism in their critique of Marx's use of the latter concept. They argue that the Victorian philosopher George Henry "Lewes, however, seems more cognizant than Marx that inside the terms of this discourse, no amount of demystification can deprive these beings of their power, which derives not from their successful impersonation of reality, but from the energy invested in them. Requiring no belief, they are invulnerable to doubt and demystification." *Practicing New Historicism*, 203–4. Marx in fact would concur: commodity fetishism is invulnerable to doubt and demystification. However, he would add the proviso: the only real way to deprive it of its power is to change the world.

38. Karl Marx, *Capital*, vol. 1, trans. Ben Fowkes (New York: Penguin, 1990), 163.

39. Ibid., 165.

40. Balibar, *The Philosophy of Marx*, 60; and also see Slavoj Žižek, *The Sublime Object of Ideology* (New York: Verso, 1989).

41. Marx, *Capital*, 899.

42. Antonio Gramsci, *Selections from the Prison Notebooks*, ed. and trans. Quintin Hoare and Geoffrey Nowell Smith (New York: International Publishers, 1971), 12. Perry Anderson argues that Gramsci is "the thinker within Western Marxism from whom Jameson has taken the least." *The Origins of Postmodernity*, 73. However, for a significant exception, see Jameson, "Architecture and the Critique of Ideology," in *The Ideologies of Theory, Essays 1971–1986*, vol. 2, especially 48–49.

43. Balibar, *The Philosophy of Marx*, 78.

44. Georg Lukács, *History and Class Consciousness: Studies in Marxist Dialectics*, trans. Rodney Livingstone (Cambridge, MA: The MIT Press, 1971), 100.

45. Jameson, "Science Versus Ideology," 288.

46. Hallward, *Badiou: A Subject to Truth*, 337.

47. Ibid., 341.

48. Jameson, *Signatures of the Visible,* 34.

49. Jameson, "Science Versus Ideology," 288.

50. Marx, *Capital,* 104.

51. Robert C. Tucker, ed., *The Marx-Engels Reader,* 2nd ed. (New York: Norton, 1978), 483.

52. Raymond Williams, *Problems in Materialism and Culture* (New York: Verso, 1980), 38.

53. For a related project, now also see Nealon, *Post-postmodernism.*

54. Alain Badiou, *Theory of the Subject,* trans. Bruno Bosteels (New York: Continuum, 2009), 54.

55. Ibid., 10.

56. Ibid., 53. In an essay on Mark McGurl's landmark study *The Program Era: Postwar Fiction and the Rise of Creative Writing* (Cambridge, MA: Harvard University Press, 2009), Jameson shows how McGurl's tripartite stuctural dialectic of "technomodernism," "high cultural pluralism," and "lower-middle class realism" can be transformed, with the addition of McGurl's repressed fourth term of Faulknerian maximalism, into a historical dialectic, one that marks the mediation between the brief "American century" and its worldwide cultural hegemony and a new global era signalled by the emergence of postcolonial magical realisms. See Fredric Jameson, "Dirty Little Secret," *London Review of Books* 34, no. 22 (November 22, 2012). For two significant meditations on the possibility of global literature, see Eric D. Smith, *Globalization, Utopia, and Postcolonial Science Fiction: New Maps of Hope* (New York: Palgrave, 2012); and Caren Irr, *Toward the Geopolitical Novel: U.S. Fiction in the Twenty-First Century* (New York: Columbia University Press, 2014).

57. Badiou, *Theory of the Subject,* 140. Also see Bosteels's discussion of this passage, *Badiou and Politics,* 101–2.

58. Lukács, *History and Class Consciousness,* 171.

59. Ibid., 197.

60. Jameson, *Representing* Capital, 2. I will return to this argument in the afterword.

61. For Jameson's specific engagement with the project of Cultural Studies, see "On 'Cultural Studies'," reprinted in *The Ideologies of Theory,* 598–635, as well as "Religion as Cultural Superstructure," in *The Hegel Variations,* 116–29.

62. See Roland Barthes, "Change the Object Itself: Mythology Today," in *Image—Music—Text,* trans. Stephen Heath (New York: The Noonday Press, 1988), 165–69. Barthes does write that "mythoclasm" needs to be "succeeded by a 'semioclasm'," but his goals are far more revolutionary, that is totalizing, in their aims: "The historical field of action is thus widened: no longer the (narrow) sphere of French society, but far beyond that, historically and geographically, the whole of Western civilization (Graeco-Judaeo-Islamo-Christian), unified under the one theology (Essence, monotheism) and identified by the regime of meaning it practices—from Plato to *France-Dimanche*" (167). If there is an error here, it is the modernist one, of believing that the transformation of the cultural practices (Eugene Jolas's "revolution of the word") would be sufficient to transform the whole of society: the idealist inversion of the modernist

materialism of economism. A postmodern cynicism would conclude that neither effort can be effective.

63. Jameson, *Marxism and Form,* 120; Ernst Bloch, *Principle of Hope,* vol. 1, trans. Neville Plaice, Stephen Plaice, and Paul Knight (Cambridge, MA: The MIT Press, 1986), 432.

64. Bloch, *Principle of Hope,* 446.

65. Ibid., 252.

66. Ibid., 254–55.

67. Ibid., 253 and 257.

68. Ibid., 260.

69. Ibid., 264.

70. Ibid., 268–69.

71. Ibid., 370.

72. Ibid., 277.

73. Ibid., 276–77.

74. Ibid., 278.

75. Ibid., 283.

76. Ibid., 273.

77. Ibid.

78. Ibid., 274. See also Badiou's comments on the role of the enemy in the condition of politics in *In Praise of Love,* 56.

79. Hardt and Negri, *Commonwealth,* 195–96.

80. Bloch, *The Principle of Hope,* 327.

81. Ibid., 315.

82. Judith Butler, *Bodies That Matter,* 137. I invoke this same passage in a discusion of the radical presentation of family that takes place in the television series *Buffy the Vampire Slayer,* in *Life Between Two Deaths.* For an indispensable project of resignification, also aimed at rethinking the foundations of a shared collective life, see Richard Dienst, *The Bonds of Debt: Borrowing Against the Common Good* (New York: Verso, 2011). Dienst writes, "indebtedness marks the Real of solidarity in several distinct senses: in the way it sustains material production, in the way it signifies a domain of dependency and sharing otherwise inaccessible, and in the way it seals our belonging to the world through our being with others (we need to know we're 'all in the soup,' as Sartre used to say)" (57).

83. Bruce Robbins, "Dive In!" *London Review of Books* 22, no. 21 (November 2, 2000): 33–34; a revised version appears as "'I Couldn't Possibly Love Such a Person': Judith Butler on Hegel," *Minnesota Review,* 52–54 (Fall 2001): 263–69. For another significant discussion of the relationship of Butler's work, and queer theory more generally, to Marxist critical theory, see Kevin Floyd, *The Reification of Desire: Toward a Queer Marxism* (Minneapolis: University of Minnesota Press, 2009).

84. Jameson, *Marxism and Form,* 142.

85. Ibid., 120.

86. Ibid., 118–19.

87. Ibid., 153–54.

88. Jameson, *The Political Unconscious,* 236.

89. Ibid., 296.

90. Ibid., 289.

91. For a fundamental elaboration on Bloch's distinction between abstract and concrete Utopianism, see Ruth Levitas, *The Concept of Utopia* (Oxford: Peter Lang, 2010).

92. Anna McCarthy, "Film and Mass Culture," *Social Text* 100 (27, no. 3) (2009): 129.

93. Jameson, *Signatures of the Visible*, 29.

94. Ibid., 25.

95. Ibid., 34.

96. I thank Roger Beebe for sharing this insight that developed in his teaching of this essay.

97. *Signatures of the Visible*, 34.

98. See Wegner, "Lacan avec Greimas."

99. Jameson, *The Modernist Papers*, xvii.

100. For another productive presentation of these two schemas in terms of a Greimasian semiotic square, see Jim Liner, "Collectivity and Form: Politics and Aesthetics of Collectivity in Michael Hardt and Antonio Negri, Amiri Baraka, and Thomas Pynchon" (PhD diss., University of Florida, 2013).

101. Jameson, *The Modernist Papers*, xix.

102. Carolyn Lesjak, "Reading Dialectically," *Criticism* 55, no. 2 (2013): 233–77.

103. Jameson, *The Political Unconscious*, 299.

CHAPTER 5

1. Jameson, *Valences of the Dialectic*, 69.

2. See Jameson, *Valences of the Dialectic*, 69–70; Jameson, "Lacan and the Dialectic," 365–97.

3. Jürgen Habermas, "Modernity—An Incomplete Project," in *The Anti-Aesthetic*, 3–15; and Jameson, "Theories of the Postmodern," in *Postmodernism*, 55–66.

4. Jameson, *Valences of the Dialectic*, 277.

5. Ibid., 222.

6. Ibid., 336.

7. Ibid., 372.

8. Ibid., 60–61.

9. Ibid., 253.

10. Anderson, "Marshall Berman: Modernity and Revolution," 34. For Jameson's utilization of Anderson's theory of modernism, see *Postmodernism*, 312; and *A Singular Modernity*, 134.

11. Jameson, *Valences of the Dialectic*, 33.

12. Ibid., 35.

13. Ibid.

14. For Jameson's own deployment of the Sartrean concept of the analogon—"that structural nexus in our reading or viewing experience, in our operations of decoding or aesthetic reception, which can then do double duty and stand as the

substitute and the representative within the aesthetic object of a phenomenon on the outside which cannot in the very nature of things be 'rendered' directly"— see *Signatures of the Visible*, 53. Moreover, Jameson's use of the concept of the analogon takes place in a 1977 essay, "Class and Allegory in Contemporary Mass Culture: *Dog Day Afternoon* as a Political Film," that is not only one of his earliest essays to deal primarily with film, but also what he later describes as a "study in what I have come to call *cognitive mapping*" (*Signatures of the Visible*, 54). For a discussion of the role of the analogon in cognitive mapping, see *Postmodernism*, 416–17.

15. Badiou, *The Century*, 150.

16. Jameson, *Valences of the Dialectic*, 174.

17. Burnham, *The Jamesonian Unconscious*, 84.

18. For a useful archive of some of the debates of this moment, see Richard Bolton, ed., *Culture Wars: Documents from the Recent Controversies in the Arts* (New York: New Press, 1992). Also see Michael Bérubé, *Public Access: Literary Theory and American Cultural Politics* (New York: Verso, 1994).

19. Jameson, *The Modernist Papers*, xvi–xvii.

20. Jameson, *Late Marxism*, 139.

21. Ibid., 140. For a vital reconsideration of Adorno's response to his years in the United States, see David Jeneman, *Adorno in America* (Minneapolis: University of Minnesota Press, 2007).

22. Jameson, *Late Marxism*, 134.

23. Ibid., 135.

24. Ibid., 130 and 131.

25. Horkheimer and Adorno, *Dialectic of Enlightenment*, 100.

26. Jameson, *Late Marxism*, 107–8. For the most significant discussion of the development and fate of this post-contemporary sense of the concept of culture, see the works of Susan Hegeman, *Patterns for America* and *The Cultural Return*.

27. Jameson, *Late Marxism*, 144.

28. Horkheimer and Adorno, *Dialectic of Enlightenment*, 95.

29. Jameson, *Late Marxism*, 147.

30. Horkheimer and Adorno, *Dialectic of Enlightenment*, 111.

31. For some significant examples of this growing body of literature, see Marc Bousquet, *How the University Works: Higher Education and the Low-Wage Nation* (New York: New York University Press, 2008); Frank Donoghue, *The Last Professors: The Corporate University and the Fate of the Humanities* (New York: Fordham University Press, 2008); The Edu-factory Collective, *Toward a Global Autonomous University* (New York: Autonomedia, 2009); Henry Giroux, *The University in Chains: Confronting the Military-Industrial-Academic Complex* (Boulder, CO: Paradigm Publishers, 2007); Randy Martin, ed., *Chalk Lines: The Politics of Work in the Managed University* (Durham, NC: Duke University Press, 1998); Masao Miyoshi, "Ivory Tower in Escrow: Ex Uno Plures," in *Trespasses: Selected Writings*, ed. Eric Cazdyn (Durham, NC: Duke University Press, 2010), 205–41; Cary Nelson, *No University Is an Island: Saving Academic Freedom* (New York: New York University Press, 2010); Christopher Newfield, *Unmaking the Public University: The Forty-Year Assault*

on the Middle Class (Cambridge, MA: Harvard University Press, 2008); Richard Ohmann, *Politics of Knowledge: The Commercialization of the University, the Professions, and Print Culture* (Middletown, CT: Wesleyan University Press, 2003); Bill Reading, *The University in Ruins* (Cambridge, MA: Harvard University Press, 1997); Michael Rothberg and Peter K. Garrett, eds., *Cary Nelson and the Struggle for the University: Poetry, Politics, and the Profession* (Albany, NY: SUNY Press, 2009); Ellen Schrecker, *The Lost Soul of Higher Education: Corporatization, the Assault on Academic Freedom, and the End of the American University* (New York: The New Press, 2010).

32. Horkheimer and Adorno, *Dialectic of Enlightenment*, 3.

33. For a brilliant rebuttal of the zero-sum logic of "comparative victimization," see Michael Rothberg, *Multidirectional Memory: Remembering the Holocaust in the Age of Decolonization* (Stanford, CA: Stanford University Press, 2009).

34. The landmark text in this revival is Giorgo Agamben, *State of Exception*, trans. Kevin Attell (Chicago: University of Chicago Press, 2005). Also see my use of this concept in *Life Between Two Deaths*.

35. Jameson, *A Singular Modernity*, 80 and 12.

36. Jameson, *Late Marxism*, 151.

37. Ibid., 152 and 153.

38. Horkheimer and Adorno, *Dialectic of Enlightenment*, 164–65.

39. Ibid., 141.

40. Eve Kosofsky Sedgwick, *Tendencies* (Durham: Duke University Press, 1993), 19. For a major reconsideration of the politicization of waged work and the Utopian potentials of postwork theories, see Kathi Weeks, *The Problem with Work: Feminism, Marxism, Antiwork Politics, and Postwork Imaginaries* (Durham: Duke University Press, 2011).

41. Horkheimer and Adorno, *Dialectic of Enlightenment*, 26–27.

42. Jameson, *Late Marxism*, 134.

43. Weeks, *The Problem with Work*, 32.

44. Jameson, *Brecht and Method*, 25 and 158.

45. Ibid., 159.

46. Ibid., 2.

47. Ibid., 132.

48. Ibid., 47.

49. Ibid., 63–64.

50. Ibid., 110.

51. Jameson, *Valences of the Dialectic*, 30–31.

52. Jameson, *Brecht and Method*, 3.

53. Ibid., 26–27.

54. See Wegner, "Lacan avec Greimas."

55. Jameson, *Brecht and Method*, 172.

56. See Barbara Herrnstein Smith, "Contingencies of Value," *Critical Inquiry* 10, no. 1 (1983): 1–36; and the book length expansion of this argument in *Contingencies of Value: Alternative Perspectives for Critical Theory* (Cambridge, MA: Harvard University Press, 1988). For other useful comments on this moment, see Jane Gallop, *Around 1981: Academic Feminist Literary Theory* (New

York: Routledge, 1991); Gallagher and Greenblatt, *Practicing New Historicism*; and Hegeman, "A Brief History of the Cultural Turn," in *The Cultural Return*, 58–75.

57. For a related periodization of the impact of theory on literary studies, see Vincent B. Leitch, *Living with Theory* (Oxford: Blackwell, 2008), 32.

58. Jacques Derrida, *The Truth in Painting*, trans. Geoff Bennington and Ian McLeod (Chicago: University of Chicago Press, 1987), 19–20. My attention was drawn to this statement by John P. Leavey, Jr., ") 1—the fractured frame, the seduction of fiction (, " in *The Archeology of the Frivolous: Reading Condillac*, by Jacques Derrida, trans. John P. Leavey, Jr. (Lincoln: University of Nebraska Press, 1987), 15.

59. Jameson, *Postmodernism*, 183. Also see Steven Knapp and Walter Benn Michaels, "Against Theory," *Critical Inquiry* 8, no. 4 (Summer, 1982): 723–42; and Steven Knapp and Walter Benn Michaels, "Against Theory 2: Hermeneutics and Deconstruction," *Critical Inquiry* 14, no. 1 (Autumn, 1987): 49–68.

60. For a useful contemporary analysis of these debates, see Bérubé, *Public Access*.

61. Kim Emery, "'Crisis Management' in Higher Education: RCM and the Politics of Crisis at the University of Florida," *Cultural Logic* (2010), http://clogic.eserver.org/2010/2010.html (accessed April 17, 2013).

62. Fredric Jameson, "Symptoms of Theory or Symptoms for Theory?" 405.

63. Ibid.

64. Ibid., 406.

65. Ibid.

66. For Jameson's own early reflections on 9/11, see "The Dialectics of Disaster," *The South Atlantic Quarterly* 101, no. 2 (2002): 297–304; and the brief comments in the special section "11 September," *The London Review of Books* 23, no. 19 (October 4, 2001): 20–25.

67. Jameson, *A Singular Modernity*, 1.

68. Ibid., 2–3.

69. Ibid., 165–66. Carolyn Lesjak similarly points out that given his presence at the 2008 New York conference, "The Way We Read Now: Symptomatic Reading and Its Aftermaths," where the "surface reading" was first announced, it becomes "all the more plausible that [Jameson's] claims regarding the status of theory and reading in *Valences* are attuned to these recent articulations of surface reading." "Reading Dialectically," 269, fn. 63.

70. Jameson, *A Singular Modernity*, 177–78.

71. Marjorie Levinson, "What Is New Formalism?" 559.

72. Marjorie Perloff, "Presidential Address 2006: It Must Change," *PMLA* 122, no 3 (2007): 662.

73. Crystal Bartolovich, "Humanities of Scale: Marxism, Surface Reading—and Milton," *PMLA* 127, no. 1 (2012): 559; Lesjak, "Reading Dialectically," 244. Also see Mathias Nilges, "Marxism and Form Now," *Mediations* 24, no. 2 (2009), http://www.mediationsjournal.org/toc/24_2 (accessed August 29, 2013).

74. Nico Baumbach, "All That Heaven Allows: What Is, or Was, Cinephilia (Part One)," *Film Comment* (March 12, 2012), http://www.filmcomment.com/

entry/all-that-heaven-allows-what-is-or-was-cinephilia-part-one (accessed April 17, 2013).

75. Jameson, *A Singular Modernity,* 179. Also see the important rebuttal to the anti-theory turn in Leitch, *Living with Theory.*

76. Lesjak, "Reading Dialectically," 237. For a not unrelated call for retrenchment and a return to standards in the realm of academic publishing, see Lindsay Waters, "A Call for Slow Writing," *Inside Higher Education* (March 10, 2008), http://www.insidehighered.com/views/2008/03/10/waters (accessed December 17, 2013).

77. Shaviro, *Connected,* 221.

78. Jameson, *The Prison-House of Language,* 196.

79. Ibid., 23–24.

80. Jameson, *Valences of the Dialectic,* 263.

81. Jacques Rancière, *The Politics of Aesthetic: The Distribution of the Sensible,* trans. Gabriel Rockhill (New York: Continuum, 2004).

82. Lesjak, "Reading Dialectically," 264.

83. Jameson, *Valences of the Dialectic,* 28–29.

84. Ibid., 28.

85. Ibid., 31. Bosteels shows that for Badiou in one of his major texts from "his Maoist years," *Théorie de la contradiction* (1975), there is a similar unity of opposites in a "conservative structuralism" growing out of Althusser's work and "the 'anarcho-desirers' who in the early 1970s flock to Deleuze's courses in Vincennes." Bosteels then cites Badiou, who maintains, "Structuralism and the ideologies of desire are profoundly coupled to one another. Far from being opposed, they are confused, in their common contradiction of the dialectic." *Badiou and Politics,* 132–33. This unity of opposites re-appears in *The Communist Hypothesis,* when Badiou discusses May '68 French radicals as "torn between a juridical reformism . . . and a Blanquist putchism masquerading as urban guerilla warfare" (87).

86. Jameson, *Valences of the Dialectic,* 29.

87. Jameson, "How Not to Historicize Theory," in *The Ideologies of Theory,* 292.

88. Ibid., 288–89.

89. Ibid., 294.

90. David Foster Wallace, *Everything and More: A Compact History of Infinity* (New York: W. W. Norton, 2010), 67.

91. Jameson, *Valences of the Dialectic,* 489–90.

92. Jameson, "How Not to Historicize Theory," 294.

93. Ibid., 287.

94. That Jameson means for *Valences of the Dialectic* to be understood as in part a response to the new late modernism is also indicated by its cover, which reproduces Diego Rivera's great mural *El Hombre En El Cruce de Caminos* (*Man at the Crossroads*). The original was commissoned for the lobby of New York City's Rockefeller Center; however, before it could be completed it was destroyed, on Nelson Rockefeller's orders, ostensibly because Rivera refused to remove the figure of Lenin from it. This event is then read as an allegory of the

transition from modernism to late modernism in Tim Robbins's brilliant film *A Cradle Will Rock* (1999). I discuss Robbins's film in "The Ends of Culture; or, Late Modernism Redux," in *Literary Materialisms,* ed. Mathias Nilges and Emilio Sauri (New York: Palgrave, 2013), 241–57.

95. Jameson, *The Modernist Papers,* 290. I draw on Jameson's insights here in my essay, "'An Unfinished Project That Was Also a Missed Opportunity': Utopia and Alternate History in Hayao Miyazaki's *My Neighbor Totoro,*" *ImageTexT* 5, no. 2 (2010): http://www.english.ufl.edu/imagetext/archives/v5_2/; reprinted in *Shockwaves of Possibility.*

96. Jameson, *Valences of the Dialectic,* 612.

97. Ibid., 434. Also see his related reading of Rem Koolhaas's notion of junk space, in "Future City," reprinted in *The Ideologies of Theory,* 563–76.

98. Jameson, *Valences of the Dialectic,* 434.

99. Jameson, *The Modernist Papers,* 404.

100. Bosteels, *Badiou and Politics,* 286.

101. Jameson, *Valences of the Dialectic,* 16–17.

102. Ibid., 26.

103. Ibid., 27.

104. Ibid., 59.

105. I discuss the lessons of Butler's work on the family and kinship in *Life Between Two Deaths,* 203–6.

106. Jameson, *Late Marxism,* 102.

107. Jameson, *Valences of the Dialectic,* 51 and 59.

108. Ibid., 190.

109. Lesjak, "Reading Dialectically," 244.

110. Jameson, *Violences of the Dialectic,* 472.

111. See Kim Emery, "Outcomes Assessment and Standardization: A Queer Critique," *Profession 2008* (2008): 255–59; and Elizabeth Freeman, "Monsters, Inc: Notes on the Neoliberal Arts Education," *New Literary History* 36, no. 1 (2005): 83–95.

CHAPTER 6

1. Jameson, *Archaeologies,* 218.

2. Jameson, *Postmodernism,* 332.

3. A first version of my discussion of *Archealogies* in this chapter was presented at a roundtable on *Archaeologies* at the Society for Utopian Studies annual meeting in 2005. For revised versions of the other contributions to the session, see Peter Fitting, "Fredric Jameson and Anti-Anti-Utopianism," *Arena Journal* 25/26 (2006), and Eric Cazdyn, "Anti-anti: Utopia, Globalization, Jameson," *Modern Language Quarterly* 68 (2007): 331–43.

4. For some of Jameson's recent work on realism, see "A Businessman in Love," in *The Novel,* vol. 2, 436–46; and *The Antinomies of Realism.*

5. However, by no means does this include everything he has written on the subject. Any full examination of this aspect of Jameson's project would also need to take into account essays and chapters not included in the present volume, such as his discussion of Susan Sontag's work on science fiction in *Marx-*

ism and Form, 402–8; his 1977 *Diacritics* essay on Louis Marin's *Utopiques,* which has been reprinted in *The Ideologies of Theory;* the extended discussions of Dick and J. G. Ballard in *Postmodernism;* the readings of science fiction films in *The Geopolitical Aesthetic;* and the sections on Andrei Platonov and cyberpunk in *The Seeds of Time.*

6. For a further discussion of this point, see Wegner, "Horizons, Figures, and Machines," and *Imaginary Communities.*

7. Jameson, *Sartre,* 190.

8. Jameson, *Archaeologies,* 44.

9. Or as Meaghan Morris effectively formulates the matter: "In an academic context, to be parochial . . . is unengaging, a failure of *spatial* tact: we fail to touch or be touched by others in a discourse 'large' enough to appeal to more than one parochialism." *Too Soon Too Late,* 6.

10. Jameson, *Archaeologies,* 54.

11. Ibid., 9.

12. Jameson, *Valences of the Dialectic,* 416. And for an even more recent deployment of this opposition, see Jameson, "A New Reading of *Capital.*"

13. See Jameson, *Marxism and Form,* 60–61.

14. Jameson, *Political Unconscious,* 29–30.

15. Ibid., 31.

16. Ibid.

17. Jameson, *Archaeologies,* 214.

18. The cultural "period" of the 1990s, one I argue that begins on November 10, 1989, and ends on September 11, 2001, is the central concern of *Life Between Two Deaths.* I discussion the concept of "late postmodernism" invoked above in the Introduction to that book.

19. Jameson, *The Hegel Variations,* 126.

20. Jameson, *The Antinomies of Realism,* 6.

21. Jameson, *Postmodernism,* 54 and 53.

22. Also see Wegner, *Life Between Two Deaths,* chapter 7.

23. Jameson, *Marxism and Form,* 195. I compare this to the more conservative sequence (Imaginary, Real, Symbolic) formed by the *Terminator* trilogy, in *Life Between Two Deaths,* chapter 3.

24. Jameson, *Archaeologies,* 11.

25. Ibid., 34–35.

26. Jameson, *Brecht and Method,* 2. This also resonates with Jameson's discussion in *The Geopolitical Aesthetic* I invoked earlier of the image of jeepney production in Kidlat Tahimik's *The Perfumed Nightmare.*

27. Jameson, *A Singular Modernity,* 215.

28. Jameson, *Archaeologies,* 72.

29. Ibid., 74.

30. Ibid., xiv.

31. Ibid., 57. For further recent discussions of fantasy and its differences from science fiction, see Darko Suvin, "Considering the Sense of 'Fantasy' or 'Fantastic Fiction': An Effusion," *Extrapolation* 41, no. 3 (2000): 209–47; and "On U. K. Le Guin's 'Second Earthsea Trilogy' and Its Cognitions: A Commentary," *Extrapolation* 47, no. 3 (2006): 488–504.

32. Jameson, *Archaeologies*, 97.

33. Ibid., 283. A similar argument is advanced in Jameson's "Third World Literature," 65–66. One less observed fact about this much discussed essay is Jameson's statement that this essay "was written for an immediate occasion—the third memorial lecture in honor of my late colleague and friend Robert C. Elliott at the University of California, San Diego" (86). Elliott is the author of the classic study *The Shape of Utopia* (1970), reprinted in 2013 in the Ralahine Utopian Studies series.

34. Darko Suvin, *Metamorphoses of Science Fiction: On the Poetics and History of a Literary Genre* (New Haven: Yale University Press, 1979), 12.

35. Jameson, *Archaeologies*, 410.

36. Ibid., 270. I discuss the specific relationship between science fiction dystopias and naturalism in *Life Between Two Deaths*, chapter 5.

37. Jameson, *Archaeologies*, 285–86. Also now see Jameson, "The Historical Novel Today, or, Is it Still Possible?" in *The Antinomies of Realism*, 259–313.

38. Jameson, *Archaeologies*, 286.

39. See Marc Angenot, "The Absent Paradigm: An Introduction to the Semiotics of Science Fiction," *Science Fiction Studies* 6 (1979): 9–19. Also see Jameson's discussion of Angenot's book, *1889: un état du discours social* (1989), in "Marc Angenot and the Literary History of a Year," reprinted in *The Ideologies of Theory*, 577–97.

40. This pair of texts by Wells functions much like the couple of Samuel Richardson and Henry Fielding in Michael McKeon's narrative of the "origins of the English novel." McKeon argues that the works of these two different authors establish the poles between which unfolds the "simple abstraction" of the genre. Mark Rose maintains that science fiction's paradigmatic encounter of the "human and the nonhuman" takes place through "four logically related categories . . . space, time, machine, and monster." Rose, *Alien Encounters: Anatomy of Science Fiction* (Cambridge, MA: Harvard University Press, 1981), 32. I would suggest that all four of Rose's coordinates have been set into place in these two novels by Wells. I develop this insight further in the opening chapter of *Shockwaves of Possibility*.

41. See Tony Pinkney, "Editor's Introduction: Modernism and Cultural Theory," in *The Politics of Modernism: Against the New Conformists*, by Raymond Williams (New York: Verso, 1989), 1–29.

42. Jameson, *Signatures of the Visible*, 156.

43. I develop this narrative in far more detail in *Shockwaves of Possibility*.

44. Jameson provides some of the tools to think about the differences between realist and modernist science fiction in his contrast of Heinlein's *Orphans of the Sky*—first serialized in 1941—and Aldiss's *Starship* (1958) (*Archaeologies*, 256–59). Moreover, later in the same essay, his earliest on science fiction reprinted here, Jameson also suggests a link between Aldiss's and Philip K. Dick's fiction and the *nouveau roman*: in both, "it is the expressive capacity of words and names that is called into question and subverted, and this is not from within but from without, by imperceptible but momentous shifts in the context of the description" (*Archaeologies*, 262).

45. Tom Moylan, *Scraps of the Untainted Sky: Science Fiction, Utopia, Dystopia* (Boulder, CO: Westview, 2001). Also see my engagements with Moylan's landmark study in *Life Between Two Deaths*, chapters 5 and 8.

46. Jameson, *Archaeologies*, 93.

47. Ibid., 177.

48. Ibid., 179.

49. Jameson, *A Singular Modernity*, 197.

50. Ibid., 209.

51. Ibid., 177.

52. Ibid., 179.

53. Jameson, *Seeds of Time*, 78.

54. Suvin, *Metamorphoses*, 64. Also now see Darko Suvin, *Defined by a Hollow: Essays on Utopia, Science Fiction, and Political Epistemology* (Peter Lang, 2009), as well as my preface to the latter, "Emerging from the Flood in Which We Are Sinking; or, Reading with Darko Suvin (Again)," xv–xxxiii.

55. Badiou, *Ethics*, 69.

56. Also see Badiou's major study of modernist culture, *The Century*.

57. Slavoj Žižek, "Afterword: Lenin's Choice" in *Revolution at the Gates: Selected Writings of Lenin from 1917*, by V. I. Lenin, ed. Slavoj Žižek (New York: Verso, 2002), 310.

58. Jameson, *Archaeologies*, 65.

59. Ibid., 66.

60. Ibid., 288–89.

61. Ibid., 118.

62. Ibid., 103.

63. Ibid., 145. I discuss these last three pairs in *Imaginary Communities*, chapter 5.

64. Jameson, *Archaeologies*, 179. Badiou too sees this ironic stance already evident in Kant, who expresses "a 'boundless admiration' for the French Revolution as a phenomenon, or historical appearance, whilst nurturing 'a boundless opposition' to its revolutionary ventures and their actors." *Metapolitics*, trans. Jason Baker (New York: Verso, 2005), 12. Jameson's discussion here also cuts to the heart of what I tried to talk about in *Imaginary Communities* as the dilemmas raised by the Utopian "resolutions" offered in Zamyatin's *We* and Le Guin's *The Dispossessed*: the by-definition unrepresented worlds of the "infinite revolution" in the former text and of the Hainish in the latter.

65. Jameson, *Archaeologies*, 181.

66. Ibid., 225.

67. See Hardt and Negri, *Empire*, 282–84.

68. Jameson, *Archaeologies*, 202.

69. Jameson, *A Singular Modernity*, 215.

70. Jameson, *Archaeologies*, xii.

71. Jameson, "Science Versus Ideology," 283.

72. Badiou, *Ethics*, 78–80.

73. See Jameson, *Archaeologies*, 196.

74. Negri, *Marx Beyond Marx*, 13.

75. Jameson, *Archaeologies,* 313.

76. Ibid., 5.

77. Ibid., 38. Richard Helgerson points toward a parallel between *Utopia* and one of the first works written in response to it: "In all combined editions, *Gargantua* precedes *Pantagruel.* Something similar happens with *Utopia.* The revolutionary depiction of the ideal anti-state, though written first, now follows an introductory dialogue replete with more moderate suggestions for piecemeal change." Helgerson, "Inventing Noplace, or the Power of Negative Thinking," in *The Power of Forms in the English Renaissance,* ed. Stephen Greenblatt (Norman, OK: Pilgrim, 1982), 115.

78. Jameson, *Archaeologies,* 202.

79. Žižek, *Tarrying with the Negative,* 97.

80. Cited in Louis Marin, *Utopiques: Jeux d'espaces* (Paris: Les éditions de minuit, 1973), 350.

81. For a brief history of Cabet's community, see V. F. Calverton, *Where Angels Dared to Tread: Socialist and Communist Utopian Colonies in the United States* (Freeport, NY: Books for Libraries, 1969), 351–56. Or take the parallel case of the California socialist Job Harriman: after failing to win the 1912 Los Angeles mayoral election—a defeat engineered by the conservative *Los Angeles Times,* which had disastrous consequences for the development of a nationwide U.S. socialist movement—Harriman and his followers relocated to the California high desert and attempted to found a utopian community, the Llano del Rio Cooperative Colony. The Llano colony failed, again in a large part due to pressures put by the *Los Angeles Times* on local landowners who controlled crucial water rights. For three different discussions of Harriman and Llano, see Aldous Huxley, "Ozymandias, the Utopia That Failed," in *Tomorrow and Tomorrow and Tomorrow* (New York: Signet, 1964), 68–81; Paul Greenstein, Nigey Lennon, and Lionel Rolfe, *Bread and Hyacinths: The Rise and Fall of Utopian Los Angeles* (Los Angeles: California Classics, 1992); and Mike Davis, *City of Quartz: Excavating the Future in Los Angeles* (New York: Verso, 1991), 3–14. I discuss this issue further, and its treatment in Octavia Butler's *Parables,* in *Life Between Two Deaths,* chapter 8.

82. Jameson, *Archaeologies,* 232.

83. Ibid., 224.

84. Robinson was a student of Jameson's at the University of California, San Diego, and he has often engaged with Jameson's ideas in his fiction—see for example his use of Greimasian semiotics in *Red Mars* and Hayden White's *Metahistory* in *The Years of Rice and Salt.* I discuss the latter in "Learning to Live in History: Alternate Historicities and the 1990s in *The Years of Rice and Salt,*" in *Kim Stanley Robinson Maps the Unimaginable: Critical Essays,* ed. William J. Burling. (Jefferson, NC: McFarland, 2009), 98–112, reprinted in *Shockwaves of Possibility.* Robinson pointed out in an email note to me that "it was *Valences* that particularly struck me while working on" *2312.* I discuss the Fall Revolution quartet in "Ken MacLeod's Permanent Revolution: Utopian Possible Worlds, History, and the *Augenblick* in the 'Fall Revolution'," in *Red Planets: Marxism and Science Fiction,* ed. Mark Bould and China Miéville (London: Pluto Press/Wesleyan, 2009), 137–55; and MacLeod's brilliant alternate

history, *The Human Front* (2002), in "Detonating New Shockwaves of Possibility: Alternate Histories and the Geopolitical Aesthetics of Ken MacLeod and Iain M. Banks," *CR: The New Centennial Review* 13, no. 2 (2013); both are also reprinted in *Shockwaves of Possibility*.

85. Jameson discusses Koolhaas's work in *The Seeds of Time*, 57–58 and 134–46, and in "Space and Congestion: Rem Koolhaas and *S,M,L,XL,*" and "Future City," both now reprinted in *The Ideologies of Theory*, 555–76. I analyze this engagement further in "Horizons, Figures, Machines;" and read Koolhaas's "theoretical novel," *S,M,L,XL,* in "'The Mysterious Qualities of This Alleged Void'."

86. Jameson, *Archaeologies*, 221.

87. Ibid., 226. I analyze the deep relationship between the nation-state and Utopia in *Imaginary Communities*.

88. Moreover, as I noted in the previous chapter, Jameson has also speculated on a "fourth moment for theory"—after those of structuralism, poststructuralism, and the political—that "has to do with the theorizing of collective subjectivities." Jameson, "Symptoms of Theory," 406.

89. E. P. Thompson, *William Morris: Romantic to Revolutionary,* rev. ed. (New York: Pantheon, 1977), 791. The importance of Thompson's work for Utopian studies is also stressed in Levitas, *The Concept of Utopia.*

90. Jameson, *Archaeologies,* 231.

91. Ibid., 231–32.

92. Ibid., 212.

93. Ibid., 416.

94. Negri, *Marx Beyond Marx,* 151.

95. I discuss further the relationships between this seemingly diverse set of interventions in *Life Between Two Deaths.*

AFTERWORD

1. Jameson, *Marxism and Form,* 306.

2. Jameson, *Valences of the Dialectic,* 70. For a fascinating study of what "*Hamlet* without Hamlet" would look like, and another demonstration of the productive possibilities of formalization, see Franco Moretti, "Network Theory, Plot Analysis," *New Left Review* 68 (2011): 80–102.

3. For his invocation of Korsch's term, see Jameson, *Representing* Capital, 128–29 and 136.

4. Jameson, *The Hegel Variations,* 18.

5. Jameson, *Representing* Capital, 135. I discuss this four-part dialectic in "Lacan avec Greimas."

6. Jameson, *The Hegel Variations,* 22.

7. Ibid.

8. Jameson, *Valences of the Dialectic,* 100.

9. Jameson, *The Hegel Variations,* 22.

10. Jameson, *Representing* Capital, 2.

11. Ibid., 141.

12. Ibid., 144.

13. Ibid., 2.

14. Ibid., 70.

15. Ibid., 71.

16. Dienst, *Bonds of Debt*, 150. Also see Shaviro, *Connected*, 159–63.

17. Jameson, *Representing* Capital, 149.

18. Ibid., 150. See also Žižek's reflections on Jameson's concepts of unemployment and exploitation in *Less than Nothing*, 100–104.

19. Jameson, *Representing* Capital, 150.

20. Ibid., 151.

21. Frantz Fanon, *The Wretched of the Earth,* trans. Constance Farrington (New York: Grove Press, 1968), 154.

22. Jameson, *Representing* Capital, 151. Also see Dienst, *Bonds of Debt,* especially his discussion of Marx's political understanding of debt found in the third volume of *Capital* (152–53).

23. Jameson, *Representing* Capital, 127.

24. Ibid., 146.

25. Ibid., 142.

26. Ibid., 13.

27. Ibid., 73.

28. Ibid., 48.

29. Ibid., 50–51.

30. Ibid., 52.

31. Ibid., 61.

32. Ibid., 61–62.

33. Jameson, *Archaeologies of the Future,* 212.

34. Jameson, *Representing* Capital, 137.

35. Badiou, *Ethics,* 51.

36. Watkins, "Generally Historicizing," in *On Jameson,* 25.

37. Jameson, *Valences of the Dialectic,* 8. For a related discussion of the "inimitability" of Derrida's style, see John P. Leavey, Jr., ") 1—the fractured frame, the seduction of fiction (," 13.

38. Watkins, "Generally Historicizing," in *On Jameson,* 25.

Index

Compiled by Derrick D. King

 FLASHPOINTS

1. *On Pain of Speech: Fantasies of the First Order and the Literary Rant,* Dina Al-Kassim
2. *Moses and Multiculturalism,* Barbara Johnson, with a foreword by Barbara Rietveld
3. *The Cosmic Time of Empire: Modern Britain and World Literature,* Adam Barrows
4. *Poetry in Pieces: César Vallejo and Lyric Modernity,* Michelle Clayton
5. *Disarming Words: Empire and the Seductions of Translation in Egypt,* Shaden M. Tageldin
6. *Wings for Our Courage: Gender, Erudition, and Republican Thought,* Stephanie H. Jed
7. *The Cultural Return,* Susan Hegeman
8. *English Heart, Hindi Heartland: The Political Life of Literature in India,* Rashmi Sadana
9. *The Cylinder: Kinematics of the Nineteenth Century,* Helmut Müller-Sievers
10. *Polymorphous Domesticities: Pets, Bodies, and Desire in Four Modern Writers,* Juliana Schiesari
11. *Flesh and Fish Blood: Postcolonialism, Translation, and the Vernacular,* S. Shankar
12. *The Fear of French Negroes: Transcolonial Collaboration in the Revolutionary Americas,* Sara E. Johnson
13. *Figurative Inquisitions: Conversion, Torture, and Truth in the Luso-Hispanic Atlantic,* Erin Graff Zivin
14. *Cosmopolitan Desires: Global Modernity and World Literature in Latin America,* Mariano Siskind
15. *Fiction Beyond Secularism,* Justin Neuman
16. *Periodizing Jameson: Dialectics, the University, and the Desire for Narrative,* Phillip E. Wegner